## MODERN PERSIAN

This book is written for all who wish to learn to speak, read and write Modern Persian, and particularly for those working by themselves. It is divided into three main parts, dealing with the Persian script, the grammar of the language and vocabulary-building respectively. There is a Key to the exercises which appear at the end of each lesson, and also a grammatical index and vocabularies each way. A transliteration in Roman characters is given for every word, phrase and sentence that is introduced.

## TEACH YOURSELF BOOKS

This excellent volume fills a gap in the material available on the language of the Persians. Mr. Mace is particularly to be congratulated upon his treatment of the grammar . . . the coverage is thorough and leaves little if anything to baffle the learner in his later, more advanced studies.

*The Incorporated Linguist*

# MODERN PERSIAN

## John Mace

TEACH YOURSELF BOOKS
Hodder and Stoughton

*First printed* 1962
*Corrected edition* 1971
*Tenth impression* 1981

*Copyright* © 1962, 1971
*Hodder and Stoughton Ltd*

This volume is published in the U.S.A. by David McKay Company Inc., 750 Third Avenue, New York, N.Y. 10017

ISBN 0 340 278420

*Printed in Great Britain for Hodder and Stoughton Paperbacks,*
*a Division of Hodder and Stoughton Ltd,*
*Mill Road, Dunton Green, Sevenoaks, Kent*
*(Editorial Office: 47 Bedford Square, London WC1 3DP)*
*by Richard Clay (The Chaucer Press), Ltd, Bungay, Suffolk*

# PREFACE

PERSIAN is an Indo-European language, that is, it is related to the tongues spoken in Western Europe. As a result of the spread of Islam after the death of the Prophet, many Arabic words were introduced into Persian, which came to be written with the Arabic alphabet; yet in its grammatical structure and its basic vocabulary Persian remains Indo-European, hence quite unlike Arabic.

Persian is therefore an easy language for us to learn to speak; at first the writing and reading of it seem difficult, but with the right approach we can learn even this quickly. This book attempts to teach the basis of the reading and writing, with the minimum of grammar, in the first dozen lessons; thereafter the grammar and idiom of the language can be explored more fully. A transliteration in Roman characters is given for the first few appearances of every word, phrase or sentence, but you should try as soon as you can to pick out the words direct from the Persian script, reading them several times over to accustom your eye to the forms. Plenty of practice is given in this, in the early lessons of the book. The book is in three main parts—Alphabet, Grammar, and Vocabulary-building, and in addition it has a Key to the exercises, an Index, and vocabularies each way.

The book is called Teach 'Yourself *Modern Persian*; this is important. Arabic forms of speech and orthography do appear in everyday Persian talking and writing, and where they do we have mentioned them; but there is no more need for the student of Modern Persian to learn Arabic than there is for the person learning, say, French to know Latin first. I do not speak, understand, read, or write Arabic beyond the half-dozen or so examples of it which appear in this book.

You ought to enjoy learning Persian—Iran is a fascinating country, unique in her long history of civilisation and art. Iran is being re-discovered by thousands of English-speaking people—British and American—and it is their need to understand and be understood among this friendly and hospitable people that has prompted the writing of this book.

I should like to take this opportunity of thanking Professor Savory, of the University of Toronto, and Mr. Leonard Cutts, the Editor-in-Chief, for their many helpful suggestions on the text.

I am also indebted to Messrs. Bruno Cassirer, of Oxford, for their kind permission to reproduce the miniatures on pp. 93 and 117, and to the Trustees of the British Museum for allowing me to reproduce drawings of the archaeological fragments on pp. 39, 79, and 201.

JOHN MACE.

---

NOTE : *Iran* is the country ; *Iranian* the nationality ; *Persian* the national language, originally the tongue of *Fars* in the south of Iran. In English *Persia* is used to mean *Iran*, but this is, really, inaccurate.

# CONTENTS

vii

# PART ONE
## Alphabet
الف با

# LESSON 1

Persian is written with the Arabic alphabet, slightly modified. We write Persian in the opposite direction to English, that is, not from left to right but from right to left. Persian books begin at what to us would be the back of the book.

ا  â  آ

The Persian â, long a, is a long open sound, halfway between the a in bar, calm, dark, and the a in wall, talk, ball. It is an a with a touch of o in it.

At the beginning of a word it is written

آ

with the long sign over it.

In the middle or at the end of a word it is written without the long sign :  ا.

ب  b  بـ

The Persian b is pronounced exactly as is b in English. When it begins a word, it is written

بـ

(to the ← left) and is joined from there to the next letter, thus :

(up ↄ)  با  bâ = with

Remember that the line of writing starts here ▬➤, on the extreme right of the page. The â ا must be struck upwards immediately from the بـ b thus :

با  با  با  با  با  با  با  (Begin here)

meaning " with " in Persian.

3

Practise a whole line of it :

با با با با با با با با با با با با

*â*, or ا *alef* as it is called, does not join to its left on to the letter following it ; in this it is irregular. If we wish to write *âb*, therefore, which means " water ", we write the initial long *â* آ and the *b* ب separately. A separate *b* ب has a longer and fuller form than the joined ﺑ *b*, which is about one-third of the length. Practise :

(from here)

آب آب آب آب آب (water) *âb* آب

با آب با آب (with water) *bâ âb* با آب

ن *n* ﻧ

Like ب *b*, the Persian *n* has a short form used at the beginning or in the middle of a word, ﻧ, and a full form ن (deeper, rounder than the flat ب *b*), used at the end of a word.

A few more words :

(from here)

آن آن آن آن آن آن (that) *ân* آن

نان نان نان نان (bread) *nân* نان

(You will recall that the initial long *alef* is always written with the long sign over it, thus آ, and that it *cannot be joined* to the letter following it. This is why, in the last two words, the final ن *n* appears separate, and in the first word the *alef* has its long sign.)

More practice. Follow the arrows :

(from here)

that *ân* آن آن آن آن آن آن 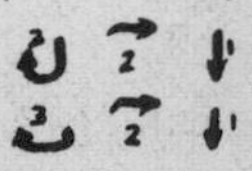

water *âb* آب آب آب آب آب

Now a whole phrase :

با آن آب (with that water) با آن آب    با آن آب    با آن آب

A useful word at this stage is

(a builder) *bannâ* بنا

because it shows us that the short forms of *b* ب and *n* ن are identical except for the position of the dot, and also it shows us that short vowels (in this case *a*, like the *a* in hat, bat, cat in English) are *not written*. We only write *long* vowels in Persian.

Practise :

(from here) ➤

a builder (*bannâ*)    بنا بنا بنا بنا بنا بنا بنا

You must be careful to pronounce double letters as in Italian, so : بنا *ban-nâ* (the *nn* is *held* before being released). Pronounce as you write, holding the *nn* and stressing the -*â* at the end : That builder *ân bannâ* بنا آن

## VOCABULARY

that آن *ân*                     builder بنا *bannâ*
water آب *âb*                    bread نان *nân*
with با *bâ*                     father, " Daddy " بابا *bâbâ*

## EXERCISES

I. Write, pronouncing as you write :

ن ب آ    ن ب آ    ن *-n*    ب *-b*    آ *â-*

آب آب آب آب آب آب    *âb* آب

آن آن آن آن آن آن آن    *ân* آن

با با با با با با با با    *bâ* با

بابا بابا بابا بابا بابا بابا بابا    *bâbâ* بابا

بنا بنا بنا بنا بنا بنا    *bannâ* بنا

نان نان نان نان نان نان نان    *nân* نان

II. Translate and write out a line of each of these, pronouncing as you write :

> (a) that bread, (b) that water, (c) that builder,
> (d) with bread, (e) with water.

III. Read your Persian for Ex. II aloud.

IV. Read aloud (without translating) :

(b) آن آب با آن نان       (a) آن بنا با آن آب

(c) با بنا (there is no word for " the " in Persian)

(d) آب با نان

V. Translate Ex. IV into English.


## LESSON 2

Persian s has a long and a short form, used in the same
way as the long and short b and n :

$$s \quad س \; ـس$$

and s with     three dots over it gives us sh :

$$sh \quad ش \; ـش$$

Practise :

(from here)

س س س س س س س س س س write it fast

ش ش ش ش ش ش ش ش ش ش

سا سا سا سا سا سا سا سا سا سا

آش آش آش آش آش آش (stew) âsh

آش با نان آش با نان : " stew with bread "

s-n looks like one letter : it is two. The n-dot tells us
that :

من سن سن سن سن سن (age) senn

The short vowel e is of course not written.

Practise :

آش آش آش *âsh*

سن سن سن *senn*

(short vowel *a* not written) " enough " *bas* بس بس

The double ـس of *s* and *sh* are tedious to write, so most Persian people leave out the " teeth ", as they are called, and write for *s* not ـس and س but ـ and س. This is a long sweeping letter, quite easy to make and easy to read.

Practise writing, pronouncing as you go :

آش آش آش آش آش *âsh*

سن سن سن سن سن سن سن *senn*

(the ؛ is there : look carefully) *bas* بس بس بس

The syllable ش *-esh* forms a very valuable suffix, meaning his, her, or its ; it is added to nouns ending in a consonant.

We have already had the nouns (read them aloud) :

نان آب آش سن

which all end in consonants. Thus we make of them

(his, her, or its bread) *nânesh* نانش

(  ,,   ,,   ,,  water) *âbesh* آبش

(  ,,   ,,   ,,  stew) *âshesh* آشش

(  ,,   ,,   ,,  age) *sennesh* سنش

Similarly, the suffix شان *-eshan* gives us the possessive *their* : it is also added to nouns ending in a consonant. Read, copy, and pronounce :

نانشان (their bread) *nâneshân* نانشان

Do a whole line of this word, pronouncing as you write :

نانشان نانشان نانشان نانشان نانشان نانشان

Now more words :

(meaning ?) *âbeshân* آبشان

آبشان get the dots right آبشان

(their stew) *âsheshân* آشان آشان

(their age) *senneshân* سنان سنان

Make your *s*'s and *sh*'s long sweeps :

سنان آشان سنان آشان

## VOCABULARY

| | |
|---|---|
| stew آش or آش *âsh* | his/her/its (suffix) ش or ـش *-esh* |
| age سن or سن *senn* | their (suffix) شان or ـشان *-eshân* |
| enough بس or بس *bas* | |

## EXERCISES

### I. Write, pronouncing as you write :

(a) بس بن *bas* بس بس بس بس بس

(b) بس بس *bas* بس بس بس بس بس

(c) سن سن *senn* سن سن سن سن سن

(d) آبش آبش *âbesh* آبش آبش آبش آبش آبش

(e) آش آش *âsh* آش آش آش آش آش

### II. Translate and write, pronouncing as you write :

(a) his bread.   (b) their bread.   (c) stew with bread.
(d) her age.

### III. Read aloud your Persian for Ex. II.

### IV. Read aloud (without translating) :

(a) آش آش آش آش آش آش

(b) نانشان نانشان نانشان نانشان نانشان نانشان

(c) آب آب آب آبش آبش آبش آبش

(d) آب با نانش آب با نانش آب با نانش

### V. Translate Ex. IV into English.

## LESSON 3

*m* in Persian has two forms, a short and a full one:

long *m* م م م م م م م short *m* مـ مـ مـ مـ مـ

As in the case of ب *b*, ن *n*, and *s-sh* س ش, the shortened form is used when a letter follows the *m* مـ, the long form when *m* م is the final letter of the word.

Practise short *m*:

ما ما ما ما ما ما "we" *mâ* ما

Don't make a long sweep between the *m* مـ and the *â* ا, or it will be read as an *s* (مسا *m-s-â*). Keep the joining short in Persian.

Again, saying it as you write:

ما ما ما ما ما ما ما ما ما *mâ* ما

شما شما شما شما "you" *shomâ* (written anti-clockwise) شما

You will notice two things about *m* مـ in the middle of a word:

(*a*) It is written anti-clockwise ـمـ . ـمـ

(*b*) We approach the *m* from the *top*: ـمـ شما. Get into the habit of writing the bead of the مـ or م in this fashion; do not write it clockwise, as certain other letters, which we shall deal with later, are always written clockwise, and confusion will arise if you do not write *m* carefully and correctly.

Now write *shomâ* with a sweeping *sh*: شما (the short *o* is unwritten) شما شما شما.

Now write the word for "I":

من من من من (I) man من

"I with you".

من با شما من با شما من با شما

Now long, final *m* :

شام شام شام    شام (dinner) *shâm*

" dinner with stew ".

شام با آش   شام با آش   شام با آش

نام نام نام نام   نام (name) *nâm*   نام

A very useful suffix is -*am* م- (short *a* unwritten),
meaning " my " :

(as the م is anti-clockwise,   آبم *âb-am*

the ب is turned round م)    (my water).

Practise :

آبم آبش   *âbesh* آبش   *âbam* آبم

نام نام   نام (meaning ?) *nânam* نانم

آشم آشم آشم   (my stew) *âsham* آشم

Just as ش- " his/her/its " became شان- " their ", so
م- -*am* " my " becomes plural مان- -*emân* " our " :

*âbemân* آبمان   *âbam* آبم

Practise :

نانمان نانمان نانمان   " our bread " *nânemân* نانمان

شام شام   " my dinner " *shâmam* شام

سنم سنم سنم   (meaning ?) *sennam* § سنم

§ Remember to hold on to the double letter : *sen-nam.*

*D.* Persian *d* has only one form ; it is not joined to the
left, i.e. to the letter following it. In this respect it is like
*alef* ا.

د *d*

Practise it. Make the hook fairly sharp, and the whole
letter resting on the line of writing :

(from here)

د   د   د   د   د   د   د   د   د   د   د   د   د

آمد آمد آمد (short *a* not written) " he came " *âmad* آمد

بد بد بد (meaning " bad " in English) *bad* بد

دم دم (*o* like *oo* in foot) " tail " *dom* دم

دمش دمش دمش " its tail " *domesh* دمش

## VOCABULARY

| | |
|---|---|
| we, us ما *mâ* | he came آمد *âmad* |
| you شما *shomâ* | my (suffix) م *-am* |
| I, me من *man* | our (suffix) مان *-emân* |
| bad بد *bad* | name نام *nâm* |
| tail دم *dom* | dinner شام *shâm* |

## EXERCISES

**I.** Write, pronouncing as you write :

(a) آمد آمد آمد بنا آمد بنا آمد

(b) سنش سنش سنش سنم سنم سنان سنان

(c) دم دم دم دمش دمش دمش

(d) بد بد بد بد بد بد .

**II.** Translate and write out, pronouncing as you write :

(a) its tail. (b) her name. (c) our dinner. (d) their bread. (e) my dinner. (f) our water.

**III.** Read aloud your Persian for Ex. II.

**IV.** Read aloud (without translating) :

(a) بنا با آن آب آمد     بنا با آن آب آمد

(b) سنم سنش سنان سنان

(c) آبم آبم آبم آبش آبش آبش آبمان آبمان

(d) نامش نامش نامش نامان نامان

(e) شام شامش شامان شامان

**V.** Translate into English Ex. IV.

## LESSON 4

The long *î* or *ee* sound heard in bean, lean, is written in Persian :

> ﻳ short (i.e. not at the end of a word)
> ی long (i.e. at the end of a word)

There is a rule which forbids the letter ﻳ *î* or *ee* to begin a word in writing : therefore if a word begins with the sound *ee* the letter ﻳ is introduced, preceded by ‍ا *alef*. This ‍ا *alef* is mute. It serves merely as a " prop ", to announce that the word is beginning with a vowel.

That is why, when *alef* is actually sounded, *â*, at the beginning of a word we take care to mark it long : آ. This tells us that the *alef* is not merely an introducing letter for another vowel, but a long vowel in its own right. Compare :

*âsh* آش    *ân* آن    *âb* آب

where the *â* آ is sounded, with

اين " this " *în*

where the *î* or *ee* is the actual vowel sounded, the *alef* being a mere dummy, an orthographic convention.

Practise, saying it as you write it :

THAT                        THIS

آن آن آن آن آن آن        اين اين اين اين اين

Do not confuse ﻳ *ee* with ﺑ *b*. *B* has one dot beneath it, *ee* has two. Note that the long form of *ee* ی has no dots at all.

ﻳ ی *ee* is also used for the sound of the English consonant *y*, as in year, yoke, you, and your. When ﻳ is used in this

manner, *as a consonant*, it needs no *alef* to introduce it at
the beginning of a word : it is only the *vocalic* ى which
must be so introduced.

Practise :

یا یا یا یا یا یا یا یا " or " *yâ*

Look now at the Persian word for "he comes ", *mî-âyad* :

مياید

*d y â î m* (reading from the *m* leftwards)

⟵

The م *m* we know from the last lesson. The first ى is *ee*.
The *alef* in the middle of the word is *â*, a long open sound
halfway between the *a* in bar, calm, dark and the *a* in
walk, talk, ball.

The second ى is a consonant, *y*. After it is pronounced
a short *a*, not written, and lastly a *d*.

Similarly : مياَم *mî-âyam* " I come ".

Practise " the builder came ".

بنا آمد (‎-مه no-)

and " the builder comes " :

بنا مياید (‎-مه no-)

The letter ب *b* gives us a useful preposition-prefix. It
means " to ".

Practise :

بشما " to you " *be-shomâ*

بمن " to me " *be-man*

بما " to us " *be-mâ*

بنا " to the builder " *be-bannâ*

When the ، be-prefix is attached to a word beginning with long *alef* آ, the resulting combination is still read as two syllables.

Pronounce :

بآب *be-âb* (two syllables) = to the water

Write :

بآب بآن بآب بآب بآن بآن آب بآن آب

When the ، *be-* is prefixed to a word beginning with another vowel introduced by a dummy *alef* ا (in words like این *in*, for example) the ، is written straight on to the *alef*, and the whole word is read with *be-* as quite a distinct syllable.

Pronounce : باین

*be-în* (two syllables) = to this

## VOCABULARY

this این *in*  
or یا *yâ*  
he/she/it comes میاید *mî-âyad*

to, towards (prefix) ، *be-*  
I come میایم *mî-âyam*

Practise :

بآن آب باین آب باین بنا بآن بنا بمن میاید بشما آمد

## EXERCISES

I. Write, pronouncing as you write :

(a) میاید میاید میاید     (b) آمد آمد آمد آمد

(c) بشما میاید بشما میاید     (d) من میایم من میایم

(e) میایم میایم

II. Translate and write, pronouncing as you write :

(a) I am coming (= I come).   (b) he is coming

III. Read aloud your Persian for Ex. II.

IV. Read, without translating:

| | |
|---|---|
| (a) بآن آب میایم | بآن آب میایم |
| (b) باین آب میاید | باین آب میاید |
| (c) آب با این آش | آب با این آش |
| (d) این بنا میاید | آن بنا آمد |

V. Translate Ex. IV.

## LESSON 5

Persian *r* is written ر. In writing it is similar to ا *alef*
and د *d* because it is not joined to the letter following it.

It is pronounced with a strong roll of the tongue, like a
Scots *r*.

Practise, following the arrow:

ر ر ر ر ر ر ر ر ر ر ر ر ر ر (down) ر

### VOCABULARY

(1) door در *dar*  I have دارم *dâram*
(2) in  head سر *sar*
man مرد *mard*  cold سرد *sard* (adjective)
has, he has دارد *dârad*  Iranian, Persian ایرانی *îrânî*
Iran, Persia ایران *îrân*

*Alef* at the beginning of a word is written:

(a) آ to signify *â*, long *a*.

(b) ا as a mute letter introducing any vowel.

You will remember how in the word این *în*, the *alef* was
a pure orthographic convention. In the same way the word

اسب *asb* or *asp* " a horse "

begins with an unwritten *short* vowel a. The *alef* is there
to introduce this initial vowel. *Do not* read the *alef* itself
as *a*—the a is not written, but introduced by the dummy
ا *alef*.

Practise :

اسب اسب اسب اسب اسب "horse" asb

This man has a horse :

این مرد اسب دارد *in mard asb dârad*

(the VERB is usually last word in a Persian sentence).

That man is coming on horseback (" with a horse ") :

آن مرد با اسب میاید *ân mard bâ asb mîâyad*

ت ؛ ت

ت ؛ t is written exactly like ب ؛ b in all respects except
that it has two dots above the letter instead of one below it.
The short and long form are used just as you have learned
to use long and short forms of :

ب ؛ b

ن ؛ n

م ه m

so : ت ؛ t

Practise :

ب b ؛ ت ؛ ت ؛ ب ت ؛ ت ؛ ت ؛ ب

## VOCABULARY

as far as, until تا *tâ*        is, he/she/it is است *ast*

he/she/it is not, isn't نیست *nîst*

Practise :

اسب اسب اسب اسب اسب horse

تا تا تا تا تا until

This is a horse :

این اسب است *in asb ast*

That isn't a horse :

آن اسب نیست *ân asb nîst*

(the verb comes last)

ﻧ *na-*. The prefix ﻧ *na-* (short *a* not written), joined to a verb beginning with a consonant, makes the verb negative :

دیدم *dîdam* I saw

ندیدم *nadîdam* I did not see

میایم *mîâyam* I am coming

نمیایم *namîâyam* I am not coming

Before a verb beginning with a vowel, the prefix is written نی *nay-* and pronounced like " nigh " in English :

آمد *âmad* he came

نیامد *nayâmad* he did not come

Notice that the ˉ long sign over the *alef* is dropped here.

Before going any further, make sure now that you know all the vocabulary we have had to date, by looking back at all the previous lessons. Then check that you know the use of the prefixes

بـ *be-* to (check its use before *alef*)

ﻧ *na-* + consonant ⎫ makes verbs negative :

نی *nay-* + vowel ⎭ " do not, does not, did not "

and of the suffixes

ش ـش *-esh* his, her, its ⎫

شان ـشان *-eshân* their ⎪ added to nouns which

م *-am* my ⎬ end in a consonant

مان *-emân* our ⎭

## EXERCISES

I. Write, pronouncing :

(a) من اسب دارم *man asb dâram* من اسب دارم

(b) من اسب دیدم *man asb dîdam* من اسب دیدم

(c) این اسب ایرانی نیست *in asb îrânî nîst* این اسب ایرانی نیست

(d) آن در است    *ân dar ast*    آن در است

(e) این نان بد است    *in nân bad ast*    این نان بد است

(f) من با شما تا دم در میایم    من با شما تا دم در میایم
*man bâ shomâ tâ dam -é dar mîâyam*

(g) آب سرد است    *âb sard ast*    آب سرد است

II. Translate, and write, pronouncing as you write :

   (a) My dinner is cold. (b) This bread is bad. (c) That
   man isn't Iranian. (d) There is no water (= water
   isn't).

III. Translate into English Ex. I.

IV. Read aloud your Persian for Ex. II.

## LESSON 6

و. The Persian letter و has two values :

   (a) long vowel : و *û* like *oo* in boot.

               *ô* like *o* in pole, but a pure vowel.

   (b) consonant : و *v* as in every.

When و is a long vowel *û* or *ô* and begins a word, of
course it must be introduced with a dummy ا *alef*. When
a consonant it can be written as first letter of a word.
There is one exception to this general rule : the word و
" and " is pronounced either *va* or *ô*, and is always spelt
without *alef*. Of the two pronunciations *va* is far more
common than *ô*.

*û*, *ô*, *v* is not joined to the letter following it. It has no
short form.

Practise :

                                  (from here)

و   و   و   و   و   و   و   و   و   و

Distinguish between ر *r*, د *d*, and و *û-ô-v*.

Practise:

ر د و   ر د و   ر د و   و و و   د د د   ر ر ر

and { و  *va*
         *ô*

face رو *rû*

he, she او *û*

two دو *dô*

I run میدوم *mídavam*

he/she/it runs میدود *mídavad*

friend دوست *dûst*

چ ح Persian *ch* is pronounced like our *ch* in church. It has a long and a short form.

Practise, following the arrows:

start it here

why? *cherá*    چرا   چرا   چرا   چ ر

If we put a dot over ر *r* we get ز *z* like our z in zoo: woman زن *zan*; from از *az* (short *a*); thief دزد *dozd*.

A very useful feature in Persian is one called the *ézâfé*. This is originally an Arabic word meaning " addition ", and it is a short vowel pronounced like *é* in the French " café ". We shall transcribe the *ézâfé* as *é*: this is to show that it is short, clipped, like *é* in French. The *ézâfé* is NEVER stressed.

This *ézâfé* has three possible meanings:

(*a*) It can mean " belonging to ":

*asb-é-mard*    اسب مرد

the horse of the man (i.e. the man's horse)

(*b*) It can join a noun to an adjective qualifying that noun (the noun always comes first, as in French):

*mard-é-îrânî*    مرد ایرانی

an Iranian man, the Iranian man

(c) It can show that the words before and after the *ézâfé* are in apposition to one another :

مرد دوستم
*mard-é-dûstam*
the man, my friend . . .

If the word before the *ézâfé* ends in a consonant, as in the examples (a), (b), and (c) above, the *ézâfé* is not written; it has to be read into the text.

If the word before the *ézâfé* ends in one of the long vowels ا *â* or و *û-ô*, the *ézâfé* is written ی *î* and is pronounced *-yé* :

ای·*â-yé* or وی *û-yé*

e.g. (a) possession : *rû-yé-mard* روی مرد
the face of the man, the man's face

(b) adjective : *bannâ-yé-îrânî* بنای ایرانی
the/an Iranian builder

(c) apposition : *bannâ-yé-dûstam* بنای دوستم
the builder, my friend . . .

If the noun before the *ézâfé* ends in the long vowel

ی *î-ee*

the *ézâfé* is not written, but is pronounced with the same *y*-glide as in the case of *â-yé* and *û-yé* above : *î-yé*.

Thus : *îrânî-yé-dûstam* ایرانی دوستم
the Persian, my friend . . .

Practise (a) unwritten *ézâfé*, pronounced *é*, after consonantal nouns :

مرد بد (meaning ?) *mard-é-bad* مرد بد  مرد بد
اسب ایرانی a Persian horse *asb-é-îrânî* اسب ایرانی اسب ایرانی

زن بنا زن بنا زن بنا   the builder's wife *zan-é-bannâ*

اسب دوستمان اسب دوستمان   our friend's horse *asb-é-dûstemân*

(b) *ézâfé* written ى after ا and و, and pronounced *â-yé* and *û-yé* ای and وى :

روى مرد   the man's face *rû-yé-mard*

بناى ایرانى   the Iranian builder *bannâ-yé-îrâní*

(c) *ézâfé* unwritten after ى itself, and pronounced *î-yé* :

ایرانى دوستم   the Persian, my friend . . . *îrânî-yé-dûstam*

Notice the difference between :

(a) The Persian, my friend, came   ایرانى دوستم آمد
*îrânî-yé-dûstam âmad*

and

(b) The Persian *is* my friend   ایرانى دوستم است
*îrânî dûstam ast*

In (a) the two nouns ایرانى and دوستم, *îrânî* and *dûstam*, are linked together by the *ézâfé*, as they agree, or are (grammatically speaking) in apposition.

In (b), although the two words ایرانى *îrânî* and دوستم *dûstam* are written as in (i), there is no *ézâfé*.

Again, distinguish in reading between

(a) I have cold water *âb-é-sard dâram* آب سرد دارم

and (b) the water is cold *âb sard ast* آب سرد است

where in (a) and (b) آب and سرد show no distinction, yet in (a) we have a noun-adjective combination (cold water) linked with an *ézâfé*, and in (b) we have the verb *to be* separating the two words in English : the water *is* cold.

The *ézâfé* is a most important and useful particle in Persian.

## VOCABULARY

| | |
|---|---|
| and { va / o و | two دو *do* |
| | woman زن *zan* |
| he, she او *û* | from از *az* |
| face رو *rû* | gold زر *zar* |
| why? چرا *cherâ* | thief دزد *dozd* |
| I run میدوم *mîdavam* | mother مادر *mâdar* |
| friend دوست *dûst* | he/she runs میدود *mîdavad* |

## EXERCISES

I. Write, pronouncing as you write :

(a) آب سرد دارم *âb-é-sard dâram*    آب سرد دارم

(b) آن اسب بد نیست *ân asb bad nîst*    آن اسب بد نیست

(c) چرا آمد؟ *cherâ âmad ?*    چرا آمد؟

(d) نام این اسب رخش رست *nâm-é-în asb Rakhsh ast*    نام این اسب رخش است

(e) *dûst-é-în mard âmad*    دوست این مرد آمد

II. Translate and write :

(a) This man is a thief. (b) I came with my friend's horse. (c) I saw the face of that man. (d) This man's wife is not Iranian. (e) I am coming to Iran.

III. Translate Ex. I.

IV. Read aloud your Persian for Ex. II.

## LESSON 7

*H.* Persian *h* has several possible forms :

(a) At the beginning of a word it is written

ه ه دہ ه

Practise :

" every " *har*    هر هر هر هر هر هر

(b) In the middle of words it is written either

(a rare form)    ٭ ڇ ۊ �ﯔ ٭

or

(a far more frequent form)    ٭ ﯔ ﯕ ﮭ ٭

Practise :

(the *h* after the vowel is sounded, } "city" *shahr* شهر
i.e. breathed upon)                      } شهر شهر شهر شهر

(c)| At the end of a word, *h* (which as a consonant is always sounded) appears as :

(a rare form in handwriting,  ٭ ٭ ٭ ٭ ٭ ﮥ
but common in print)

or

(in handwriting but never  ﮫ ﮫ ﮫ
in print)

Practise writing both ways :

"the bottom, the end" *tah* ﺗﮫ or ﺗﻪ

(d) Standing alone, *h* is written ﻩ or ﻩ :

(1) moon, (2) month *mâh* ماه ماه

A final or lone *h*, ﮥ ﮫ or ﻩ is used also to indicate a short vowel, *é*, or occasionally *a*, at the end of a word. This is the only case of a short vowel being written in Persian :

"three" *sé* ﺳﻪ ﺳﻪ ﺳﻪ ﺳﻪ
"having come" *âmadé* آمده

This *h*-vowel is *not* used to indicate the *ézâfé*. We shall, however, use the same *é* letter to transliterate it, as it is exactly the same *sound* as the *ézâfé*.

## VOCABULARY

nine } نه نُه { *noh*
no } { *na*

three سـه/ـه *sé*

everything هر چیز *har chíz*

four چهار *chahár*

every هر *har*

thing چیز *chíz*

fish ماهی *máhí*

glass شیشه/ـشـیـشـه *shíshé*

ten ده *dah*

moon, month ماه *máh*

I give میدهم *mídeham*

After a short vowel-*h* the *ézâfé* sounds like *éyé*. It is not written:

$$\text{shíshéyé dar} \quad شیشه در$$

the glass (i.e. window) of the door

*P* in Persian is written پ (short) and پ (long). It belongs to the *b*-family, of which we now know

     بـ ب *b*

     تـ ت *t*

     نـ ن n (written deep ن in its full form)

     پـ پ *p*

As you see, it is important to get the dots right. *P* has three dots below it پـ پ *p*. Do not confuse it with چـ چ *ch*.

## VOCABULARY

screw پیچ *pích*

hand دست *dast*

on the right hand

    دست راست *dast-é-râst*

on the left hand

    دست چپ *dast-é-chap*

then پس *pas*

the right foot

    پای راست *pâ-yé-râst*

the left foot پای چپ *pâ-yé-chap*

eye چشم *cheshm*

father پدر *pedar*

right-hand راست *râst*

left-hand چپ *chap*

foot پا *pâ*

what ? چه چیز *ché chíz*

wool پشم *pashm*

brother برادر *barâdar*

Tehran تهران *tehrân*

Practise :

this thing is a screw *in chîz pîch ast* این چیز پیچ است

این چیز پیچ است get the dots right این چیز پیچ است

this month is cold *in mâh sard ast* این مه سرد است

این ماه سرد است این ماه سرد است این ماه سرد است

in this town everything is bad در این شهر هر چیز بد است

*dar in shahr har chîz bad ast* در این شهر هر چیز بد است

## EXERCISES

I. Write, pronouncing as you write :

در دست چپ مادرم و در دست راست پدرم است (*a*)

*dar dast-ê-chap mâdaram va dar dast-ê-râst pedaram ast*

*be-shomâ har chîz mîdêham* بشما هر چیز میدهم (*b*)

برادرمان هر ماه بشهر میاید (*c*)

*barâdaremân har mâh be-shahr mîâyad*

II. Translate and write out :

(*a*) I saw all three of (از) you in town.

(*b*) The door is on the left.

(*c*) In my glass there is no water (= water isn't).

(*d*) Every glass has water (in it).

III. Translate Ex. I.

IV. Read aloud your Persian for Ex. II.

## LESSON 8

Persian *k* has a short form ک and full forms :

کـ (printed, when preceded by a joined letter)

ك (printed, when alone)

It is handwritten ــکـ ـل ک *k*

and ــکـ ـل ک *k*

Hard Persian *g* (as in English gun) is written like *k* but with a double headstroke ⌐ instead of a single one :

(short)    ک     ﯕ     ﯖ     گ     ک    *g*

(full)     ک     ﯕ     ﮕ     گ     ک    *g*

(The full form is often ک in print. The ◦ is not important and is never written in handwriting.)

Practise :

    somebody, *kasî* (write the headstroke last) کسی

کسی    کسی    کسی    کسی    کسی    کسی    کسی

    butter, *karé* کره    کره    کره    کره

    plaster, *gach* گچ    گچ    گچ    گچ    گچ

    warm, *garm* گرم    گرم    گرم    گرم    گرم

*L.* Persian *l* is similar to ک ک *k* :

                   (short) ل

                   (full) ل

Two differences : (*a*) there is *no* headstroke ⌐ ; (*b*) ل full-form *l* is deeper than full-form *k* ک.

Practise :

     *k*   ک    ک    ک      ک    ک    ک

     *l*   ل    ل    ل      ل    ل    ل

   بله   بله   بله   بله   بله    " yes " *balé*     بله

   پل   پل   پل   پل   پل    " bridge " *pol*     پل

   پول   پول   پول   پول   پول    " money " *pŭl*     پول

Special joinings for these new letters:

(a) k-â and g-â are thus:

| WRITTEN | | | PRINTED |
|---|---|---|---|
| kâ | کا |
| gâ | گا |

(b) l-â is thus:

| WRITTEN | | | | PRINTED |
|---|---|---|---|---|
| lâ | لا or لا |

(c) k-l and g-l:

| WRITTEN | | | | | PRINTED |
|---|---|---|---|---|---|
| kl | کل کل |
| gl | گل گل |

(d) k-l-â and g-l-â:

| WRITTEN | | | PRINTED |
|---|---|---|---|
| klâ | کلا |
| glâ | گلا |

ا â is easily distinguishable from ل short l because short l joins to the next letter, whereas ا â does not, and from ل long l because long l has the ل final flourish to it, which ا â has not.

Practise:

(a) " work " kâr کار کار کار کار کار کار کار کار

"place " gâh گاه گاه گاه گاه گاه گاه گاه

(b) " good-morning " salâm سلام سلام سلام سلام سلام سلام سلام

(c) " chief, supreme " koll کل کل کل کل کل کل کل

"rose, flower " gol گل گل گل گل گل گل گل

(d) " class " kelâs کلاس کلاس کلاس کلاس کلاس

"pear " golâbi گلابی گلابی گلابی گلابی گلابی

## VOCABULARY

somebody کسی kasî

never هرگز hargez

butter کرهٔ karé

warm گرم garm

bridge پل pol

work کار kâr

pear گلابی golâbî

no, not a, none هیچ hîch

principal, head, supreme

   (adjective) کل koll

everybody هرکس harkas

did, he did کرد kard

plaster گچ gach

yes بله balé

money پول pûl

place گاه gâh

flower, rose گل gol

class کلاس kelâs

nothing هیچ چیز hîch chîz

nobody هیچ کس or میچکس hîchkas

## EXERCISES

I. Write, pronouncing as you write :

(a) او از کار آمد اواز کار آمد   û az-kâr âmad

(b) این گل در آب است این گل در آب است   în gol dar âb ast

(c) harkas bâ asb be-shahr mîâyad   هرکس با اسب بشهر میاید

(d) پول ندارم پول ندارم   pûl nadâram

II. Translate :

   (a) What am I giving him ?

   (b) I am giving him bread and butter.

   (c) Is he coming to work ? Yes, he is coming.

   (d) Has he money ? No, but he has work.

III. Translate Ex. I.

IV. Read aloud your answers to Ex. II.

## LESSON 9

خ kh خ. Persian kh, like the sound of ch in the Scots
word loch or the German ach, has a short form خ and a
full form خ. It is one of the چ ch- family. Be careful not
to confuse خ خ kh with چ چ ch.

Practise :

خوب   خوب   خوب   خوب "good" *khûb*

مرد خوب   مرد خوب   مرد خوب a good man *mard-é-khûb*

خیل "very" *khêili* (*êi* as in weight)

این خیل خوب است This is very good *în khêili khûb ast*

این خیل خوب است   این خیل خوب است

In the written combination خوا *kh-v-â* the و *v* is silent in modern Persian, hence we pronounce only *khâ* :

خوا = *khâ*

Write, pronouncing as you write :

خواب   خواب   خواب   خواب (sleep) *khâb*

میخوابم   میخوابم   میخوابم (I sleep) *mîkhâbam*

خواهش،   خواهش (a request) *khâhesh*

خواست   خواست (he wanted) *khâst*

Don't confuse خواب *khâb*, sleep (where the و is silent and the following ا is sounded, *â*) and خوب *khûb*, good, where the *û* و is sounded.

خواب   *khâb*

خوب   *khûb*

ف ف *f*. Persian *f* is written ف in full and ف in short form. Full ف is long and flat like ب *b* but it has a ring at its beginning, which ب *b* has not.

Practise :

ف ف ف ف ف ف ف ف ف ف ف *f*

(the dot is always over the ring : ف)

هفت   هفت   هفت   هفت *haft* seven

گرفت   گرفت   گرفت *gereft* took, he took

فردا   فردا   فردا   فردا *fardâ* tomorrow

The letter " 'ain " ع.

This letter is used in Persian to mark a break in the flow of speech, or, technically speaking, a glottal stop. If we pronounce " bottle " as it is pronounced in the Cockney dialect, we say " bo'l ". The " ' " represents here a glottal stop, a catch in the breath.

Those who speak German need only to think of their *Kehlkopfverschlusslaut* in such expressions as *die Arbeit, geeignet,* and *der Beamte.*

(*a*) In the middle of a word, *'ain* is written ﻊ (a triangle) :
　　　" afterwards " *ba'ad* بعد
　　　" meaning " *ma'ani* معنی

(*b*) Alone, it is written ع

(*c*) At the beginning of a word, it is written ﻋ (the ﻋ is a
　　　*consonant*) :
　　　　　" holiday " *'êid* عید
　　　　　(*êi* as in weight)

(*d*) At the end of a word it is written ع

Practise :

عید *'êid* عید عید عید عید
ساعت *sâ'at* an hour ساعت ساعت ساعت
معنی *ma'ani* معنی معنی معنی معنی
بعد *ba'ad* بعد بعد بعد بعد

ج چ. Another member of the چ خ *ch-kh* family is ج ج *j*, pronounced like our *j* in jewel.

| | | |
|---|---|---|
| ج | چ | *ch* |
| خ | خ | *kh* |
| ج | ج | *j* |

Do not confuse ج *j* with خ *kh*. The place of the dot is the only difference in writing.

Do not confuse the sound of ج *j* with گ *g*. ج *j* is soft, گ *g* is hard.

## VOCABULARY

took, he took گرفت *gereft*
good خوب *khûb*
request خواهش *khâhesh*
tomorrow فردا *fardâ*
sleep خواب *khâb*
holiday عید *'eid*
total, sum جمع *jam'*
meaning معنی *ma'ant*

seven هفت *haft*
I sleep میخوابم *mîkhâbam*
(he) wanted خواست *khâst*
very خیل *khêilî*
afterwards بعد *ba'ad*
Friday جمعه or جمع *jom'é*
place جا *ià*

## EXERCISES

I. Write, pronouncing as you write :

(a) من خواهش دارم *man khâhesh dâram* من خواهش دارم

(b) فردا جمعه است *fardâ jom'é ast* فردا جمعه است

(c) این مرد خیلی خوب است *în mard khêilî khûb ast*

(d) این جای خوب است *în jâ-yé-khûb ast*

(e) جمع سه و چهار هفت است *jam'-é-sé o chahâr haft ast*

II. Translate :

(a) I sleep well (= good). (b) That place is bad. (c) What (thing) has he in his (omit) hand ? (d) The water is not warm.

III. Translate Ex. I.

IV. Read aloud your answers to Ex. II.

## LESSON 10

*GH.* In Persian there is a guttural *gh*-sound, like a very heavily and thickly pronounced French *r*. It is the voiced equivalent of the letter خ *kh* which we had in the last lesson.

This *gh*-sound is spelt in one of two ways :

(*a*) ق *q̈ gh* like ف *f* but with two dots, and ‏ﻮ‏ deeper in the full form :

ق̈ق ق̈ق ق̈ق ق̈ق ق̈ق *gh* ق̈ق

(*b*) غ *ġ gh* like ع *'ain* with a dot :

غ̇غ غ̇غ غ̇غ غ̇غ *gh* غ̇غ غ̇غ

Practise :

، قبل از  قبل از  قبل از  قبل از before *ghabl az*

غیر از  از  غیر از other than *ghêir az*

تغیر  تغیر  تغیر change *taghyîr*

باغ  باغ  باغ  باغ garden *bâgh*

بقیه remainder, rest *baghîyé*

قرمز red *ghermez*

Learn carefully which words have غ and which words have ق in them, to avoid errors of spelling later.

Numerals in Persian are written → left to right, i.e. in the opposite direction to words. The reason for this is that the Arabic (from which both letters and numerals were taken into Persian) numerals are spoken in order of increasing size, i.e. smallest first. An Arab reads 1959 as nine and fifty and nine hundred and one thousand; a Persian reads them as one thousand and nine hundred and fifty and nine, as we do in English.

Here are the numerals 1–10, with their names in Persian:

| | | | | | | |
|---|---|---|---|---|---|---|
| ١ | yek | 1 | یک | ۶ or ٦ | shesh 6 | شش |
| ٢ | do | 2 | دو | ٧ | haft 7 | هفت |
| ٣ | sé | 3 | سه | ٨ | hasht 8 | هشت |
| ٣ or ٤ | chahâr 4 | چهار | | ٩ | noh 9 | نه |
| ٥ or ٥ | panj 5 | پنج | | ١٠ | dah 10 | ده |

$$١٩٥٩ = 1959$$

When the numbers are used with a noun or an under-stood noun, in conversation we use the word

نفر *nafar* following the number, to indicate people, and

تا *tâ* following the number, to indicate things or animals.

نفر *nafar* and تا *tâ* are not used if the noun denotes an abstract idea or a measure of time:

دو ساعت two hours       سه روز three days (*rûz* = day)

The noun itself is always used in the *singular* form after a number:

two friends *dô nafar dûst* دو نفر دوست

three requests *sé khâhesh* سه خواهش

two horses *dô tâ asb* دو تا اسب

four builders *chahâr nafar bennâ* چهار نفر بنا

I have five (of them) *panj tâ dâram* پنج تا دارم

I saw six thieves *shesh nafar dozd dîdam* شش نفر دزد دیدم

## Vocabulary

before قبل از *ghabl az*　　　　other than غیر از *ghêir az*
garden باغ *bâgh*　　　　　　change تغییر *taghyîr*
red قرمز *ghermez*　　　　　rest, remainder بقیه *baghîyé*

(The numerals 1 to 10, given earlier this lesson, should also be learned.)

## Exercises

I. Write, pronouncing as you write :

١ شش با چهار ده است　　٢ من سه تا گل دارم
٣ هرکس آمد　　　　　٤ او آب گرم خواست

II. Translate :

1. He didn't want money.
2. Three glasses have (= has) warm water (in them), and two have (= has) cold water.
3. I gave (to-) him bread and butter.
4. In his (omit) hand he has three loaves of bread (*sé tâ nân*).

III. Translate Ex. I.

IV. Read your Persian for Ex. II.

## LESSON 11

*Arabic letters.* The Arabic alphabet contains letters which have distinct and different sound-values in Arabic, but which, when used in Persian, have the same sound as each other.

For example, Arabic has four letters *z* :

ز (which we have had already)
ذ like د *d* with a dot
ض　ظ

and ظ which only has a full form but which joins to its left, nevertheless.

ز, ذ, ض, and ظ have different sounds in Arabic. They all have *one and the same sound* in Persian—z.

woman *zan* زن      some *ba'azî* بعضى
paper *kâghaz* كاغذ      noon, midday *zoɦr* ظهر

A native Persian word is usually spelt with ز for *z*, though not always. Most words containing ذ, ض, and ظ are foreign words, usually Arabic.

$$ ذ \ ض \ ظ = ز $$

There are in Arabic three letters *s* :

     ـس س (we know already)
     ـص ص like ض *z* undotted
     ـث ث like پ *p* but dotted above

$$ ض \ ث = س $$

half *nesf* نصف      cause, reason *bâ*es باعث
        dirty *kasîf* كثيف

Two letters *t* :

     ت ة (see lesson 5)
     ط undotted

$$ ط = ت $$

direction *taràf* طرف      electric battery *bâtrî* باطرى
and two letters *h* :

     ه ه ه ه ه (see lesson 7)

ح ‎ ← like چ ، خ ، ج but undotted :

morning *sobh* صبح       letter (of the alphabet) *harf* حرف

$$\boxed{\text{ح} = \text{ه}}$$

To summarize the new letters :

ذ ض ظ = ز

ص ث = س

ط = ت

ح = ه

The last letter we have to learn is not in the Arabic alphabet—it has been added by the Persians to represent a sound never found in Arabic, and not often found in Persian. It is :

ژ *zh*

This is an ر *r* with three dots, and gives the sound of *s* in our word pleasure, or of French *j* in *je, jour.*

     lampshade (French *abat-jour*) *âbâzhûr* آباژور

     agency (French *agence*) *âzhâns* آژانس

     *Zhâlé* (a Persian girl's name) ژاله

This completes the alphabet, with the exception of a few orthographic signs (not letters), which we shall deal with later in the book.

Here now is the whole alphabet, in the order used in Persian dictionaries, and with their Persian names :

| | | | | | |
|---|---|---|---|---|---|
| ا | *alef* | â | ت | *té* | t |
| ب | *bé* | b | ث | *sé* | s |
| پ | *pé* | p | ج | *jîm* | j |

| | | | | | |
|---|---|---|---|---|---|
| چ | chîm | ch | ظ | zâ | z |
| ح | hé hotî | h | ع | 'ain | ' |
| خ | khé | kh | غ | ghain | gh |
| د | dâl | d | ف | fé | f |
| ذ | zâl | z | ق | ghâf | gh |
| ر | ré | r | ک | kâf | k |
| ز | zé | z | گ | gâf | g |
| ژ | zhé | zh | ل | lâm | l |
| س | sîn | s | م | mîm | m |
| ش | shîn | sı | ن | nûn | n |
| ص | sâd | s | و | vâv | v, û, ô |
| ض | zâd | z | ه | hé havaz | h, é |
| ط | tâ | t | ی | yé | y, î |

ا is called *alef maddé*. ⁻ the long sign is called *maddé*.

Of the above, you must remember that :

ا
د ذ
ر ز ژ
و
} are not joined to the letter following them,
i.e. they have no short form.

ع     is a consonant.

ا     is used to introduce vowels beginning words,
whether the vowel is short or long.

و
ی
} are both consonants and long vowels.

ه   { at the end of a word is either *h* or a short
vowel, *é*, or *a*.
anywhere else : is *h*.

Of the sounds for which there is more than one letter,
س *s* is far more common than ث and ص

| ز *z* | „ | „ | „ | ذ, ض, and ظ |
| ت *t* | „ | „ | „ | ط |
| ه *h* | „ | „ | „ | ح |

The two letters غ *ghain* and ق *ghâf*: both are found
very frequently, غ in native Persian words and ق in
Arabic loan-words.

## VOCABULARY

| | |
|---|---|
| some بعضی *ba'azî* | half نصف *nesf* |
| noon, midday ظهر *zohr* | cause, reason باعث *bâ'es* |
| paper کاغذ *kâghaz* | dirty کثیف *kasîf* |
| direction طرف *taraf* | dirt کثافت *kesâfat* |
| morning صبح *sobh* | electric battery باطری *bâtrî* |
| agency آژنس *âzhens* | lampshade آبازور *âbâzhûr* |

## EXERCISES

I. Copy out the alphabet, without any explanation or
names of any letters; arrange the letters in families,
thus:

| ك | ف | ع | ط | ص | س | ر | د | ج | ب | ١ |
| گ | ق | غ | ظ | ض | ش | ز | ذ | چ | پ | |
| | | | | | | ژ | | ح | ت | |
| | | | | | | | | خ | ث | |

ل   م   ن   و   ه   ی

II. (a) Which letters are never joined to their left, i.e.
have no short form?

    (b) List the letters for *z*, *s*, *t*, and *h* which are mostly
used for foreign words.

(c) What is the commonest way of writing (i) *s*, (ii) *z*, (iii) *t*, (iv) *h* ?

(d) A word beginning with a vowel other than *alef maddé* must be introduced by . . . ?

(e) Is *'ain* a vowel or a consonant ?

(f) What is the short form of ی *ye* ?

III. Translate :

1. My friend came to the bridge.
2. I am coming before you.
3. What did I give him ?  Nothing.
4. He has bread and water.

IV. Read :

۱ من بشما این سه تا نان را دادم و آن آب را

۲ غیر از این ندارم    ۳ یک دوست از تهران آمد

۴ در این شهر آب خوب نیست    ۵ او فردا از پل با پول میاید

V. Read your Persian for Ex. III.

VI. Translate Ex. IV.

# PART TWO

## Grammar

صرف

# LESSON 12

The personal pronouns in Persian are :

| 1st | من | man | I | ما | mâ | we |
| 2nd | شما | shomâ | you | شما | shomâ | you |
| 3rd | او | û | he or she | ایشان | îshân | they (people) |
| | آن | ân | it | آنها | ânhâ | they (things) |

You will notice that (1) شما shomâ "you", like its English
equivalent, is used for one person or several; (2) there is
no "gender" whatsoever in Persian words. Hence we use
او û for both "he" and "she". The plural of او û is
ایشان îshân "they", only used when speaking of people;
(3) things are designated by آن ân "it" (literally "that")
whose plural is آنها ânhâ "they" (literally "those things").

When speaking of animals, we can use either او û and
ایشان îshân or ân and ânhâ آن آنها, though we usually use
strictly آن ân and آنها ânhâ for the lower animals.

The Persian verb is a very simple thing to master: there
are a mere handful of irregulars, and even they follow a
clear pattern. Those students who have studied French or
German or Russian will find the Persian verb refreshingly
simple.

The infinitive of Persian verbs always ends in either دن-
-dan or تن- -tan:

| to get or take | گرفتن | gereftan |
| to eat or drink | خوردن | khordan |
| to see | دیدن | dîdan |
| to give | دادن | dâdan |

43

If we take the ن- -*an* off these verbs we have :

-گرفت *gereft-*  خورد- *khord-*

-دید *díd-*  داد- *dâd-*

which is the Past Stem.

To the Past Stem we add the personal endings, and this gives us the Past Tense :

|  |  |  |  |  |
|---|---|---|---|---|
| 1st | م- | -*am* | یم- | -*ím* |
| 2nd | ید- | -*íd* | ید- | -*íd* |
| 3rd | { (no ending) | | ند- | -*and* |
|  | (no ending) | | (no ending) | |

The conjugation in the past tense of the verb گرفتن *gereftan* to take or to get, is therefore :

(1) I took  گرفتم (من) (*man*) *gereftam*

(2) you took  گرفتید (شما) (*shomâ*) *gereftíd* } singular

(3) { he took  گرفت (او) (*û*) *gereft*

{ it took  گرفت (آن) (*ân*) *gereft* }

(1) we took  گرفتیم (ما) (*mâ*) *gereftím*

(2) you took  گرفتید (شما) (*shomâ*) *gereftíd* } plural

(3) { they (people) took گرفتند (ایشان) (*íshân*) *gereftand*

{ they (things) took گرفت (آنها) (*ânhâ*) *gereft* }

You will notice here that (*a*) the you-person (2nd) ending is the same for singular and plural, as in English ; (*b*) the 3rd person singular has no ending—the past stem *itself* is used, with no further ending ; (*c*) in the 3rd person plural, if the subject is *inanimate* (i.e. if we use آنها *ânhâ*) the verb is used in the 3rd person singular form. We only use the plural 3rd person ending ‫ند‬- -*and* with ‫ایشان‬ *ishân*, i.e. in referring to people or higher animals.

The -ِ- vowel in ‫ـِ‬- and ‫ید‬- is long : -*im, id*.

The unwritten vowel in ‫م‬- and ‫ند‬- is a short *a* : -*am*, -*and*.

Here are the past tenses of the other three verbs, ‫دیدن‬ to see, ‫دادن‬ to give, and ‫خوردن‬ to eat or drink : ·

*dîdan* ‫دیدن‬ to see, past stem -‫دید‬ *dîd*-

|     | | |
| --- | --- | --- |
| (1) | I saw (‫من‬) ‫دیدم‬ <br> (*man*) *dîdam* | we saw (‫ما‬) ‫دیدیم‬ <br> (*mâ*) *dîdîm* |
| (2) | you saw (‫شما‬) ‫دیدید‬ <br> (*shomâ*) *dîdîd* | you saw (‫شما‬) ‫دیدید‬ <br> (*shomâ*) *dîdîd* |
| (3) | he/she saw ‫دید‬ (‫او‬) <br> (*û*) *dîd* <br> it saw ‫دید‬ (‫آن‬) <br> (*ân*) *dîd* | they (people) saw (‫ایشان‬) ‫دیدند‬ <br> (*îshân*) *dîdand* <br> they (things) saw ‫دید‬ (‫آنها‬) <br> (*ânhâ*) *dîd* |

*dâdan* ‫دادن‬ to give, past stem -‫داد‬ *dâd*-

|     | | |
| --- | --- | --- |
| (1) | (*man*) *dâdam* ‫دادم‬ (‫من‬) | (*mâ*) *dâdîm* ‫دادیم‬ (‫ما‬) |
| (2) | (*shomâ*) *dâdîd* ‫دادید‬ (‫شما‬) | (*shomâ*) *dâdîd* ‫دادید‬ (‫شما‬) |
| (3) | (*û*) *dâd* ‫داد‬ (‫او‬) <br> (*ân*) *dâd* ‫داد‬ (‫آن‬) | (*îshân*) *dâdand* ‫دادند‬ (‫ایشان‬) <br> (*ânhâ*) *dâd* ‫داد‬ (‫آنها‬) |

*khordan* ‫خوردن‬ to eat or drink, past stem -‫خورد‬ *khord*-

|     | | |
| --- | --- | --- |
| (1) | (*man*) *khordam* ‫خوردم‬ (‫من‬) | (*mâ*) *khordîm* ‫خوردیم‬ (‫ما‬) |
| (2) | (*shomâ*) *khordîd* ‫خوردید‬ (‫شما‬) | (*shomâ*) *khordîd* ‫خوردید‬ (‫شما‬) |
| (3) | (*û*) *khord* ‫خورد‬ (‫او‬) <br> (*ân*) *khord* ‫خورد‬ (‫آن‬) | (*îshân*) *khordand* ‫خوردند‬ (‫ایشان‬) <br> (*ânhâ*) *khord* ‫خورد‬ (‫آنها‬) |

If the subject of the verb is emphasized, then we use the verb together with the personal pronoun (which we have bracketed in the tables above)—otherwise, the ending of the verb itself indicates who the subject is :

گرفتم I got    دادند they gave    خوردیم we ate

For the next few lessons, until we deal with the Present Tense in Lesson 14a, we shall give verbs in the Vocabularies first in the Infinitive, then the Past Stem, thus :

to see دید- دیدن dîdan, dîd-

The Past Stem is not given in dictionaries written for Persians, as it is always regularly formed. Note that the verb usually stands last in its clause.

## VOCABULARY

I من man
you شما shomâ
he/she او û
it آن ân
we ما mâ
they ایشان îshân (people)
آنها ânhâ (things)

to take/get گرفتن gereftan, past stem گرفت- gereft-
to eat/drink خوردن khordan, past stem خورد- khord-
to see دیدن dîdan, past stem دید- dîd-
to give دادن dâdan, past stem داد- dâd-

## EXERCISES

I. Translate orally into Persian :

(1) You gave bread to that man.

(2) We saw a friend with his horse in town.

(3) He got bread and water.

(4) They ate bread with butter.

(5) I gave (to-) him everything.

II. Write out Ex. L

III. Read Ex. II.

IV. Read aloud :

| | |
|---|---|
| ۲ ما ماهی با آب و نان و کره خوردیم | ۱ در شهر اسب دیدم |
| ٤ ایشان آن آب و نان را خوردند | ۳ آن مرد سه تا اسب در شهر گرفت |
| ٦ اسب دیدیم | ۵ بنا پول گرفت |
| ۸ این اسب آب خورد | ۷ بمرد پول دادم |
| ۱۰ ایشان دو نفر را دیدند | ۹ در تهران هر چیز دیدم |

V. Translate Ex. IV.

VI. Copy Ex. IV.

## LESSON 12*a*

### فرهنگ *farhang*, Vocabulary

| | |
|---|---|
| then پس *pas* | to go رفتن – رفت *raftan, raft-* |
| bus اتوبوس *otóbús* | to be بودن – بود *búdan, búd-* |
| late دیر *dír* | to come آمدن – آمد *ámadan, ámad-* |
| office دفتر *daftar* | early, quickly زود *zúd* |
| bath حمام *hammám* | cause, reason سبب *sabab* |
| yesterday دیروز *dírúz* | air, weather هوا *havá* |
| coffee قهوه *ghahvé* | (at) night, شب *shab* |
| for this reason باین سبب *bé-ín sabab* | (in the) evening }  |

Using this vocabulary, read aloud the following text :

### دیروز

دیروز هوا خیلی گرم بود. من زود حمام گرفته و قهوه و نان و کره خوردم.
پس بشهر رفتم. با اتوبوس رفتم. اتوبوس دیر آمد و باین سبب من بدفتر
دیر آمدم. شب من بمنزل آمدم و شام خوردم.

Take each sentence again slowly, practising its pronunciation:

*dîrûz havâ khêîlî garm bûd.*　　١ دیروز هوا خیلی گرم بود.

٢ من زود حمام گرفتم و قهوه و نان وکره خوردم

*man zûd hammâm gereftam va ghaḥvé va nân va karé khordam.*

*pas bé-shaḥr raftam.*　　٣ پس بشهر رفتم

*bâ otôbûs raftam.*　　٤ با اتوبوس رفتم

٥ اتوبوس دیر آمد و باین سبب من بدفتر دیر آمدم

*otôbûs dîr âmad va bé-în sabab man bé-daftar dîr âmadam.*

٦ شب من بمنزل آمدم و شام خوردم

*shab man bé-manzel âmadam va shâm khordam.*

In this lesson we have three new verbs:

to go رفتن　 to come آمدن　 to be بودن

These verbs all form their past tenses regularly, by first taking ن- -*an* off their infinitives to get the past stem:

رفت-　　آمد-　　بود-

and adding the regular endings.

All Persian verbs, without a single exception, form their past tenses regularly in this way.

|  | to come آمدن *âmadan* |  | to be بودن *bûdan* |
|---|---|---|---|
|  | past stem -آمد *âmad-* |  | past stem -بود *bûd-* |
| (1) | آمدیم　 آمدم | بودیم　 بودم |  |
| (2) | آمدید　 آمدید | بودید　 بودید |  |
| (3){ | آمدند　 آمد | بودند　 بود |  |
|  | آمد　 آمد | بود　 بود |  |

to go رفتن *raftan*

past stem رفت- *raft-*

| | | | |
|---|---|---|---|
| (1) | رفتم | | رفتیم |
| (2) | رفتید | | رفتید |
| (3) { | رفت | | رفتند |
| | رفت | | رفت |

تمرین *tamrín*, EXERCISES

I. Conjugate گرفتن and رفتن in the past tense.

II. Fill in the blank spaces in these past tenses :

(a) to come : آمدن *âmadan*     to be : بودن *bûdan*

past stem -آمد *âmad-*     past stem — -

| | | | | | |
|---|---|---|---|---|---|
| (1) | — آمدم | — آمدیم | من بودم | | ما — |
| (2) | شما — | — آمدید | شما — | | — بودید |
| (3) { | او — | — آمدند | او — | | ایشان — |
| | آن — | آنها — | آن — | | — بود |

III. Answer orally, in complete Persian sentences, these questions on the text :

۱ دیروز هوا خیلی گرم بود؟

۲ من چه زود گرفتم؟

۳ من چه طور (how ? = *ché-tour*) قهوه و نان و کره خوردم؟

٤ و چه طور من بدفتر رفتم؟

۵ دیروز اتوبوس دیر آمد یا زود آمد؟

IV. Write out your answers to Ex. III.

V. Translate into Persian :

Yesterday I went late to the office. The weather in Teheran was very warm, and the bus was (came) late. In the evening I went home and had (ate) supper.

## LESSON 13

*Negative verbs.* Any verb, irrespective of tense, is made negative by prefixing to it نـ *na-*. The prefix نـ *na-* is *always stressed* in pronunciation.

> you didn't get شما نگرفتید *shomâ nàgereftîd*
>
> I didn't see ندیدم *nàdîdam*
>
> he/she/it wasn't نبود *nàbûd*

(Occasionally during this book a grave ' accent will be put over the stressed syllable, to remind you that the stress falls there.)

Pronounce :

(1) *man pûl nàgereftam* I didn't get any money. ۱ من پول نگرفتم

(2) *shomâ shâm nàkhordîd* ۲ شما شام نخوردید

> You didn't eat supper.

(3) *îshân bé-man pûl nàdâdand* ۳ ایشان بمن پول ندادند

> They didn't give me money.

Before a verb beginning with a vowel, نـ *nà-* becomes نیـ *này-* (pronounced like English " nigh ") :

> He didn't come او نیامد *û nàyâmad*

In Persian we use *double negatives*, for example :

> او هیچ چیز نگرفت *û hîch chîz nàgereft*
>
> literally : he didn't take nothing ( هیچ چیز ).

Here are some more negative expressions. They all require the verb prefixed with نـ *na-* or نیـ *nay-* :

| | |
|---|---|
| هیچ جا nowhere (" no place ") | جا place *jâ* |
| هیچ وقت never (" no time ") | وقت time *vaght* |
| هیچ کس nobody (" no person ") | کس person *kas* |

هیچ کدام none (of them) ("no which")   کدام which ? *kodâm*

هیچ no, not a single

هیچ چیز nothing (" no thing ")      چیز thing *chîz*

In all these cases the هیچ *hîch* may be written on as one word with its successor, but the separate forms are more common :

هیچجا or هیچ جا      هیچوقت or هیچ وقت

هیچ چیز or هیچچیز      هیچکس or هیچ کس

Practise :

۱ من شما را دیروز هیچ جا ندیدم

(1) I didn't see you anywhere (" nowhere ") yesterday.

۲ در دفترش هیچوقت نبودم

(2) I was (" wasn't ") never in his office.

۳ دیروز هیچکس بمنزل نیامد

(3) Nobody came (" didn't come ") home yesterday.

٤ کدام مرد رفت؟ هیچ کدام نرفت

(4) Which man went ? None of them went (" didn't go ").

۵ دیروز هیچ پول نگرفتم

(5) I didn't get any (" no ") money yesterday.

۶ هیچ چیز نخوردیم

(6) We ate (" didn't eat ") nothing.

*The Definite Direct Object.* If we use a verb with a *direct object* in Persian, and that direct object is a definite known one, we usually suffix را -*râ* to the object. This را -*râ* can be written on to the word, or written separately. را is *not* a word, it is a particle, a suffix. But because it indicates something definite, we can often translate it into English as " the ", using the definite article. There is of course no definite article as such in Persian.

Compare :

I got money *man pûl gereftam* ۱ من پول گرفتم
(i.e. some money—any money—an unknown quantity) with

I got the money *man pûl-râ gereftam* ۲ من پول را گرفتم
(i.e. a particular, known sum which we have already mentioned).

In sentence ۲ above we could write پول را as پولرا one word, if we wished. It is usually a matter of personal choice.

Similarly, in the negative, compare :

I didn't get the money ۳ من پولرا نگرفتم
*man pûl-râ nàgereftam*

with

I didn't get (any) money ۳ من پول نگرفتم
*man pûl nàgereftam*

را *-râ* can never be suffixed to هیچ *hîch* or its compounds :

I didn't get any money at all من هیچ پول نگرفتم
*man hîch pûl nàgereftam*

را *-râ* is also suffixed to the personal pronouns :

| | | |
|---|---|---|
| *marâ* مرا (the ن is omitted) | me |
| *shomârâ* شمارا | you (object) |
| *ûrâ* اورا | him, her |
| *ânrâ* آنرا | it (object) |
| *mârâ* مارا (note : two long *â*'s) | us |
| *îshânrâ* ایشانرا | them (people) |
| *ânhârâ* آنهارا | them (things) |

Note : (a) مرا = را + من. The n ن is always dropped and the result is always written as one word.

(b) In مارا us, both â's are long.

In مرا me, the first a is short, the second long.

Pronounce : (a as in " hand ") marâ مرا me.

(â as in " father ") mârâ مارا us.

These pronouns denote the *direct object* of the verb. Don't use them for the *indirect object*. Compare :

The man saw us مرد مارا دید

with

The man gave us (= *to* us) money مرد بما پول داد

The *indirect object* (= to me, to us, etc.) is of course expressed with the بِ bé prefix :

| | | | |
|---|---|---|---|
| to me بمن bé-man | | to us بما bé-mâ | |
| to you بشما bé-shomâ | | to you بشما bé-shomâ | |
| to him<br>to her } باو bé-û | | to them { | بایشان bé-îshân (people) |
| | | | بآنها bé-ânhâ (things) |
| to it بآن be-ân | | | |

In English the " to " in " The man gave (to) us money " is usually omitted. In Persian we *must* use بِ bé- " to ".

*mard bé-mâ pûl dâd* The man gave us money مرد بما پول داد

and

*mard pûl-râ bé-mâ dâd* مرد پولرا بما داد

The man gave us *the* money (پولرا money is here the definite direct object, with را -râ suffixed, and بما (to) us is an indirect object, with بِ bé- prefixed). The direct object normally precedes the indirect one in Persian.

## فرهنگ *farhang*

| | |
|---|---|
| no, not a هیچ *hich* | nowhere هیچ جا *hich jâ* |
| place جا *jâ* | none of them هیچ کدام *hich kodâm* |
| which ? کدام *kodâm* | never هیچ وقت *hich vaght* |
| time وقت *vaght* | father پدر *pedar* |
| mother مادر *mâdar* | brother برادر *barâdar* |
| sister خواهر *khâhar* (*v* silent) | daughter, girl دختر *dokhtar* |
| boy, son پسر *pesar* | |

Note : (*a*) Do not confuse پدر father with پسر son. (*b*) پدر, برادر, مادر, and دختر are historically the same words as their English counterparts, of course.

## تمرین *tamrîn*

I. Translate into Persian :

(1) My father didn't give me any money.

(2) He didn't give me the money.

(3) My brother didn't go anywhere yesterday.

(4) I gave him nothing.

(5) My mother gave my sister nothing (را or به ?).

(6) His daughter never came to the office.

(7) Nobody went.

(8) His father came to the office late yesterday.

(9) That bus never comes early.

(10) I saw the bus. We saw a bus.

II. Translate into English :

١ باو هیچ چیز ندادم     ٢ شما با اتوبوس آمدید؟

٣ هوا خیلی گرم نبود     ٣ هیچوقت در این شهر نبودم

٥ باران رفت     ٤ من در شهر هیچکس ندیدم

٧ شما شام نخوردید     ٨ پولش را هیچ وقت نگرفتم

٩ دخترش و برادرش دیروز در شهر بودند     ١٠ این چیز را هیچ جا ندیدند

III. Read aloud your answers to Ex. I and Ex. II.

IV. Complete these conjugations in the past tense :

| not to take نگرفتن | not to eat نخوردن |
|---|---|
| past stem –نگرفت | past stem –نخورد |

| من نگرفتم | — نگرفتیم | — نخوردم | ما — |
| شما — | — نگرفتید | — نخوردید | شما — |
| او — | ایشان — | — او | ایشان — |
| آن — | — نگرفت | — آن | آنها — |

V. Put an appropriate negative with هیچ in these sentences : (e.g. شما هیچ جا نرفتید ← شما نرفتید)

١ کدام مرد را دیدند؟ — — ندیدند

٢ ما — در شهر نبودیم

٣ دیروز ایشان — — نرفتند

٤ چه گرفتید؟ — — نگرفتم

٥ — — ندیدم

## LESSON 13*a*

The word هیچ and its compounds answer questions. These questions are usually introduced by special question words.

هیچ itself, with a noun, answers the question چه *ché* (colloquially *chî*) what ?

Similarly,

| هیچوقت | answers the question | | | کی *kêi* when ? |
|---|---|---|---|---|
| هیچ جا | ,, | ,, | ,, | کجا *kojâ* where ? |
| هیچکس | ,, | ,, | ,, | کی *ki* who ? |
| هیچ کدام | ,, | ,, | ,, | کدام *kodâm* which ? |
| هیچ چیز | ,, | ,, | ,, | چه چیز *ché chîz* what (thing) ? |

Note: ‌کی *kêi* when ? and کی *kî* who ? are written alike. In all of these cases هیچ and its compounds give a *negative* answer : where ? nowhere ; who ? nobody ; when ? never.

When we make a question in Persian, we do not alter the order of the words. All we need to do is to raise the voice towards the end of the question.

In print, we sometimes find a European question mark used in reverse ؟. But this is by no means compulsory : in fact we should get accustomed to reading Persian without any punctuation at all, or at most the full stop . , question mark ؟, and parentheses ( ).

As well as هیچ *hîch,* which is a negative answer, we have several positive answer words, some of which can be pre-fixed, like هیچ, to the answer. We shall deal for the moment with just a few :

هر *har* any, every    آن *ân* that    این *în* this

| Question | Negative Answer | Positive Answers | | |
|---|---|---|---|---|
| چه what ? | هیچ no, none | هر every | آن that | این this |
| کی when ? | هیچوقت never | هروقت every time | آنوقت then | حالا now * |
| کجا where ? | هیچجا nowhere | هرجا every-where | آنجا there | اینجا here |
| کی who ? | هیچکس nobody | هرکس every-body | این شخص this person / آن شخص that person | |
| کدام which ? | هیچکدام none of them | هریکی each one | آن یکی that one / این یکی this one | |
| چه چیز what ? | هیچ چیز nothing | هرچیز everything | آن چیز that thing / این چیز this thing | |

Note: (*a*) * " now " is a special word, حالا ـ حالا *hâlâ*. (*b*) اينشخص this person and آنشخص that person do not form with كس a person ; they form with the Arabic word شخص *shakhs*, written separately or as one word. (*c*) اين يكى *in yekî* this one and آن يكى *ân yekî* that one do not form with كدام, but with يكى " one ".

In addition to the above list, we can add an entirely new word :

چه طور *ché tôur ?* or چطور *chétôur ?* how ? in what way ?

negative answer : هيچ طور   in no way, in no manner, by no means.

positive answers :   هر طور in any way, in every way.

اينطور or اين طور in this way, like this, thus, so.

آنطور or آن طور in that way, like that, thus, so.

چطور or چه طور has also another meaning : as an adjective it means what sort of ?, what kind of ? It takes no *ézâfé*.

What sort of house is it ?   چه طور منزلى است؟
*ché tôur manzeli ast ?*

and the answer : This kind   اين طور *întôur*.

Also : of another kind   طور ديگر *tôur-é-dîgar* (*ézâfé* here)

of every kind   هر طور *har tôur*

(of) that kind   آن طور *ân tôur*

Two other expressions meaning " what kind of ? " :

چگونه *chégûné* (one word) ) " what kind of ? "

چه جور *ché jûr* (two words) ) (no *ézâfé*)

We do not usually employ the answer forms corresponding to these expressions ; instead we use the constructions with طور above.

را. The particle را, used for the definite direct object, comes after the whole group of words denoting the object. For example :

من آن مرد را دیدم   I saw that man

آن مرد دوستم را دیدند .   They saw that man, my friend

It is not necessary, as you see, to use را after every word : را is a particle which appears only *once* after the last word-unit of the definite direct object. Even if we have a complicated direct object such as a string of words connected with the *ézâfé* (see Lessons 6 and 16), we merely put one را, written either as a separate word or on to the last consonant of the last word :

حسن پدر احمد را دیدند

*hasan-é-pedar-é-ahmad-râ dîdand*

They saw Hassan, the father of Ahmad

or if the objects are several, linked together with and, the same rule applies :

پدر و مادر و خواهر و برادر را ندیدم

*pedar o mâdar o khâhar o barâdar râ nàdîdam*

I didn't see (my) father, mother, brother and sister.

## فرهنگ

| | | | |
|---|---|---|---|
| now حالا | | here اینجا | |
| then آن وقت | | there آنجا | |
| every time } | | everywhere هرجا | |
| whenever } هروقت | | nowhere هیچ جا | |
| always } | | that one آن یکی | |
| never هیچ وقت | | where ؟ کجا | |
| this time این وقت | | that person آن شخص *ânshakhs* | |
| this person این شخص *înshakhs* | | nobody هیچکس | |
| everybody هر کس | | this one این یکی | |

| | | | |
|---|---|---|---|
| none هیچ | each one هریکی | |
| that one آن یکی | morning صبح *sobh* | |
| afternoon بعد از ظهر *ba'ad az zohr* | noon ظهر *zohr* | |
| motor car ماشین *mâshin* | tea چای *châi* | |
| lunch ناهار *nâhâr* | no نه *na*, خیر *khêir*, نخیر *ndkhêir* | |
| taxi تاکسی *tâksî* | | |

### Text

Note: In this text, and throughout most of the book, an unwritten *ézâfé* (*é*, *éyé*, or *îyé*) will be shown with an * asterisk. This is merely as an aid to accurate reading—it is of course never there in a Persian text.

حسن دیروز کجا رفت؟ حسن دیرور هیچ جا نرفت ــ حسن منزل بود.
حسن کی بتهران رفت؟ هیچ وقت بتهران نرفت. کی باحسن منزل بود؟ هیچ کس
نبود. صبح احمد کجا بود؟ اینجا نبود ــ اورا ندیدم؟ نه ندیدم. پدر * احمد
را دیدم و او در دفتر بود. احمد اینجا با مادر و خواهر خود بود.

### تمرین

I. Answer orally these questions on the text :

١ دیروز حسن کجا بود؟

٢ دیروز احمد کجا بود؟

٣ دیروز احمد را دیدید؟

٤ حسن کی بتهران رفت؟

٥ کی باحسن منزل بود؟

II. Write out your answers to Ex. I.

III. Read aloud the questions in Ex. I, reading the appropriate answer from Ex. II after each question.

IV. Write in Persian :

(1) Did nobody come yesterday ?

(2) I saw where he went. Where did he go ? He went there.

(3) How did they go home? They went home this
way: by bus and by taxi.

(4) I have never been (= I wasn't never) in Tehran.
Were you there?

(5) Which bus did you take? This one or that one?

(6) I never saw this person at the office. I never saw
anybody (= didn't never see nobody) there.

(7) Where was his brother at that time? His brother
was at that time in Tehran.

V. Read aloud your Persian for Ex. IV.


## LESSON 14

*Plurals.* In classical Persian, the rule for forming plurals
of nouns was:

(a) add ان- *-ân* to animate nouns (people or higher
animals).

(b) add ها- *-hâ* to inanimate nouns (lower animals or
things).

But in modern Persian we can use ها- or ان- for most
animate nouns. We always use ها- for inanimate ones.

دوست a friend

دوستان or دوستها friends

زن woman

زنان or زنها women

چیز thing

چیزها things

ماشین car (*mâshîn*)

ماشینها cars

ان- after a long ا â becomes یان- -yân for reasons of euphony :

| | |
|---|---|
| آقا gentleman | بنا builder |
| آقایان gentlemen | بنایان builders |

and in nouns ending in a vowel ه- -é, the ه- -é is dropped and we add گان -égân :

| | |
|---|---|
| بنده slave, bandé | پرنده bird, parandé |
| بندگان slaves, bandégân | پرندگان birds, parandégân |

Some animate nouns have retained exclusively ان- -ân as their proper plural suffix, and never take ها- -hâ, even in modern Persian. Among these few are most animates ending in ا -â and ه- -é, such as those above.

The easiest way to learn Persian plurals is to study these few rules :

(a) All inanimates take ها- -hâ.

(b) A *few* animates take exclusively ان- or یان- or گان- : these can be learnt as they occur.

(c) Most animates can take either ان- or ها- indiscriminately.

(d) A certain number of words borrowed from Arabic form their plurals as in Arabic, but these *nearly always* have in addition a ان- or ها- Persian plural, which is universally accepted by educated Iranians. Thus :

منزل manzel, house, is an Arabic word borrowed into Persian.

Its Arabic plural is منازل manâzel (a medial â is inserted).
Its Persian plural is منزلها or منزلها manzelhâ.
Both the native and the Arabic plurals are acceptable.

Do not attempt yet to learn Arabic plurals as such: they will be dealt with later.

The ending ‎ان‎- is always, if possible, joined to its word. The ending ‎ها‎- can be written either joined or disjoined. After a vowel ‎ه‎- -é it *must* be disjoined, to avoid the confusion of having two letters ‎ه‎ together.

For example:

| | | |
|---|---|---|
| woman | ‎زن‎ | *zan* |
| women (animate plural) | ‎زنان‎ | *zanân* |
| women (inanimate plural) | { ‎زنها‎ | *zan-hâ* |
| | or | |
| | ‎زنها‎ | *zanhâ* |

but

| | | |
|---|---|---|
| child | ‎بچه‎ | *bachché* |
| children | ‎بچهها‎ | *bachché-hâ* |

### ‎تلفظ‎ *talaffoz* PRONUNCIATION

The plural endings ‎ان‎- and ‎ها‎- are always *stressed*.

Pronounce
| | |
|---|---|
| *âghâyǎn* | ‎آقایان‎ |
| *zanǎn* | ‎زنان‎ |
| *zanhǎ* | ‎زنها‎ |

*Hold* the double } *bachché-hǎ* ‎بچهها‎
chch

*chîz-hǎ* ‎چیزها‎

The grave ‘ accent shows where the heavy stress falls. Stress is *very important* in Persian.

The plural noun can take the usual prefixes and suffixes: in the case of suffixes, the plural ending is added before any other suffix:

| | |
|---|---|
| child بچه | gentleman آقا |
| to the child بچه | to the gentleman بآقا |
| to the children بچه‌ها | to the gentlemen بآقایان |
| a house منزل | my house منزلم |
| my houses منزلهایم or منازلم | |
| our house منزلمان   our houses منازلمان or منزلهایمان | |

(after و- and ا- -*am* and -*emân* become -*yam* and -*yemân*
یمان ـیم)

his friend دوستش     their friend دوستشان
his friends دوستهایش or دوستانش
their friends دوستهایشان or دوستانشان

(after و- and ا- -*esh* and -*eshân* become -یش -*yesh* and
یشان -*yeshân*).

In the case of a definite direct object in the plural, the
usual suffix را-, coming right at the end of the whole object
expression, is used :

۱   من دوسترا دیدم
I saw the friend

۲   من دوستش را دیدم
I saw his friend

۳   من دوست‌ها را دیدم
I saw the friends

۴   من دوستهایش را دیدم
I saw his friends

۵   من دوستانشان را دیدم
I saw their friends

۶   من دوستشان را دیدم
I saw their friend

You will notice that the combination in no. ۵ :

دوستانشان را

*dûstâneshânrâ*

has as its first element دوست friend ; the first ـان- is the
plural, friends ; ـش- *-esh* is his, which is itself made plural
شان- *eshân*, their ; and را is the suffix of the definite direct
object. There are two separate syllables ـان- *-ân-* in the
word. The first is a plural sign transforming " friend "
into " friends " ; the second makes the possessive " his "
into " their ".

After ان-, یان-, and گان- the *ézâfé* is unwritten and pronounced *é*. After ها- it is written ی- and pronounced *-yé*.

good boys (animate pl.) پسران خوب *pesarân-é-khûb*

good boys (inanimate pl.) پسرهای خوب *pesarhâ-yé-khûb*

little children بچه‌های کوچک *bachchéhâ-yé-kûchek*

big birds پرندگان بزرگ *parandégân-é-bozorg*

این this and آن that do not change to mean these and
those when used before plural nouns :

| | |
|---|---|
| آن ماشین | این ماشین |
| that car | this car |
| آن ماشین‌ها | این ماشین‌ها |
| those cars | these cars |

but when these and those have no noun after them, or
when the noun is understood but not expressed, then they
take the plural inanimate ending ها, invariably :

Which women did you see ? کدام زنان را دیدید

I saw these (ones) اینها را دیدم

I saw those (ones) آنها را دیدم

Do not confuse آنها those ones (animate or inanimate) with the subject-pronoun آنها they (inanimate only), which we had in Lesson 12.

In Lesson 12 we learned that آنها, referring to inanimate subjects (i.e. lower animals and things) takes the verb in the 3rd person *singular* form. This rule applies when the subject of the verb is an inanimate plural noun. Compare

The women came زنان آمدند     They came ایشان آمدند

with

These things were (= was) bad این چیزها بد بود

They were (= was) bad آنها بد بود

## فرهنگ

| | |
|---|---|
| child بچه *bachché* | cat گربه *gorbé* |
| bird پرنده *parandé* | to read (خوانـ) خواندن *khândan,* |
| to pull (کشیـد-) کشیدن *kashídan,* | *khând-* |
| *kashíd-* | tail دم *dom* |
| book کتاب *ketâb* | to write (نوشتـ) نوشتن *neveshtan,* |
| dog سگ *sag* | *nevesht-* |
| pen قلم *ghalam* | leaf برگ *barg* |
| tree درخت *derakht* | letter نامه *nâmé* |
| small کوچک *kúchek* | paper کاغذ *kâghaz* |
| line, writing خط *khatt* | take, carry (بر-) بردن *bordan* |
| pencil مداد *medâd* | |

## تمرین

### I. Put into the plural:

زن – پرنده – سگ – درخت – باغ – قلم – مداد – منزل – کتاب – آقا

– بچه – اتوبوس – ماشین – خط – گربه – اسب – این سگ – آن گربه

– این – آن

II. Put into the plural :

١   این آقا اینجا آمد

٢   شما نامه نوشتید؟ نه من نامه ننوشتم. او نامه بدوست نوشت

٣   کتاب پدر داد

٤   در منزل برادرم بود

٥   دوستم بتهران رفت و بمن نامه نوشت

٦   این سگ خیلی بد بود

٧   پسر خیلی بد نوشت

٨   در باغم درخت بود

٩   باغ خیلی بزرگ بود. منزل خیلی کوچک بود

١٠   خط * آن نامه خیلی بد بود. نخواندم. شما آنرا خواندید؟ نه نامه را نخواندم

III. Translate :

1. Did you read the letters ?  Which letters ?  These.

2. My books were not very big.

3. He took pens, papers, and pencils (*singular*) to the office.

4. Yesterday I wrote a letter.  Which letter ?  This one.

5. These children came late.  How did they come, by bus or by car ?

6. These houses were big, but those were small.

7. I saw the birds in the trees.

8. These bad boys pulled that dog's tail.

9. He drew a (یک) line with a big pencil. (کشیدن to pull also means to draw, in all senses.)

10. His dog and our cat went in(to) our garden.

IV. Read aloud your answers to Ex. II.

V. Read aloud your answers to Ex. III.

VI. In the spaces in the sentences on the right, put the correct form of the past tense of the verb on the left :

| | |
|---|---|
| بودن | ۱  در باغ درخت‌های بزرگ —— |
| آمدن | ۲  گربه‌ها در منزل —— |
| رفتن | ۳  آن ماشین‌ها خوب —— |
| نوشتن | ٤  این قلم‌ها خوب نـ— |
| بودن | ٥  گلها در آن باغ بزرگ —— |
| رفتن | ۶  احمد و حسن دیروز خیلی زود بدفتر —— |
| بودن | ۷  آنوقت منزل‌ها آنجا نـ— |
| نوشتن | ۸  پسران با مداد —— |
| نوشتن | ۹  این قلم‌ها خوب —— و آنها بد —— |
| آمدن | ۱۰  دیروز پسرها دیر بمنزل ——؟ بله اتوبوس‌ها دیر —— |

VII. How is the *ézâfé* pronounced in the following, *é* or *yé* ?

۲  منزل‌های * دوستمان        ۱. منزل * دوستم

٤  پسران * مرد            ۳  پسر * آن مرد

٥  ایرانی * خوب

VIII. How is the *ézâfé* expressed in the following, unwritten or ی ?

۲  دوستها —— آن مرد        ۱  دوستان —— آن مرد

٤  منزلها —— حسن         ۳  منزل —— حسن

٥  بچه —— این زن

## LESSON 14a

فرهنگ

| | |
|---|---|
| how old is he/she ? سنش | big بزرگ *bozorg* |
| *sennesh chist ?* چیست ؟ | is است *ast* |
| I haven't ندارم *nàdâram* | I have دارم *dâram* |
| twenty بیست *bîst* | how much ? |
| but ولی *vali* | how many ? چند ؟ *chand ?* |
| you have دارید *dârîd* | we have داریم *dârîm* |

### TEXT

این مرد پدرم است. آن زن مادرم است. من یک پدر و یک مادر دارم.
چند برادر و خواهر دارید؟ من برا در ندارم ولی یک خواهر دارم. و سنش
چیست؟ سن* خواهر* من بیست است. شما چند برادر و خواهر دارید؟
من خواهر ندارم ولی دو برادر دارم. ما یک منزل در تهران داریم. منزل
بزرگ است. منزل* شما بزرگ است؟ بله منزلمان خیلی بزرگ است.

Take each sentence individually, and read it slowly,
making sure (use the vocabulary where necessary) that you
understand it :

۱ این مرد پدرم است

*în mard pedaram ast*

This man is my father

۲ آن زن مادرم است

*ân zan mâdaram ast*

That woman is my mother

۳ من یک پدر و یک مادر دارم

*man yek pedar va yek mâdar dâram*

I have one father and one mother

٤ چند برادر و خواهر دارید؟

*chand barâdar o khâhar dârîd ?*

How many brothers and sisters have you ?

۵ من برادر ندارم ولی یک خواهر دارم

*man barâdar nàdâram vali yek khâhar dâram*

I have no brother (I don't have a brother) but I have
one sister

۶ و سنش چیست؟    *va sennesh chist ?*

And what (how much) is her age ?

۷ سن * خواهر * من بیست (۲۰) است.

*senn-é-khâhar-é-man bîst ast*

My sister's age is twenty

۸ شما چند برادر و خواهر دارید؟

*shomâ chand barâdar o khâhar dârîd ?*

How many brothers and sisters have *you* got ?

۹ من خواهر ندارم ولی دو برادر دارم.

*man khâhar nddâram vali do barâdar dâram*

I have no sister, but I have two brothers

۱۰ ما یک منزل در تهران داریم    *mâ yek manzel dar tehrân dârîm*

We have a house in Tehran

۱۱ منزل بزرگ است.    *manzel bozorg ast*

The house is big

۱۲ منزل * شما بزرگ است؟    *manzel-é-shomâ bozorg ast ?*

Is your house (the house of you) big ?

۱۳ بله منزلمان خیلی بزرگ است

*balé manzelemân khêîlî bozorg ast*

Yes, our house is very big

Practise reading the text till you can do it fluently, before continuing with this lesson.

بودن

The verb بودن *bûdan* to be is itself very rarely used in the Present Tense. Instead we use this Present Tense :

(for I am, you are, he is, etc.)

1 (man) hastam   (من) هستم    (mâ) hastîm   (ما) هستیم
2 (shomâ) hastîd   (شما) هستید    (shomâ) hastîd   (شما) هستید

3 {
(*û*) *ast* (او) است     (*îshân*) *hastand* هستند (ایشان)
(*ân*) *ast* (آن) است     (*ânhâ*) *ast* (آنها) است
}

You will notice (*a*) the endings for the 1st and 2nd persons singular and plural, and the 3rd plural animate (ایشان) are those we have already met in the Past tense ; (*b*) the 1st and 2nd persons singular and plural and the 3rd plural animate (ایشان) begin with ه *h*. The او, آن, and آنها forms have no ه *h*.

There *is* a 3rd singular and plural (او, آن, and آنها persons) which goes with an *h* : هست *hast*. This form means there is, there are (it is an emphatic form). Compare :

It is a house    *manzel ast*    منزل است

with

There is a house    *manzel hast*    منزل هست

The negative of all these forms is :

1   *nîstam*   نیستم     *nîstîm*   نیستیم
2   *nîstîd*   نیستید     *nîstîd*   نیستید
3 {
  *nîst*   نیست     *nîstand*   نیستند
  *nîst*   نیست     *nîst*   نیست
}

نیست is used as the negative of هست as well :

It isn't a horse
There isn't a horse
} اسب نیست   *asb nîst*

داشتن *dâshtan*, to have

The verb داشتن *dâshtan* means to have. In the Past Tense it is regular, i.e. we take off the ن-*an*, leaving داشت- *dâsht-* as the Past Stem.

To the Past Stem we add the regular past endings to get the Past Tense :

1   *dâshtam*   داشتم     *dâshtîm*   داشتیم

2 *dâshtîd* داشتید     *dâshtîd* داشتید

3 { *dâsht* داشت     *dâshtand* داشتند

   { *dâsht* داشت     *dâsht* داشت

= I, you, he, she, it, we, you, they had

The present tense endings for all verbs except بودن, which we have just learned, are the same except in one person (3rd singular, and hence also 3rd inanimate plural) as the past tense endings. The difference lies not in the endings but in the *stem* to which those endings are added.

Of داشتن, داشت- is the Past Stem and دار- the Present Stem.

The present tense of داشتن to have is:

stem دار- *dâr-*

1 *dâram* دارم     *dârîm* داریم

2 *dârîd* دارید     *dârîd* دارید

3 { *dârad* دارد     *dârand* دارند

   { *dârad* دارد     *dârad* دارد

You will notice that (*a*) the 1st singular and plural, 2nd singular and plural, and the 3rd animate plural (من, ما, شما, and ایشان forms) have the same personal endings as has the past tense, but (*b*) for the 3rd singular and 3rd inanimate plural (او, آن, and آنها) the ending is د- -*ad*; (*c*) the stem vowel of this verb is pronounced long, *â*; the م- -*am*, د- -*ad*, and ند- -*and* endings are pronounced with a short *a*, while, as in the past tense, the *î* of ید- -*îd* and یم- -*îm* is long.

The endings given above are the same in spelling and pronunciation for all verbs in the present tense except بودن to be.

*nà-* is added to the present tense to negate it just as it is to the past tense:

نداشتن *nàdâshtan*, not to have

past stem -نداشت-      ندار- present stem

past tense:              present tense:

| | | | | |
|---|---|---|---|---|
| 1 | نداشتم | نداشتیم | ندارم | نداریم |
| 2 | نداشتید | نداشتید | نداری | ندارید |
| 3 { | نداشت | نداشتند | ندارد | ندارند |
| | نداشت | نداشت | ندارد | ندارد |

The present tense of all verbs is normally used to indicate the *future* also. This is especially the case when the context of the verb tells us that the future is intended.

I am (I shall be) here tomorrow    فردا اینجا هستم

We shan't have (haven't) a lesson tomorrow    فردا درس نداریم

تمرین

I. Read again the text and the vocabulary, to refresh your mind on the words and constructions, and then answer orally the following questions, with reference to yourself:

١ شما برادر یا خواهر دارید؟

٢ مادر و پدر دارید؟

٣ سن * شما چیست

٤ منزل * شما کوچک یا بزرگ است؟

٥ باغ دارید؟

II. Write out your answers to Ex. I.

III. Put in each space the correct past tense form of بودن:

١ این آقایان دیروز در منزلم ——.

۲ شما دیروز در دفتر ——؟

۳ این کتاب بزرگ ——.

٤ خواهر و برادر \* شما در منزل ——؟

٥ نه ولی مادرم آنجا ——.

IV. Translate and write out :

1. Tomorrow I shall be at the office early.

2. Yesterday I had two gentlemen at the house.

3. I didn't have the money—did you have (it) ?

4. This room has four windows (پنجره *panjeré*) and one
   door.  The windows have six panes (شیشه *shîshé*)
   each (one).

5. These aren't my books.  Where are they ?  I didn't
   see them anywhere.

V. Write the negative of these sentences :

۱ این مرد دوستم است.      ۲ آن زن مادر \* خوب است.

۳ من خیلی وقت اینجا هستم §.      ٤ آب هست؟

٥ ایرانی هستید.

§ " I have been here . . . " literally in Persian, " I *am*
here a long time "—the *present*, not the perfect or past, is
used when the action continues from the past into the
present.  Cf. exactly the same construction in three major
European languages :

> Je suis ici depuis longtemps ⎫
> Ich bin hier seit langer Zeit ⎬ because I *am*
> Я давно вдесь ⎭      *still here*

## LESSON 15

### *The indefinite suffix* ی- -*î*

When we wish to use a noun and to make clear that it is indefinite, we add to it the suffix ی- -*î* :

مرد *mard* man, the man

مردی *mardî* a man, some man or other, any man

The suffix can be added to a compound, i.e. to a noun followed by a qualifying adjective :

خوبی * مرد *mard-é-khûbî* some good man or other

بزرگی * شهر *shahr-é-bozorgî* any big city

It can be attached to certain pronouns, and to the word یک *yek* one :

یکی *yekî* someone

شخصی *shakhsî* somebody

کسی *kasî* somebody, anybody

هیچی *hîchî* none, nothing (at all)

If we wish, we can add it to the noun and not to the adjective :

مردی خوب *mardî khûb* any good man

in which case the *ézâfé* is *dropped*. It is most important to remember that if ی- -*î* is added in the middle of an *ézâfé* compound, such as مرد * خوب *mard-é-khûb*, then that interrupted *ézâfé* is dropped. We have thus several good ways of expressing, for example, " some good man or other " :

| | |
|---|---|
| مرد * خوبی<br>یک مرد خوب<br>یک مرد * خوبی<br>مردی خوب<br>یک مردی خوب | In each of these combinations, the ی- -î is added to a different word. They all mean much the same thing, but the one we dealt with first, |

| |
|---|
| مرد * خوبی |

is by far the most common.

If the noun ends in ی- -î already, we cannot add a further ی- to it:

صندلی *sandalî* chair, or any chair, or the chair
کشتی *kashtî* boat, any boat, the boat

If the noun or adjective ends in و- -*û* or ا- -*â* we pronounce a glottal stop (see Lesson 9) between this final vowel and the *î*. We have already had, in Lesson 9, the letter ع *'ain*. But ع *'ain* is only found in Arabic loan words, and this -*î* suffix is purely Persian. Instead of *'ain* in this case we use the sign ٔ, called *hamzé*. *Hamzé* is not a letter, it is a sign. It is written over what we call a *bearer*, which looks like a ب *b* without its dot, thus:

ئـ or ئ

Thus آقا *âghâ* with ی- -*î* indefinite added looks like
آقائی "some gentleman or other"

and is pronounced *âghâ'î*. *Do not*, in pronouncing this word and others like it, run the ا into the ی. The ئ is there expressly to prevent this tendency. Pronounce a clear stop, a catch of the breath, between the ا and the ى : آقائ *âghâ'î*.

Exactly the same thing happens with a word ending in و -*û* :

> بو　*bû* smell
>
> بوی بد　*bû-yé bad* the bad smell
>
> بوئ　*bû'î* some smell
>
> بوئ بد　*bû'î bad*　⎫
>
> or　　　　⎬ some bad smell or other
>
> بوی بدی　*bû-yé badî*　⎭

Similarly :

> بنا　*bannâ* the builder
>
> بنائ　*bannâ'î* any builder
>
> جا　*jâ* place
>
> جائ　*jâ'î* some place, somewhere

An indefinite -*î* added to a word ending in ه -*é* (vocalic *h*) is written either with a *hamzé* over the ه and nothing else :

> خانه　*khâné* house
>
> خانۀ　*khâné'i* a house

or the *hamzé* can be left off, giving a form identical with the definite form :

> خانه　*khâné* house, or *khâné'î* a house

or the syllable -*î* is written ای :

> خانهای　*khâné'i* a house

It goes without saying that as ى is an indefinite suffix,

one very seldom finds را the definite direct object suffix
connected to it.  Compare :

بنا دیدم    I saw a builder

بنا را دیدم    I saw the builder

بنائی دیدم    I saw some builder (or other)

Nor can ی be found in conjunction with such definite words
as این this and آن that and هر every. There are exceptions
to this :

این یکی    means this one

آن یکی    „    that one

هریکی    „    every one or everyone

ی- is often found with negatives, and especially with هیچ
no, none, not a.  In this case the ی- is best expressed in
English by " any ", with the verb in the negative :

کسی دیدید؟    Did you see anybody ?

نه هیچ کسی ندیدم    No, I didn't see anyone (at all)

which could also be (without هیچ) :

نه کسی ندیدم    No, I didn't see anyone

When the word immediately before the verb است " is "
ends in ی-, the ا of است is not pronounced.  The ا may be
dropped in writing, or it can be retained, but in pronunciation it *must* be dropped.  If the ا is dropped in writing,
then we run the ست- -st straight on to the ی- -i, which is
shortened from ی- to -ِ- :

این چه چیز است؟    *in ché chîz ast ?*  ⎫
این چه چیزی است؟                          ⎪
    or                ⎬ *in ché chîzîst ?*  ⎬ What is this ?
این چه چیزیست                              ⎭

After a word ending in long *â* ا-, the ا of است is dropped, both in speech and in writing.

کجاست؟ *kojâst ?* Where is it ?

این آب نیست ودکاست *în âb nîst, vodkâst*

This isn't water, it's vodka

After the question ک *kî* who ?, the verb هستید you are is joined on in the same way. These two words are almost invariably written as one when they occur together :

کیستید؟ *kîstîd ?* Who are you ?

The unblended *kî hastîd* ک هستید؟ form does exist, but it is very rare.

*Something, somewhere, somebody, someone,* followed by an adjective, are regularly expressed by using the ی- suffix on the first word and dropping the *ézâfé* link. Learn :

چیزی خوب    something good

چیزی بد    something bad

کسی خوب    someone (somebody) good

جائی دیگر    somewhere else

یکی دیگر one more, another one, a different one (دیگر *dîgar* is an adjective meaning other, different).

تمرین

I. Give the indefinite form of these words :

۴ گاه     ۳ رو     ۲ آقا     ۱ بنا

۸ کوچه     ۷ درخت     ۶ کتاب     ۵ کس

۱۲ صندلی     ۱۱ بچه     ۱۰ مرد     ۹ چیز

II. Write in Persian:

1. I saw that man yesterday. He had some book or other in (his) hand.

2. Which bus came late? I didn't see: sometimes (گاهی *gâhî*) the buses are late, sometimes early.

3. A gentleman came to the house today.

4. Did you take anything from the table? No sir, I didn't see or (= and) take anything.

5. Who is this? It isn't his brother, it's someone else.

III. Pronounce:

(voice rising) *kojâst?*   کجاست

*în chîst?*   این چیست

$\left.\begin{array}{l}\text{این چیز خوبیست} \\ \text{این چیز خوبی است}\end{array}\right\}$ *în chîzé khûbîst*

IV. Read:

۱ در این منزل کسی دیگر هست؟ نه آقا کسی دیگر نیست.

۲ چرا این مرد دوستی ندارد؟ این مرد بدی است و هیچکس دوستش نیست.

۳ از دفتر دیروز ظهر جائی دیگر نرفتم.

٤ شما چرا بمنزل رفتید؟ وقت نداشتم.

٥ شما کتاب * خوبی دارید. چه کتابی؟ من کتابی ندارم.

V. Translate Ex. IV.

## LESSON 15a

*Possessive pronoun endings.* We have already had the
endings م- my, مان- our, ش- his/her/its, and شان- their. Here
now is the full table of possessive suffixes:

(اسب a horse)

(1) اسبم *asbam*           اسبمان *asbemân*
    my horse                 our horse
(2) اسبتان *asbetân*       اسبتان *asbetân*
    your horse                your horse
(3) اسبش *asbesh*         اسبشان *asbeshân*
    his/her/its horse         their horse

We can add these endings to a plural noun:

(دوستان friends)

(1) دوستانم *dûstânam*      دوستانمان *dûstânemân*
    my friends                our friends
(2) دوستانتان *dûstânetân*    دوستانتان *dûstânetân*
    your friends              your friends
(3) دوستانش *dûstânesh*     دوستانشان *dûstâneshân*
    his/her/its friends       their friends

If we add these endings to a word ending in a vowel,
for example an inanimate plural in ها- *-hâ*, we put in a
ـِ- *-y-* to make it possible to pronounce the word:

(اسبها horses)

(1) اسبهایم *asbhâyam*     اسبهایمان *asbhâyemân*
    my horses               our horses
(2) اسبهایتان *asbhâyetân*    اسبهایتان *asbhâyetân*
    your horses             your horses
(3) اسبهایش *asbhâyesh*     اسبهایشان *asbhâyeshân*
    his/her/its horses      their horses

These are the possessive endings we usually write and
speak : they are unstressed. If, however, we wish to *stress*
the fact of ownership of something, then we often use the
noun followed by the *ézâfé* followed by the *personal pronoun*
(not the possessive) :

این اسب * شما نیست اسب * من است

*in asb-é-shomâ nîst, asb-é-man ast*

This isn't *your* horse (= the horse of you), it's *my* horse
(= the horse of me)

صندلی * شما را ندیدم ولی صندلی * او را دیدم

*sandalî-yé-shomâ-râ nàdîdam vali sandalî-yé-û râ dîdam*

I didn't see *your* chair, but I saw *his* chair

If the possessive pronoun refers to the subject of the
verb, e.g. in such constructions as

> I took my (own) money
> He has his (own) house
> They saw their (own) friends

we cannot use either the ـم -تان ـش-, etc., endings or the
*ézâfé* construction shown above. We have to use the particle

---

*khod* خود " own "

---

خود can either be used by itself, linked like any other
adjective by the *ézâfé* to the noun possessed :

۱ من پول * خود را گرفتم

*man pûl-é-khod râ gereftam*

I took my (own) money

in which case the خود *khod* is invariable, and does not
change for person :

۲ ما پول * خود را گرفتیم

We took our money

۳ او پول * خود را گرفت

He took his money

and so on, the context showing us to whom the خود refers,
or we can, for special emphasis, add the م- تان- ش- etc.,
possessive endings to the خود, depending on the person
concerned:

| | |
|---|---|
| *pûl-é-khodam râ gereftam* | ۱ پول * خودم را گرفتم |
| *pûl-é-khodemân râ gereftîm* | ۲ پول * خودمان را گرفتیم |
| *pûl-é-khodesh râ gereft* | ۳ پول * خودش را گرفت |

خود, with or without the م- تان- ش-, etc., possessive
endings suffixed to it, can take the را definite object ending
if desired:

| | |
|---|---|
| *pûl-é-khod-râ gereftam* | ۱ پول * خودرا گرفتم |
| *pûl-é-khodam-râ gereftam* | ۱ پول * خودم را گرفتم |
| *pûl-é-khod-râ gereftîm* | ۲ پول * خودرا گرفتیم |
| *pûl-é-khodemân-râ gereftîm* | ۲ پول * خودمانرا گرفتیم |
| *pûl-é-khod-râ gereft* | ۳ پول * خودرا گرفت |
| *pûl-é-khodesh-râ gereft* | ۳ پول * خودش را گرفت |

and so on for all persons. This structure is used whenever
the possessive refers to the subject of the verb itself.
Compare:

۴ اسبش را گرفتم

I took his (i.e. somebody else's) horse

and

۵ اسبش را گرفت

He took his (somebody else's) horse

with

۶ اسب * خودش را گرفت

He took his (i.e. his own) horse

## فرهنگ

| | |
|---|---|
| ambassador سفیر safîr | country کشور keshvar |
| embassy سفارت sefârat | corner گوشه gûshé |
| war جنگ jang | as well همچنین hamchonîn |
| minister وزیر vazîr | the Persian Language زبان* فارسی zabân-é-fârsî |
| Ministry of War وزارت* جنگ vezârat-é-jang | tongue, language زبان zabân |
| Ministry of Justice وزارت* دادگستری vezârat-é-dâdgostarî | king پادشاه pâdeshâh |
| square میدان méidân | queen ملکه maleké |
| lane کوچه kûché | court دربار darbâr |
| beautiful قشنگ ghashang | ministry وزارت vezârat |
| tile کاشی kâshî | mosque مسجد masjed |
| mosaic کاشیکاری kâshîkârî | justice دادگستری dâdgostarî |
| to drive راندن راند- rândan, rând- | street خیابان khîâbân |
| various مختلف mokhtalef | name اسم esm |
| to pass (by) گذشتن گذشت- (از) gozashtan, gozasht- (az) | taxi تاکسی tâksî |
| | building عمارت 'emârat |
| Ferdousi (a Persian poet) فردوسی Ferdôusî | colour رنگ rang |
| | green سبز sabz |
| to stop ایستادن ایستاد- îstâdan, îstâd- | bank بانک bânk |
| | blue آبی âbî |
| driver شوفر shôfer | yellow/golden زرد zard |
| | not yet هنوز ... نه hanuz ... na- |

Read:

### خیابانهای * شهر

دیروز یک تاکسی گرفتم و از خیابانهای * بزرگ و کوچک * شهر گذشتم. گاهی تاکسی می ایستاد و ما عمارت‌های * قشنگ را می دیدیم. در این شهر هر خیابان و هر کوچه چیزی دارد و هنوز همه چیز را ندیده ایم. این میدان * کوچک * قشنگ را دیدید؟ در هریکی از گوشه‌هایش یک در* بزرگ هست. این چهار در درهای * دربار * پادشاه است. دربار * پادشاه و ملکه * ایران است. در خیابانهای * دیگر* شهر عمارت‌های * دیگر هست. اینجا وزارت * جنگ - وزارت‌های * دیگر را دیدید؟ دیروز وزارت‌های * دادگستری و فرهنگ را دیدم. همچنین منزل * وزیر * فرهنگ را.

در ته * این خیابان یک مسجد * بزرگ هست. مسجدهای * § ایران
خیلی قشنگ است. این کاشیکاری چه قشنگ است! رنگ‌های * آبی
و زرد و سبز دارد. تاکسی همچنین از سفارت‌های * مختلف در خیابان *
فردوسی گذشت. سفارت‌ها خیلی بزرگ است و باغهایش خیلی قشنگ.
هر سفارت باغ * خودش را دارد.

§ ایرانی * یک مسجد

§ مسجد masjed also has an Arabic plural: مساجد masâjed.

## تمرین

**I.** Fill in the space with the correct possessive, either
suffix or خود * as appropriate :

۱ دیروز پسرتان را دیدم. شما پسر ——‌ را دیدید؟

۲ قبل از درس هر یکی از پسرها کتاب ——‌ را گرفت. من کتابها ——‌ را
بایشان دادم.

۳ هر سفارت باغ ——‌ را دارد.

٤ پادشاه در دربار ——— بود.

٥ این قلم * این پسر است. پسر قلم ——— را بمن داد.

II. Write in Persian :

    1. He passed through his (own) garden.

    2. I passed through his garden.

    3. I passed through my garden.

    4. He passed through my garden.

    5. He passed through her garden.

III. Answer orally and in writing :

١ زبان * فارسی زبان * خودتان است؟ کدام زبان زبان * خودتان است؟

٢ شما باغ * خودتان را دارید؟

٣ کاشیکاری را دیدید؟ کجا در مسجد بودید؟

٤ منزل * خودتان را دارید یا منزل * کسی دیگر است؟

٥ قلمتان کجاست؟ قلم خودتان را در دست دارید؟

## LESSON 16

### اضافه Ezâfé

It is time to revise the *ézâfé*.

The *ézâfé* is a short syllable, pronounced *é* after consonants and *yé* after vowels. It is used to show :

(*a*) possession :

| | | |
|---|---|---|
| اسبهای * مرد | اسب * مرد | |
| اسب * پادشاه | اسب * آن مرد | اسب * این مرد |
| اسب * کدام مرد؟ | اسبهای * آن مرد | اسبهای * این مرد |

(*b*) noun + qualifying adjective :

| | | |
|---|---|---|
| اسبهای * ایرانی | دست * راست | مرد * بزرگ |
| کتاب * فارسی | کتاب‌های * فارسی | باغ * قشنگ |

(c) apposition (agreement) :

حسن * شوفر     بنای * دوستم     آقای سفیر
حسن * ایرانی

Note : (1) it can be used to denote any combination of
(a), (b), and (c) above :

... اسب * دوست * ایرانیم

the horse of* my friend* the Iranian . . .

(2) If we use the indefinite suffix ی- after a noun linked
by an ézâfé to the next word, that ézâfé is dropped and
replaced by the ی- :

مرد * خوب

but

(no ézâfé) مردی خوب

*The writing and pronunciation of the ézâfé*

(a) It is unwritten, and pronounced as a short vowel -é- ;
after a word ending in a consonant :

اسب * بزرگ

Remember that a breathed ه h, that is to say, one following
a written or unwritten vowel, is a *consonant* :

شاه * ایران shâh-é-îrân the Shah of Persia

(b) It is written ی- and pronounced -yé- ; after a word
ending in a long vowel ا or و :

ای â-yé     وی û-yé
my books کتابهای * من    big houses منزلهای * بزرگ
بوی * بد the bad smell

(c) After the long vowel ی- î and after ه é (h) *as a vowel,* the *ézâfé* is pronounced -*yé*. It is usually in these cases unwritten, but it is occasionally written, to avoid possible ambiguity, with a ' *hanzé* over the ى or the ه :

good fruit    میوۀ خوب or   میوه خوب   *mivé-yé-khúb*

a big ship    کشتیِ بزرگ or   کشتی بزرگ   *kashtî-yé-bozorg*

this gentle-   صندلیِ این آقا or صندله این آقا   *sandalî-yé-în âghâ*
man's chair

If we wish to add the definite direct object suffix را to a compound linked by an *ézâfé* (or with many *ézâfés*) we add the را to the *last element only*. It is either written on to this last word, or written separately; more often separately.

this big chair این صندلیه بزرگ *în sandalî-yé-bozorg*

این صندله بزرگ را کجا گرفتید؟

*în sandalî-yé-bozorg râ kojâ gereftíd?*

Where did you get this big chair?

The possessive *ézâfé* (see Lesson 15a) is often used, especially in conversation, with the noun مال *mâl* " property " thus : \* مال *mâl-é-* " the property of ". We use \* مال *mâl-é-* when the *possessing* is the thought uppermost in the mind of the speaker. Compare :

This is my book این کتاب \* من است

*în ketâb-é-man ast*

with

This book is mine این کتاب مال \* من است

*în ketâb mal-é-man ast* (literally, is my property)

The question " whose ? " can only be asked by using \* مال : کی بود؟ \* مال آن ماشین Whose car was that ? (literally, That car, the property of whom was it ?). " Whose is

. . . ? " as a question comes last in its sentence. It is written :

مال . . . کی است؟

or

مال . . . کیست؟

and is in both cases pronounced *mâl-é-kîst ?*

Whose is this book ?

این کتاب مال * کیست؟    or    این کتاب مال * کی است؟

*în ketâb mâl-é-kîst ?*

The answer could be

مال * من است

*mâl-é-man ast* It's mine

or

مال * من

*mâl-é-man* mine

مال *

can be used to great emphatic effect. Compare

آمد و کتاب * من را گرفت

He came and took my book

with

آمد و کتابی را که مال * من بود گرفت

He came and took the book which was mine

## فرهنگ

| | |
|---|---|
| easy آسان *âsân* | bazaar بازار *bâzâr* |
| fruit میوه *mîvé* | cherry گیلاس *gîlâs* |
| tree درخت *derakht* | Hassan حسن *hasan* |
| several, many, much زیاد *zîâd* | fire آتش *âtesh* |
| apple سیب *sîb* | teacher آموزگار *âmûzegâr* |
| village ده *déh* | capital city پایتخت *pâ-yé-takht* |
| interesting (literally noteworthy) قابل * توجه *ghâbel-é-tavajjoh* | Firoozan (an Iranian name) فیروزان *fîrûzân* |
| lesson درس *dars* | national ملی *mellî* |
| worthy (of) قابل * *ghâbel-é-* | lamp, light چراغ *cherâgh* |
| director رئیس *ra'îs* | painting نقاشی *naghghâshî* |
| bright روشن *rôushan* | education, vocabulary, diction- |
| painter نقاش *naghghâsh* | ary فرهنگ *farhang* |
| | Esfahan (city in S. Iran) اصفهان *esfahân* |

تمرین

I. In these sentences, mark the *ézâfé*, if any, with an *
(asterisk). Use also ' *hamzé* where appropriate :

١   این عمارت بزرگ قشنگ مال بانک ملی ایران است

٢   زبان فارسی آسان نیست

٣   دیروز چه چیز گرفتید؟ کتابی فارسی گرفتم

٤   حسن شوفر شوفر خوبی است

٥   چیزی خوب بمن داد

٦   در خیابانهای مختلف شهر تهران ماشینهای زیاد هست

٧   این اسب مال کیست؟ مال برادر این آموزگار است

٨   سیب و گلابی و گیلاس میوه خوب است

٩   یک پرنده بزرگ در درخت دیدم

١٠   از آتش برقی بد آمد

II. Read the above sentences when you have marked in
the *ézâfé*, taking care to pronounce it correctly.

III. Write in Persian :

    1. Whose car is that ? Which one ? That one.

    2. That is the Minister of Education's car.

    3. Tehran is the capital of Iran. It is a big city.

    4. There are not many big cities in Iran : but there
       are many small villages.

    5. As the car passed through the streets of Esfahan
       we saw something interesting.

IV. Explain the *ézâfé* in these phrases by placing each one
in one or other of these columns, thus:

(آقای * فیروزان رئیس * بانک * ملی بود : example)

| Apposition | Noun + Adjective | Possession |
|---|---|---|
| آقای * فیروزان | بانک * ملی | رئیس * بانک |

١ حسن * شوفر کجاست؟　٢ این عمارت * بزرگ چیست؟

٣ اسب * این آقا اسب * قشنگی است. ٤ چراغهای * این ماشین روشن است

٥ فرش و نقاشی * قشنگ در بازار دیده؟

## LESSON 16a

*The present tense of verbs.*　We have already had the
present tense of بودن and داشتن.　When we conjugated to
have in the present, we took the Present Stem, which for
داشتن was دار- *dâr-*, and added the endings

|  |  |  |  |
|---|---|---|---|
| (ما) یم- | (من) م- | 1 |  |
| (شما) ید- | (شما) ید- | 2 |  |
| (ایشان) ند- | (او) د- | 3 { | |
| (آنها) ند- | (آن) د- | | |

For the present tense of all other verbs, we take the
present stem, as we did with داشتن above, add the same
personal endings as we did to دار- above, and *also* (this is
most important) add the Present Prefix:

می- or می- *mî-*

To form the present stem of most verbs, we take the
تن- *-tan,* دن- *-dan,* or یدن- *-îdan* endings off the infinitive;
for example :

| Infinitive | Past Stem | Present Stem |
|---|---|---|
| read خواندن *khândan* | خواند- *khând-* | خوان- *-khân-* |
| pull کشیدن *kashîdan* | کشید- *kashîd-* | کش- *-kash-* |
| weave بافتن *bâftan* | بافت- *bâft-* | باف- *-bâf-* |

To these present stems we add (1) the personal endings
as for the present of داشتن to have, and (2) مِ- *mi-* the
prefix for the present tense. Here now in full are the
present tenses of these three model verbs:

(*a*) to read : خواندن, past stem خواند- *khând-*.

Present Stem خوان- *-khân-*

|   |   |   |   |   |   |
|---|---|---|---|---|---|
| (1) | I read | میخوانم | we read | میخوانیم | |
|  | *mîkhânam* | | *mîkhânîm* | | |
| (2) | you read | میخوانید | you read | میخوانید | |
|  | *mîkhânîd* | | *mîkhânîd* | | |
| (3) | he reads | میخواند | they read | میخوانند | |
|  | *mîkhânad* | | *mîkhânand* | | |
|  | it reads | میخواند | they read | میخواند | |
|  | *mîkhânad* | | *mîkhânad* | | |

(*b*) to pull : کشیدن, past stem کشید- *kashîd-*.

Present Stem کش- *-kash-*

| (1) | *mîkasham* | میکشم | *mîkashîm* | میکشیم |
|---|---|---|---|---|
| (2) | *mîkashîd* | میکشید | *mîkashîd* | میکشید |
| (3) | *mîkashad* | میکشد | *mîkashand* | میکشند |
|  | *mîkashad* | میکشد | *mîkashad* | میکشد |

(*c*) to weave : بافتن, past stem بافت- *bâft-*

Present Stem باف- *-bâf-*

| (1) | *mîbâfam* | میبافم | *mîbâfîm* | میبافیم |
|---|---|---|---|---|
| (2) | *mîbâfîd* | میبافید | *mîbâfîd* | میبافید |
| (3) | *mîbâfad* | میبافد | *mîbâfand* | میبافند |
|  | *mîbâfad* | میبافد | *mîbâfad* | میبافد |

Apart from بودن to be and داشتن to have, there are *no* irregular verbs as such in Persian. We can put it this way :

(*a*) *All verbs*, including even بودن and داشتن, are completely regular in the past tense.

(*b*) بودن is seldom used in the present—the forms هستم, etc., are used instead.

(*c*) داشتن is without the -می *mi-* prefix in the present, otherwise its present is regular.

(*d*) For all remaining verbs, it is necessary to find the present stem. This is got in most cases by taking تن- or دن- or یدن- off the infinitive, but in many cases the present stem is irregular.

Note that : the *present stem* is the only irregularity ever encountered ; once we have the stem, we add -می *mi-* and suffix the regular present tense endings. And even then, most so-called " irregular " present stems can be grouped together. We shall study some of these groups from time to time.

Here are the present stems of the verbs we know so far (irregular present stems are marked §) :

| Infinitive | English | Present Stem | Present 1st Singular |
|---|---|---|---|
| رفتن | go | -رو- *-rav-* § | میروم |
| دیدن | see | -بین- *-bîn-* § | میبینم |
| دادن | give | -ده- *-deh-* § | میدهم |
| گرفتن | take, get | -گیر- *-gîr-* § | میگیرم |
| خوردن | eat, drink | -خور- *-khor-* | میخورم |
| خوابیدن | sleep | -خواب- *-khâb-* | میخوابم |

| | | | |
|---|---|---|---|
| خواندن | read | -خوان- | -khân- | میخوانم |
| بافتن | weave | -باف- | -bâf- | میبافم |
| نوشتن | write | -نویس- | -nevîs- § | مینویسم |
| گذشتن | pass by | -گذر- | -gozar- § | میگذرم |

The negative prefix can be added to the present tense :

نمیروم    *nàmîravam* I'm not going

نمیبینید    *nàmîbînîd* you don't see

### تلفظ *talaffoz*

The vowel of مِی- is long : *mî*. It is stressed when it is the only prefix.

The vowel of نَ- is short : *nà*. It is stressed whenever it appears. Practise pronouncing :

you go میروید *mîravîd* (prefix stressed)

you aren't going نمیروید *nàmîravîd* (first prefix stressed)

اسفندیار          رستم

جنگِ * رستمِ و اسفندیار (از شاهنامهٔ فردوسی)

The battle of Rustam (right) and Esfandyâr, an episode from Ferdousi's poem " Shâhnâmé " (Book of Kings) which is the Persian national epic.

(*Drawn from B. W. Robinson's " Persian Miniatures ", by kind permission of the publishers, Bruno Cassirer, Ltd., Oxford.*)

We have learnt a verb meaning *to be* in the present ;
هستم , هستید, etc. There is also a form of the present of this
important verb which appears as a suffix.

(1) *-am* -م          *-îm* -یم

(2) *-îd* -ید          *-îd* -ید

(3) $\begin{cases} \text{*-ast* ست} \\ \text{*-ast* ست} \end{cases}$      *-and* -ند

                         *-ast* ست

Examples :

(1) singular من خیلی خوشم    *man khêilî khosham*
                                   I am very happy

(2) singular/plural دیر کردید؟    *dîr kardîd ?* Are you late ?

(1) plural ما راحتیم    *mâ râhatîm*
                                     We are comfortable

(2) plural بلدند    *baladand*
                                     They are *au fait*

(*balad* بلد adjective = informed, *au fait*)

If we wish to suffix -م *-îm* or -ید- *-îd* to a word ending
in ا- *-â* or و- *-û*, we write a *hamzé* on a bearer first and
pronounce the glottal stop, thus :

راستگوئیم *râstgû'îm* We are truthful

بنائید؟ *bannâ'îd ?* Are you a builder ?

In the same situation the suffixes -م *-am*, -ند *-and* are
written separately, with their own ا *alef* : ام, اند.

After a final ه *é* all these suffixes must be written with
their own introductory ا *alef* :

خسته ام    *khasté am* I'm tired

خیلی گرسنه اند *khêilî gorosné and* They are very hungry

(گرسنه) *gorosné* = hungry ; خسته *khasté* = tired ;

راستگو *râstgû* = truthful)

شما خسته اید؟ *shomâ khasté îd ?* Are you tired ?

Note : There is a negative short form of this verb " to be ", but it is very seldom used. We need not bother with it here.

فرهنگ

| | |
|---|---|
| today امروز *emrûz* | restaurant رستوران *restôrân* |
| last night دیشب *dîshab* | window پنجره *panjeré* |
| at home منزل *manzel* | room اطاق *otâgh* |
| tonight امشب *emshab* | garage گاراژ *gârâzh* |
| time وقت *vaght* | servant نوکر *nôukar* |
| work کار *kâr* | tired خسته *khasté* |

TEXT

دیروز ببازار رفتم. امروز کجا میروید؟ من امروز ببازار نمیروم میروم § دفتر . دیشب منزل شام خوردم ولی امشب وقت ندارم و باین سبب در رستوران شام میخورم. شما کجا شام میخورید؟

از پنجرهٔ اطاق خودتان چه چیزها میبینید؟ از پنجره گاراژ * بزرگ را میبینم و همچنین یک میدان. ماشینها از میدان میگذرد و در خیابانها میرود.

من فارسی میخوام شما فارسی میخوانید؟ نه من فارسی نمیخوانم ونمینویسم. چه چیز بنوکر خودتان میدهید؟ من باو پول میدهم و او از من پولرا میگیرد. شما دیشب زود خوابیدید یا دیر؟ دیشب من خیلی دیر خوابیدم – کار * زیاد داشتم ولی امشب خیلی زود میخوابم – خسته ام.

§ After the verbs رفتن to go and آمدن to come, we can omit به- *to-*, which is then understood :

میروم دفتر *mîravam daftar* I go to the office

تمرین

**I.** Write in Persian :

   1. I am tired. (Short form.)

   2. Do you write ?

   3. Are you going ?

   4. He doesn't read.

   5. We are happy. (one word.)

   6. They are going.

   7. They came.

   8. Who sees ?

   9. What happens ? (= passes).

 10. You give.

**II.** Put into the Present Tense :

| | | |
|---|---|---|
| ۳ کی گذشت؟ | ۲ ما دیدیم | ۱ من رفتم |
| ۶ شما خواندید؟ | ۵ او نوشت | ٤ ایشان خوردند |
| ۹ زود خوابیدند | ۸ اینجا رفت | ۷ هیچ کس ندید |
| | ۱۰ آنها گرفت | |

**III.** Conjugate گرفتن and دیدن in the Present.

**IV.** Change the long forms of " to be " in these examples
to the suffix form (e.g. من بزرگم to من بزرگ هستم) :

   ۱ تازه هستم     ۲ بلد هستند     ۳ کجا هستید؟

   ٤ در آب هستند     ٥ خسته هستیم

**V.** Complete, in the Present Tense :

| | |
|---|---|
| بافتن | ۱ در ایران فرشهای * خیلی قشنگ ——. |
| رفتن | ۲ او فردا باصفهان ——. |
| نوشتن | ۳ ما نامه ——. |
| گذشتن | ٤ کی از اینجا ——؟ |
| خواندن | ٥ هیچ کدام از این آقایان فارسی نـ——. |

## LESSON 17

*Prepositions.* Prepositions in Persian fall into two groups :
those used without being connected to their noun by an
*ézâfé* link, and those which require an *ézâfé* after them.
The ones without an *ézâfé* are pure Persian prepositions
proper ; those linked by an *ézâfé* to their noun are usually
adverbs, nouns, adjectives, or foreign words borrowed and
used as prepositions.

(*a*) Prepositions which do not take the *ézâfé* :

     به -ب‍ *bé* (written joined or separate) to

     در *dar* in     با *bâ* with

     بی *bî* without     از *az* from

     جز *joz* instead of, except for

(*b*) Prepositions always joined by an *ézâfé* to the noun
they govern :

| | | |
|---|---|---|
| * طرف | *taraf-é-* | towards |
| * داخل | *dâkhel-é-* | inside |
| * بیرون | *bîrûn-é-* | outside |
| * برای | *barâ-yé* | for (colloquially *bar-é*) |
| * بدون | *bedûn-é-* | without |
| * بین | *béin-é-* | between |
| * پیش | *pîsh-é-* | in front of |
| * پشت | *posht-é-* | behind |
| * پهلوی | *pahlû-yé-* | in the presence of |
| * روی | *rû-yé-* | on |
| * زیر | *zîr-é-* | under |
| * توی | *tû-yé-* | in, on |
| * نزدیک | *nazdîk-é-* | near (to) |

Note :

(a) پشت " behind " will be familiar to Latin scholars.

(b) در dar has two meanings : (1) a door, and (2) in.

(c) There are many more *ézâfé* prepositions—those given above are merely the most important.

Compound prepositions are common in Persian. They all take the *ézâfé* :

| | | |
|---|---|---|
| از توی * | *az tu-yé-* | from out of |
| از روی * | *az ru-yé* | off |
| از زیر * | *az zîr-é-* | from under |
| بطرف * | *bétaraf-é-* | in the direction of |
| بجای * | *béjâ-yé-* | in place of, instead of |
| از پشت * | *az posht-é-* | from behind |
| از نزدیک * | *az nazdîk-é-* | away from (" from near to ") |
| از طرف * | *az taraf-é-* | from the direction of, on behalf of |
| در میان * | *dar mîân-e-* | among |
| از میان * | *az mîân-é-* | from among |
| از بین * | *az bêin-é-* | from between |

## فرهنگ

| | | |
|---|---|---|
| table میز *mîz* | | pan دیگ *dîg* |
| carpet فرش *farsh*, قالی *ghâlî* | | light چراغ *cherâgh* |
| to stand ایستادن -ایست- *îstâdan,* | | plate بشقاب *boshghâb* |
| pres. stem -*îst-* | | spoon قاشق *ghâshogh* |
| to sit نشستن -نشین- *neshastan,* | | furniture اثاثیه *asâsîyé* |
| pres. stem -*neshîn-* | | tea چای *châî* |
| rug قالیچه *ghâlîché* | | lunch ناهار *nâhâr* |
| balcony بالکن *bâlkon* | | bed تخت خواب *takht-é-khâb* |
| key کلید *kelîd* | | placed, situated واقع *vâghé'* |
| wall دیوار *dîvâr* | | seated نشسته *neshasté* |
| stove بخاری *bokhârî* | | cup فنجان *fenjân* |

floor, ground زمین *zamín*  
a glass لیوان *livân*  
letter of the alphabet حرف *harf*  
street door, front door درب *darb*  
lock قفل *ghofl*  
picture نقش *naghsh*  
bowl ظرف *zarf*  

knife کارد *kârd*  
lampshade آبازور *âbâzhúr*  
fork چنگال *changâl*  
consisting of عبارت از *'ebârat az*  
breakfast ناشتائی *nâshtâ'î*  
translation ترجمه *tarjomé*  

Note : (a) عبارت از consisting of, is always used with the verb بودن to be. which is always placed after the عبارت *'ebârat* :

١ این کتاب عبارت است از ترجمه

*în ketâb 'ebârat ast az tarjomé*

This book consists of translation(s)

٢ اثاثه اش از چه عبارت بود؟

*asâseash az ché 'ebârat bûd ?*

What did his furniture consist of ?

(b) ظرف bowl and حرف letter of the alphabet are Arabic words. We can either use their Arabic plurals ظروف *zorûf* and حروف *horûf* or else the Persian ones ظرفها *zarfhâ* and حرفها *harfhâ*. With Arabic plurals we always have the choice of using the Persian plural. It is of course considered more educated to use the original Arabic one, though no foreigner would be criticized for not doing so.

تمرین

I. Translate and write out :

1. A plate, a knife, and a cup are on the table.
2. What is near the table ?
3. In this house there are three people (نفر). Outside the house is a garden, and in the garden there are flowers.

4. Did you see the key in the door ? Yes, it was in the door, but I pulled it out.

5. What do you have (= take) for lunch every day ?

6. Do you drink coffee with breakfast ? In England they drink tea out of cups, but in Iran we drink it out of glasses. (Use the singular for " cup " and " glass ".)

7. Who was standing behind the door ?

8. I saw my friend with his father yesterday.

9. Did he say this in your presence ?

10. No, he said it to his friends outside.

11. Inside this house there is a lot of furniture.

12. His house is situated near the Embassy.

13. What does his furniture consist of ? Of chairs, tables and beds.

14. He goes to work without me, but it is very near.

15. Is the stove near the front door ? Yes, it is situated behind the front door.

16. I went towards the mosque.

17. My brother was sitting inside the bank. He had a book in (his) hand.

18. I never have a hat on (my) head.

19. Who put the picture on that wall, near the window, under the light ?

20. We took the rug off the carpet, and under it we put our money.

21. This is your room, and this big bed is for you.

II. From the examples below, pick out the prepositional
constructions requiring the *ézâfé*. Then mark that *ézâfé*
with an * asterisk. Say how the *ézâfé* is pronounced
in each case :

| | | |
|---|---|---|
| ۳ از زیر زمین | ۲ توی اطاق | ۱ در اطاق |
| ۶ بدون اضافه | ۵ بی ناهار | ٤ در میان این بچهها |
| ۹ با اتوبوس | ۸ بطرف تهران | ۷ از پشت درب |
| | ۱۰ جز من | |

## LESSON 17*a*

The stressed prefix of the Present Tense, -می *mî-* can be
written separate in most verbs. There is no difference in
the pronunciation :

میروم or می روم *mîravam* I go

When this prefix is attached to a verb beginning with
آ *â*, the ˉ long sign over the ا *alef* is dropped when the
-می *mî-* is joined ; thus from آوردن *âvardan* to bring, present
stem -آور- *-âvar-*, we have

میاورم or میآورم *mîâvaram* I bring

We *must* write as one word, dropping the ا dummy *alef*,
all verbs beginning in short *a*. Thus from انداختن *andâkhtan*
to throw, we have میندازم *mîandâzæn* I throw.

We *must* write separately the Present of ایستادن *îstâdan*,
to stand. This is to avoid the clash of two long *î*'s :

می ایسم *mî-îstam* I stand

*Irregular Present Stems—1st group : kh-z, kh-s, kh-sh.*

Verbs whose infinitives end in the guttural combination
ختن *-khtan* change this ending into a sibilant sound, *z*, *s*, or
*sh*, to form their Present Stem.

(Note : In the following list, instead of quoting the Past Stem after the infinitive, we shall omit this Stem and quote instead the Present Stem. This system of quoting verbs is the usual one found in Iranian grammars and dictionaries, so we shall keep to it for the rest of this manual, omitting the Past Stem which is always regularly formed.)

## GROUP 1a. *kh-z*

| Infinitive | | English | Present Stem | |
|---|---|---|---|---|
| آموختن | *âmûkhtan* | teach | آموز- | *-âmûz-* |
| آمیختن | *âmîkhtan* | mix | آمیز- | *-âmîz-* |
| آویختن | *âvîkhtan* | hang | آویز- | *-âvîz-* |
| ساختن | *sâkhtan* | make | ساز- | *-sâz-* |
| سوختن | *sûkhtan* | burn (to be on fire) | سوز- | *-sûz-* |
| ریختن | *rîkhtan* | pour | ریز- | *-rîz-* |
| انداختن | *andâkhtan* | throw | انداز- | *-andâz-* |
| پرداختن | *pardâkhtan* | pay | پرداز- | *-pardâz-* |
| پختن | *pokhtan* | cook | پز- | *-paz-* |

(root vowel also changes here)

## GROUP 1b. Others

| شناختن | *shenâkhtan* | know a person, "*connaître*" | شناس- | *-shenâs-* |
|---|---|---|---|---|
| فروختن | *forûkhtan* | sell | فروش- | *-forûsh-* |

Note : (*a*) شناختن *shenâkhtan* to know is used only like the French *connaître* or the Spanish *conocer* or the German *kennen* : to know a person, to be acquainted with. To know a thing or a fact is a different verb.

(*b*) In پختن *pokhtan* to cook, the vowel also changes in forming the Present Stem : -پز- *-paz-*.

| | |
|---|---|
| ice یخ *yakh* | seed تخم *tokhm* |
| wind باد *bâd* | grass سبزه *sabzé* |
| world جهان *jahân*, دنیا *donyâ* | sea دریا *daryâ* |
| fall افتادن (-افت) *oftâdan, -oft-* | river رود *rûd*, رودخانه *rûdkhâné* |
| hill, } کوه or کوُه *kûḥ* | it's raining باران میاید *bârân* |
| mountain } که *koh* |   *miâyad* |
| rain باران *bârân* | snow برف *barf* |
| a plain دشت *dasht* | winter زمستان *zemestân* |
| it's snowing برف میاید *barf* | autumn پائیز *pâ'ïz* |
|   *miâyad* | climate آب و هوا *âb o havâ* |
| summer تابستان *tâbestân* | village ده *déḥ* |
| spring بهار *bahâr* | iron آهن *âhan* |
| little, few کم *kam* | season, chapter (book) فصل *fasl* |
| country کشور *keshvar* | seasons, chapters فصول (Ar. pl.) |
| road راه *râḥ* |   *fosûl* فصلها (Pers. pl.) *faslhâ* |
| railway راه آهن *râḥ-é-âhan* | tree درخت *derakht* |
| beside * کنار *kenâr-é-* | flour آرد *ârd* |
| salt نمک *namak* | desert بیابان *bîâbân* |
| | guest مهمان *mehmân* |

## TEXT

### فصول (فصلها)

در تابستان زمین خشک است ولی گاهی باران میاید. در ایران باران کم

میاید ولی در کشورهای دیگر باران * زیاد میاید. تابستان گرم است یا

سرد؟ تابستان گرم است. برف در فصل * تابستان و پائیز میاید؟

نخیر برف در زمستان میاید و گاهی در بهار.

در تابستان * خشک ما روی * درختها و روی * سبزهٔ باغ آب

میریزیم. دوست * ما پارسال درخت در باغ نداشت و در بهار تخم در زمین

کاشت و آب روی * تخمها ریخت: حالا درختهای * خیلی کوچک دارد.

زمستان گرم نیست ــ سرد است. در شهرهای * ایران و در دشت برف *

زیاد میاید. کشورهائی در دنیا هست که (which) در زمستان برف ندارد ولی

در ایران برف * زیاد و باد * سرد میاید. روی * رودخانه‌ها یخ هست.

فصل * بهار — در پای * کوه * دماوند (۵۳۳٤ متر)

(دماوند *damâvand*, highest mountain in Iran)

## تمرین

I. Answer each of these questions orally in Persian, then write your answer out :

۱ در کشورتان تابستان خیلی گرم است یا نه؟

۲ در کدام فصل برف میاید؟

۳ روی تخمهای کوچک چه میریزید؟

٤ در بیابان درخت هست؟ درخت. — (i.e. "trees" in general)

۵ منزلتان در ده واقع است یا در شهر؟

۶ در پائیز باد گرم است یا سرد؟

۷ ما در کشور * خودمان دشتهای بزرگ داریم؟

٨ شما در ایران بوده اید؟

٩ در ایران در فصل \* تابستان باران کم میاید یا زیاد؟

II. Translate orally and in writing :

1. He mixes flour, water, and salt and pours it into a cup. He cooks this on the fire.
2. He is standing near the door.
3. The fire is burning well.
4. What are you making? Will you sell it?
5. I know that man. He teaches my son Persian.
6. Why did he throw this paper out? I paid for it myself.
7. He is hanging the picture on the wall.
8. When did he sell his car?

III. Put into the Present Tense :

| | | |
|---|---|---|
| ٣ من شناختم | ٢ آنها سوخت | ١ شما پرداختید |
| ٦ انداختید | ٥ پخت | ٤ ایستادم |
| ٨ فروختیم | ٧ آوردند | |

## LESSON 18

*Present Stems ending in long vowels*

Some present stems end in long vowels, ١- *â* or و- *û*. e.g. The present stem of آمدن *âmadan* to come is -١- -*â*- and of گفتن *goftan* to say is -گو- - *gû*-.

In these verbs, because of the final vowel, the present undergoes slight changes, for phonetic reasons, before the addition of the personal endings م- -یم -د- -یم etc. We shall take آمدن and گفتن as models. All verbs whose present stems end in -١- -*â*- go like آمدن, and all verbs with present stems ending in -و- -*û*- go like گفتن.

| To come | | | To say | |
|---|---|---|---|---|
| آمدن *âmadan* | | | گفتن *goftan* | |
| آمد- *âmad*- past stem | | | گفت- *goft*- past stem | |
| -آ- -*â*- pres. stem | | | -گو- -*gû*- pres. stem | |

| | | | | |
|---|---|---|---|---|
| (1) | میانیم | میایم | میگوئیم | میگویم |
| | *miâ'îm* | *miâyam* | *migû'îm* | *migûyam* |
| (2) | میائید | میائید | میگوئید | میگوئید |
| | *miâ'îd* | *miâ'îd* | *migû'îd* | *migû'îd* |
| (3) | مایند | مایید | میگویند | میگوید |
| | *miâyand* | *miâyad* | *migûyand* | *migûyad* |
| | مایید | مایید | میگوید | میگوید |
| | *miâyad* | *miâyad* | *migûyad* | *migûyad* |

You will notice that (*a*) it is not the *endings* which are irregular, but the *stems*, (*b*) where the personal ending has the short vowel *a*, i.e. in the cases of the 1st singular and 3rd singular and plural :

$$(1)\ \text{م-} \quad\quad ———$$
$$(2)\ ——— \quad\quad ———$$
$$(3)\begin{cases} \text{د-} & \text{ند-} \\ \text{د-} & \text{د-} \end{cases}$$

we put the consonant -*y*- -ﻳ- between the stem and the personal ending. It is easier to say the word with this -ﻳ- glide-vowel put in. (*c*) Where the personal ending has the long vowel ﻴ *î*, i.e. in the cases of the 1st plural and 2nd singular and plural :

$$(1)\ ——— \quad\quad \text{م-}$$
$$(2)\ \text{ید-} \quad\quad \text{ید-}$$
$$(3)\ ——— \quad\quad ———$$

we put a ˈ *hamzé*, resting over a " bearer ", a bearer being, you will remember, like an undotted ‍ ب *b*, thus :

ٔ

This ٔ is pronounced as a glottal stop, like the letter ع ˈ*ain*.

Pronounce :

(Catch your breath on the *hamzé*) *mîgûˈîd* میگؤید

     *mîâˈîd* میائد      *migûˈîm* میگؤیم

But pronounce *a* -*y*- glide in these ones :

     *mîâyam* میایم      *mîgûyam* میگویم

     *mîâyad* میاید      *mîgûyand* میگویند

There is no glottal stop, no catch of the breath, in these last four examples. Be careful to see and hear the difference in :

| Glottal Stop | | -*y*- Glide | |
|---|---|---|---|
| میائد | میگؤید and | مياید | میگوید |
| *mîâˈid* | *mîgûˈid* | *mîâyad* | *mîgûyad* |
| you come | you say | he comes | he says |
| میائیم | میگؤیم and | میایم | میگویم |
| *mîâˈim* | *mîgûˈim* | *mîâyam* | *mîgûyam* |
| we come | we say | I come | I say |

*Irregular Present Stems—2nd group : ûdan-â*

Verbs whose infinitive ends in ‍ ودن- -*ûdan* take a Present Stem in ‍ ا- -*â*- and conjugate exactly like آمدن *âmadan* above in the present tense :

| Infinitive | English | Present Stem |
|---|---|---|
| فرمودن *farmûdan* | command | ‍ فرما- -*farmâ*- |
| نمودن *namûdan* | show | ‍ نما- -*namâ*- |

| افزودن afzûdan | increase | ‑افزا- -afzâ- |
| آزمودن âzmûdan | test, examine | ‑آزما- -âzmâ- |
| پیمودن pêimûdan | measure | ‑پیما- -pêimâ- |
| زادن zâdan | bear young (animals) | ‑زا- -zâ- |

(the infinitive has the present stem vowel here)

Note that the irregularities we are listing concern the present tense only: the past tense of *all* verbs is *always regular* in Persian.

## عبارات EXPRESSIONS 'ebârât

(a)　　چه فرمودید؟ *ché farmûdîd ?*

چه فرمودید خانم؟ *ché farmûdîd khânom ?* (to a lady)

چه فرمودید آقا؟ *ché farmûdîd âghâ ?* (to a gentleman)

These expressions, meaning literally " What did you command ? " are used in polite conversation to mean " What did you say ? ".

(b) بله؟ *balé ?* (" Yes ? ") said with a rise in the voice: *balé ?* means " I beg your pardon—what did you say ? ".

We can use (i) and (ii) together :

بله چه فرمودید؟

*balé, ché farmûdîd ?* Excuse me, but what did you say ?

(c) خواهش میکنم *khâhesh mîkonam* Please (requesting something) :

خواهش میکنم راه * شمیران کجاست؟

*khâhesh mîkonam — râh-é-shemirân kojâst ?*

Excuse me—where is the Shemirân road ? (Shemirân is a northern suburb of Tehran)

تمرین

I. In the following verbs in the present tense, a ـ " bearer "
has been written without its necessary mark, ٔ *hamzé* or
ـ two dots (-*y*- glide) as the case may be. Fill in the
*hamzé* or the -*y*- glide as necessary :

(e.g. شما میائد should be شما میائد
(من میگؤم should be من میگوم)

١ ایشان میگؤند       ٢ کی میأد؟

٣ ما مینأیم       ٤ آن میفزأد

٥ شما چه میفرمأید؟       ٦ او میگؤد

٧ ما نمیگؤیم       ٨ او نمینأد

٩ هیچکس نمی آزمأد

II. Now check your answers to Ex. I with the Key at the
back of the book : correct your mistakes.
Now pronounce carefully each example of Ex. I :

ٔ = a glottal stop

ـ = -*y*-

III. Put into the present tense :

١ چه فرمودید؟       ٢ نیامدند

٣ او نیاموخت       ٤ آمدیم

٥ گفتید

## LESSON 18a

*Numbers*

  Cardinal :

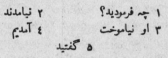

| | | | | | | |
|---|---|---|---|---|---|---|
| 3 | سه *sé* ٣ | | | 1 | یک *yek* ١ | |
| 4 | چهار *chahâr* ٤ or ٣ | | | 2 | دو *do* ٢ | |

| | | | | | |
|---|---|---|---|---|---|
| 8 | هشت | hasht | ۸ | | |
| 9 | نه | noḥ | ۹ | | |
| 10 | ده | daḥ | ۱۰ | | |

| 5 | پنج | panj | ۰ or ۵ |
|---|---|---|---|
| 6 | شش | shesh | ۶ or ۶ |
| 7 | هفت | haft | ۷ |

0   صفر   sefr   ۰

Ordinal :

| 6th | ششم | ۶م | sheshòm | 1st | اول | — | avval |
|---|---|---|---|---|---|---|---|
| 7th | هفتم | ۷م | haftòm | 2nd | دوم | ۲م | dovvòm |
| 8th | هشتم | ۸م | hashtòm | 3rd | سوم | ۳م | sevvòm |
| 9th | نهم | ۹م | nohòm | 4th | چهارم | ۳م | chahâròm |
| 10th | دهم | ۱۰م | dahòm | 5th | پنجم | ۵م | panjòm |

Note : (a) Apart from اول 1st avval, which is taken from Arabic, all ordinal numbers are formed by adding the syllable م -òm to the cardinal number. This م- -òm is stressed. (b) The ordinals are adjectives, and are joined to the noun they qualify, by the ézâfé :

چهارم * درس   dars-é-chahâròm the fourth lesson

صفحهٔ پنجم   safḥé-yé-panjòm the fifth page

جلد هشتم   jeld-é-hashtòm   the eighth volume

(c) The cardinals are always used with the noun in the singular. We say اسبها asbhâ horses, but with a number it is singular, thus : چهار اسب chahâr asb four horses.

شش کتاب وپنج قلم   shesh ketâb va panj ghalam

" six book and five pen "

When the noun denotes *people*, we often use the word

نفر nafar persons

between the number and the noun. When the noun denotes things or animals, we can use

تا tâ pieces

in the same position :

۱ پنج نفر ايرانی و دو نفر انگليسی هفت نفرند

*panj nafar îrânî va do nafar inglîsî haft nafarand*

Five Iranians and two Englishmen are seven people

۲ اين شش تا قلم و آن سه تا کتاب را بايشان دادم

*în shesh tâ ghalam va ân sé tâ ketâb râ bé-îshân dâdam*

I gave them these six pens and those three books

The cardinal numbers answer the questions

چقدر؟ *chéghadr ?*    چند؟ *chand ?*    چند نفر؟ *chand nafar ?*

چند تا؟ *chand tâ ?* How many ?

چقدر؟ *chéghadr ?* also means the singular : How much ?
This expression never takes نفر *nafar* or تا *tâ* after it.

The ordinal numbers answer the question, untranslatable
into English :

چندمين؟ *chandomîn ?* " the how-manyeth ? "

cf. the German adjective *der Wievielte ?*

چندمين *chandomîn* is an adjective, but it always precedes
its noun and has no *ézâfé*.

Read these examples for practice :

۱ ديروز چند نفر دوست آمدند؟ شش نفر آمدند

۲ چند تا کتاب خوانديد؟ من دو تا خواندم ولی دوستم سه تا خواند

۳ اين چندمين درس است؟ ششم يا هفتم؟ اين درس هفتم است

٤ چقدر پول داريد؟ من هيچ پول ندارم

تمرين

I. Write in Persian numerals (e.g. 6 + 4 = 10 becomes
۱۰ = ٤ + ۶) :

    (*a*) 2 × 3 = 6  (*b*) $6\frac{1}{2} + 3\frac{1}{2} = 10$  (*c*) 6th, 7th, and 8th

II. Write in words in Persian :

    (*a*) eighth  (*b*) first  (*c*) second  (*d*) third

III. Fill in the blank with نفر or تا as necessary:

۱ در این اطاق شش —— صندلی و دو —— میز است

۲ چند —— فنجان داریم؟

۳ دو —— ایرانی رفتند

٤ چند نفر مهمان میایند؟ پنج —— مهمان میایند

۵ چند —— فرش فروخت؟

(مهمان *mehmân* = a guest)

## LESSON 19

*The Subjunctive*

The subjunctive mood is used a great deal in Persian. By itself, a subjunctive verb has the meaning " may " or " might " or " let me (do) —— ".

The Present Subjunctive is formed by taking the Present Tense, dropping the میـ *mi*- prefix, and substituting the Subjunctive Prefix بـ *bé*. This بـ *bé* is usually *joined* in writing.

Compare, for example, the Present Tense with the Present Subjunctive Tense of

رفتن *raftan* to go

Present Stem ‑رو‑ *-rav-*

| Present Tense | Present Subjunctive Tense |
|---|---|
| SINGULAR | |

(1) میروم *míravam* I go     بروم *béravam* I may go

(2) میروید *míravíd* you go     بروید *béravíd* you may go

(3) { میرود *míravad* he goes     برود *béravad* he may go

     میرود *míravad* it goes     برود *béravad* it may go

PLURAL

(1) میرویم *mîravîm* we go          برویم *béravîm* we may go

(2) میروید *mîravîd* you go          بروید *béravîd* you may go

(3) { میروند *mîravand* they go          بروند *béravand* they may go

میرود *mîravad* they go          برود *béravad* they may go

The بِ *bé* is always stressed. Pronounce:

بروم *béravam*      بگویم *bégûyam*      بخوانیم *békhánîm*

بفروشد *béjorûshad*      بنمائید *bénamâ'íd*      بفرمایند *béfarmâyand*

When the verb begins with آ long *â* or ا short *a*, the بِ becomes بی, and the whole combination is pronounced بیا *bîâ* or بیا *bîa* (the ‾ *maddé* is dropped):

آ verbs : بیاموزند *bîâmûzand*      بیایم *bîâyam*

ا verbs : بیافزوئیم *bîafzû'îm*      بیاندازد *bîandâzad*

Before ایستادن *îstâdan* to stop, the به *bé*- is separated:

به ایستم *bé-îstam* I may stop

To make the negative of the Subjunctive, we first remove the بِ-بی *bé*- or *bî*-, and then replace it with the negative prefix نَ *na*-, or نَی *nay*- before a vowel. This negative prefix is stressed here as elsewhere. Remember that the بِ *bé* or بی *bî* is *dropped* in the Negative Present Subjunctive. So, for گفتن for example :

Present Subjunctive                    Present Subjunctive
Affirmative                            Negative

بگویم *bégûyam* I may say          نگویم *nagúyam* I may not say

بگوئید *bégû'îd* you may say          نگوئید *nagú'îd* you may not say

بگوید *bégûyad* he may say          نگوید *nagúyad* he may not say

بگوئیم *bégû'îm* we may say          نگوئیم *nagú'îm* we may not say

بگوئید *bégû'îd* you may say　　　نگوئید *nagû'îd* you may not say

بگویند *bégûyand* they may　　　نگویند *nagûyand* they may not
say　　　　　　　　　　　　　　　　　　　　　say

The second person of the Subjunctive (both affirmative and negative) is used by itself as the Imperative or command form :

من بگوئید *béman bégû'îd* Tell me

باو نگوئید *bé-û nagû'îd* Don't tell him

منزل بروید *manzel béravîd* Go home

اینجا نیائید *înjâ nayâ'îd* Do not come here

آن کتاب را بدهید *ân kitâb râ bédehîd* Give that book

Similarly, other persons (without pronouns) can be used to express the idea " let . . . " :

برود *béravad* let him go, he may go, may he go

نگوئیم *nagû'îm* let us not say, may we not say

and the question form of the 1st person singular is very common, thus :

چه بگویم؟ *ché bégûyam ?* What am I to say ? What can I say ?

*Suffix* ش- *-esh.* Besides meaning his, her, or its (possessive), the suffix ش- *-esh* can be added to prepositions. This usage is particularly common in colloquial speech :

| What did you | { *ché bé-û goftîd ?* | ۱ باو چه گفتید؟ |
| tell him/her ? | { *ché besh goftîd ?* | ۲ چه بش گفتید؟ |
| I asked him/her | { *az û nâmesh porsîdam* | ۳ از او نامش را پرسیدم |
| his/her name | { *azesh nâmesh porsîdam* | ٤ ازش نامش را پرسیدم |

(پرسیدن *porsîdan,* ـپرس- *-pors-* = to ask)

Prepositions normally taking the *ézâfé* after them drop their *ézâfé* if this ش- -*esh* suffix is added:

| He stood behind him/her | { *posht-é-û îstâd* *poshtesh îstâd* | ٥ پشت * او ایستاد ٦ پشتش ایستاد |
| Did you go in front of it? | { *pîsh-é-ân raftîd?* *pîshesh raftîd?* | ٧ پیش * آن رفتید؟ ٨ پیشش رفتید؟ |

If the preposition ends in a vowel, we put a -ی- -*y* glide between it and the ش- -*esh* to facilitate pronunciation:

| Is the book on the table? | { بله روی * آن است *balé rûyé ân ast* } | ٩ کتاب روی * میز است؟ *ketâb rûyé mîz ast?* |
| Yes, it is on it | { بله رویش است *balé rûyesh ast* } |

My friend went instead of him/her

*dûstam bejâyesh raft*        ١٠ دوستم بجایش رفت

The ش- -*esh* suffix can also be added to verbs, to indicate the direct object of that verb:

> آن را or اورا = here ش-

| No, I didn't see him/her | { نه اورا ندیدم *na ûrâ nadîdam* نه ندیدمش *na nadîdæmesh* |

In all the uses of ش- -*esh* outlined above, we can use the corresponding plural suffix شان- -*eshân* = them (animate *and* inanimate). This use is similarly colloquial:

I told him/her *besh goftam*        ١ بش گفتم
I told them *beshân goftam*        ٢ بشان گفتم

۱ شما پهلویش بودید؟

Were you at his/her house ? *shomâ pahlûyesh bûdîd ?*

۲ شما پهلویشان بودید؟

Were you at their house ? *shomâ pahlûyeshân bûdîd ?*

I didn't see him/her *nadîdamesh* ندیدمش ۱

I didn't see them *nadîdameshân* ندیدمشان ۲

Note : بودن *bûdan* and داشتن *dâshtan*. Do not attempt yet to form the Present Subjunctives of these two verbs. They have special Subjunctive forms which we shall deal with later.

تمرین

I. Put into the Present Subjunctive :

| | | |
|---|---|---|
| ۱ میروم | ۲ نمیایم | ۳ میپرسید |
| ٤ میکنند | ۵ میگوید | ۶ نمیخوریم |
| ۷ مینویسیم | ۸ نمیکشد | ۹ میپردازیم |
| | ۱۰ نمیپزد | |

II. Make your answers to Ex. I Nos. ۱, ۳, ٤, ۵, ۷, and ۹ *negative subjunctive.*

III. Make your answers to Ex. I Nos. ۲, ۶, ۸, and ۱۰ *affirmative subjunctive.*

IV. Write in Persian and then read aloud, paying attention to the stressed prefixes :

1. May I go out ?
2. What am I to say ?
3. Come here.
4. Where is he to go ?
5. Let's see him. (One word.)
6. Don't take his money.

7. Let him not take his (own) money.
8. Say this after (= with) me.
9. Don't cook my dinner late tonight.
10. Why may I not pay ?

V. Put into the form using the suffix ش- -esh or شان-
-eshân :

۲ باو گفتم

۴ روی * آن بود

۱ چرا آنرا نکردید؟

۳ باو نگئید

۵ توی * اطاق نرود

VI. Translate Ex. V.

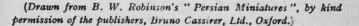

(Drawn from B. W. Robinson's " Persian Miniatures ", by kind
permission of the publishers, Bruno Cassirer, Ltd., Oxford.)

### LESSON 19a

*Questions.* We said in Lesson 13a that we make a question in Persian by raising the voice towards the end of the sentence (in speech) and (in writing) we occasionally, though by no means always, use a European question-mark reversed ؟. Not all Persian books, and very few Persian writers, bother about the ؟ mark. Persian books printed in Europe usually do, of course, use ؟.

The *order of words* of the statement is not changed to make a question :

They saw him    *ûrâ didand*    ۱ اورا دیدند

(falling tone)

Did they see him ?    *ûrâ didand ?*    ۲ اورا دیدند؟

(rising, inquiring tone)

*Question-words.* Many questions in Persian, as in English, are introduced by question-words :

why ?    *chérâ ?*    چرا

what ?    *ché ?*    چه    (colloquially *chî ?*) *ché chîz ?*    چه چیز

which ?    *kodâm ?*    کدام

who ?    *kî ?*    کی

when ?    *kêi ?*    کی

where ?    *kojâ ?*    کجا

how ?    *chétôur ?*    چطور

how much/many ? *chand ?*    چند    *chéghadr ?*    چقدر

and the many compounds we can form from these words :

whose ?    *mâl-é-kî ?*    کی * مال

for what ?    *barâ-yé-ché ?*    چه * برای

from where ?   *az kojâ ?*   از کجا

until when ?   *tâ kêi ?*   تا کی

and so forth.

When these words are used to form questions in Persian, we can put them at the beginning of the question, as in English :

Where did Hassan come from ?   ۱ حسن از کجا آمد؟

To whom did he say this ?   ۲ به کی این چیز را گفت؟

When are you coming tomorrow ?   ۳ شما فردا کی میائید؟

Why did you come today ?   ٤ چرا امروز آمدید؟

But it is far more usual to put the question-word immediately before the verb, i.e. nearly at the end of the question :

۱ حسن از کجا آمد؟

۲ این چیز را به کی میگفت؟

۳ شما فردا کی میائید؟

٤ امروز چرا آمدید؟

In good conversational Persian this latter order is much better.

*Indirect Speech.* In English, we have two ways of indicating speech. We have Direct Speech :

(*a*) He said " I am ill "

and we have Indirect Speech or Reported Speech :

(*b*) He said that he was ill

These two sentences both mean exactly the same thing, but in (*a*) the *exact words* of the speaker, with no alteration in tense or person, are used. In (*b*) we merely get a *report* of what the speaker said : the tense of the verb and the person of its subject are both changed to fit the report.

In Persian there is no distinction between Direct and Indirect Speech : we always use the *exact* words of the speaker.

« » Inverted commas are occasionally used in Persian : they are not obligatory.

Speech is usually introduced by the conjunction که *ke* " that ". This word, like the inverted commas, is not obligatory.

Examine :

My brother said " I am ill "      ۱ برادرم گفت «مریضم»

        OR               ۲ برادرم گفت مریضم

My brother said that he was ill    ۳ برادرم گفت که مریضم

(مریض *mariz* ill)             ٤ برادرم گفت که «مریضم»

Exactly the same method is used to express questions in speech :

Ahmad asked " Where are you going ? "    ۱ احمد پرسید «شما کجا میروید؟»

        OR            ۲ احمد پرسید شما کجا میروید؟

Ahmad asked where I/he/ she was OR we/you/they were going    ۳ احمد پرسید که شما کجا میروید؟

                 ٤ احمد پرسید که «شما کجا میروید؟»

In the questions ۱, ۲, ۳, and ٤ above the ؟ may also be omitted.

The *context* of the speech usually indicates who is meant by the " شما ", but the exact words of the speaker are always used. As you see, the conjunction "که" is not always translatable into English.

A question which requires an answer "yes" or "no" may be introduced by آیا. This is an untranslatable question particle. It always appears as first word in the question clause:

Are you going out? 

{
shomá birûn mîravîd ?    ۱ شما بیرون میروید؟

OR

áyâ shomá birûn mîravîd ?    ۲ آیا شما بیرون میروید؟
}

If we wish to quote a yes-no question as speech, we usually introduce this question by که آیا, which is then translated as "whether" in English. Again, neither the که nor the آیا is obligatory:

Ahmad asked "Are you going out?"

OR

Ahmad asked whether I/ he/she was OR we/you/ they were going out

{
۱ احمد پرسید شما بیرون میروید

۲ احمد پرسید آیا شما بیرون میروید

۳ احمد پرسید که شما بیرون میروید

٤ احمد پرسید که آیا شما بیرون میروید
}

All the above, ۱, ۲, ۳, and ٤, can take either « » or ؟ or both together; and the *context* of the question tells us who is indicated by شما shomá.

Again, the same method is used to express commands as quoted speech:

| | | |
|---|---|---|
| Go! | béravîd | بروید |
| He said "Go" | goft béravîd | ۱ گفت بروید |
| OR | goft béravîd | ۲ گفت «بروید» |
| He told me/him/her/us/ | goft ké béravîd | ۳ گفت که بروید |
| you/them to go | goft ké béravîd | ٤ گفت که «بروید» |

*Irregular Present Stems—3rd group : -stan verbs*

Verbs whose infinitive ends in ـستن ‎ -*stan* nearly all have irregular Present Stems. Here are the most important irregularities encountered :

### GROUP 3a. s-h

| Infinitive | | English | Present Stem |
|---|---|---|---|
| كاستن | *kâstan* | lessen | ‑كاه‑ ‑*kâh*‑ |
| خواستن | *khâstan* | wish, want | ‑خواه‑ ‑*khâh*‑ |
| جستن | *jastan* | jump | ‑جه‑ ‑*jah*‑ |
| رستن | *rastan* | escape | ‑ره‑ ‑*rah*‑ |

### GROUP 3b. s-nd

| | | | |
|---|---|---|---|
| بستن | *bastan* | tie, bind, close | ‑بند‑ ‑*band*‑ |
| پیوستن | *pêivastan* | unite | ‑پیوند‑ ‑*pêivand*‑ |

### GROUP 3c. s-n

| | | | |
|---|---|---|---|
| شکستن | *shekastan* | break | ‑شکن‑ ‑*shekan*‑ |
| نشستن | *neshastan* | sit | ‑نشین‑ ‑*neshîn*‑ |

(vowel change also here)

### GROUP 3d. Others

| | | | |
|---|---|---|---|
| گسیختن | *gosîkhtan* ⎫ | break | ‑گسل‑ ‑*gosel*‑ |
| گسستن | *gosîstan* ⎭ | | |
| شستن | *shostan* | wash | ‑شو‑ ‑*shû*‑ |
| جستن | *jostan* | look for, seek | ‑جو‑ ‑*jû*‑ |
| خاستن | *khâstan* | arise | ‑خیز‑ ‑*khîz*‑ |

In Group 3d above, note (*a*) گسستن *gosîstan* to break has an alternative form in the infinitive only—the present stem has only the one form. This verb is not as common as 3c شکستن *shekastan*. (*b*) In all these four verbs there is a vowel change as well as a consonant change. (*c*) Do not confuse

3a خواستن khâstan = to wish (pres. stem -خواه- --khâh-) with
3d خاستن khâstan (no mute -و- v here, N.B.) whose meaning
is to arise, with the pres. stem خیز -khîz-.

## TEXT

### مرد * دانا و مرد * پیاده

مردی دانا روزی بر سبزه کنار * راهی نشسته بود. دید شخصی پیاده
میاید. وقتی که این شخص نزدیک مرد * دانا رسید پرسید «از اینجا تا شهر
چند ساعت راه است؟» مرد دانا گفت «راه بروید» آن شخص تعجب کرد
و پرسید «چه فرمودید؟» مرد * دانا جواب داد «گفتم راه بروید» مرد *
پیاده فکر کرد «این مرد دیوانه است» و بدون اینکه حرف بزند بطرف شهر
راه افتاد وقتی که قدری راه رفت مرد * دانا صدایش کرد و گفت «شها دو
ساعته بشهر میرسید» شخص * پیاده گفت «پس چرا زود تر نگفتید» مرد *
دانا گفت «چون اول نمیدانستم تند یا یواش راه میروید نمیتوانستم بگویم دیر
یا زود بشهر میرسید ولی حالا که دیدم چطور راه میروید میدانم که دو
ساعته بشهر میرسید».

## فرهنگ

| | | | |
|---|---|---|---|
| sick, ill مریض *marîz* | | but ولی *valî* | |
| seated نشسته *neshasté* | | now that حالا که *hâlâ ké* | |
| a few چند *chand* | | centre مرکز *markaz* | |
| walk { پیاده رفتن *piâdé raftan* / راه رفتن *râh raftan* | | wise دانا *dânâ* | |
| | | fellow شخص *shakhs* | |
| be surprised تعجب کردن *ta'ajjob kardan* | | walking, on foot پیاده *piâdé* | |
| surprise تعجب *ta'ajjob* | | when وقتی که *vaghtî ké* | |
| a second time دفعهٔ دوم *daf'é-yé-dovvóm* | | after بعد از *ba'd az* | |
| | | moment موقع *móughé* | |
| ask (of) پرسیدن -پرس- (از) *porsîdan, -pors-* | | grass سبزه *sabzé* | |
| | | a time دفعه *daf'é* | |
| then پس *pas* | | think فکر کردن *fekr kardan* | |
| | | as چون *chún* | |

mad دیوانه *dîvâné*

earlier, sooner, quicker زودتر *zûdtar*

arrive رسیدن -رس- *rasîdan, -ras-*

speak حرف زدن *harf zadan*

voice صدا *sedâ*

call صدا کردن *sedâ kardan*

know (a fact) دانستن -دان- *dânestan, -dân-*

minute } دقیقه *daghîghé*
moment }

without a word* بدون* حرف زدن *bedûn-é-harf-zadan*

slow(ly) یواش *yavâsh*

hour, watch ساعت *sâ'at*

civilization تمدن *tamaddon*

answer جواب *javâb*

تمرین

### I. Answer these questions orally and in writing in Persian:

۱ مرد * دانا کجا نشسته بود؟     ۲ کی دید؟

۳ مرد * پیاده از مرد * دانا چه پرسید؟     ٤ و مرد * دانا چه جوابش داد؟

۵ مرد * دانا چرا این جواب را داد؟ چه چیز را نمیدانست؟

### II. Translate:

1. I don't know what his name is.
2. Did he say where he was going?
3. Tell him to go.
4. Hassan said he had seen someone in the village, but he didn't know who it was.
5. Tell him to wash his hands.

### III. Translate (a) into English Direct Speech, then (b) into English Indirect Speech:

e.g.

بش گفت که بروید.

(a) He said to him: " Go."

(b) He told him to go.

۱ ازش پرسیدم که چرا اینجا هستید     ۲ بایشان فرمود بیائید

۳ مرد فکر کرد که این شخص دیوانه است     ٤ گفت دیر است

۵ امروز آموختیم چند سال * پیش ایران مرکز * تمدن بود

## LESSON 20

After the verbs " can, to be able to " and " want to "
in English, we use the infinitive of the verb:

$$\left.\begin{array}{l}\text{I can go}\\ \text{I am able to go}\\ \text{I want to go}\end{array}\right\} \text{(in the Present)}$$

$$\left.\begin{array}{l}\text{I could go}\\ \text{I was able to go}\\ \text{I wanted to go}\end{array}\right\} \text{(in the Past)}$$

In all these examples, " go " and " to go " are infinitives
in English.

In Persian, we do not use the infinitive in such cases,
but the Present Subjunctive Tense (the ـبِ *bé-* tense) in the
appropriate person, thus, for example:

بروم   *béravam*   that I may/might go

*can, to be able to* :

> Infinitive :   توانستن   *tavânestan*
> Past Stem :   ـتوانست-   *tavânest-*
> Present Stem : ـتوان-   *-tavân-*

Thus the Present 1st person singular is میتوانم (من) (*man*)
*mîtavânam* I can, I am able to. The Past 1st person singular
is (من) توانستم (*man*) *tavânestam* I could, I was able to.

*to want to* :

> Infinitive :   خواستن   *khâstan*
> Past Stem :   ـخواست-   *khâst-*
> Present Stem : ـخواه-   *-khâh-*

Present 1st singular میخواهم (من) (*man*) *mîkhâham* I want
to.   Past 1st person singular (من) خواستم (*man*) *khâstam*
I wanted to.

Examine:

> *man mîtavânam ânjâ béravam* ‏۱ من میتوانم آنجا بروم‏
>
> I am able to go there (literally, I am able that I go there)

> *shomâ tavânestîd ânjâ béravîd* ‏۲ شما توانستید آنجا بروید‏
>
> You were able to go (literally, that you might go) there

> *îshân namîtavânand înjâ bîâyand* ‏۳ ایشان نمیتوانند اینجا بیایند‏
>
> They can't come (literally, They cannot, that they may come) here

> *kî mîkhâhad bâ man béravad ?* ‏۴ کی میخواهد با من برود؟‏
>
> Who wants to go (literally, that he go) with me ?

> *hîchkas nakhâst bédaftar béravad* ‏۵ هیچکس نخواست بدفتر برود‏
>
> Nobody wanted to go to the office

> ‏۶ دوستم گفت که نمیخواهد دیر برسد‏
> *dûstam goft ké namîkhâhad dîr bérasad*
>
> My friend said he didn't want to arrive late
>
> (OR: My friend said: " I don't want . . . ")

The ‏توانستن‏ or ‏خواستن‏ form (called the auxiliary verb) can come just before the subjunctive verb :

> *shomâ înjâ mîkhâhîd beneshînîd ?* ‏۷ شما اینجا میخواهید بنشینید؟‏
>
> Do you want to sit here ?

*or* just after its own subject :

> *shomâ mîkhâhîd înjâ beneshînîd ?* ‏۸ شما میخواهید اینجا بنشینید؟‏
>
> Do you want to sit here ?

The subjunctive verb can be *understood*, of course, just as the corresponding infinitive can in English :

> *mîkhâham bégûyam valî namîtavânam* ‏۹ میخواهم بگویم ولی نمیتوانم‏
>
> I want to speak, but I can't

*râh namîravand. ramîkhâhand*   ۱۰ راه نمیروند. نمیخواهند

They aren't walking.  They don't want to

After the verb " want to " in English, we often have an *object* before the infinitive :

I want him to write (i.e. I don't want to write myself)

This is translated by putting the object between the خواستن auxiliary and the subjunctive verb, but in the *subject* form : i.e. no را- *-râ* particle attached to the noun or pronoun.  For further clarity a که *ké* particle can be used :

I want him to write
(literally. I want that
he should write)
$$\left\{ \begin{array}{l} \text{۱۱ من میخواهم او بنویسد} \\ \textit{man mîkhâham û bénevîsad} \\ \text{OR} \\ \text{۱۲ من میخواهم که او بنویسد} \\ \textit{man mîkhâham ké û bénevîsad} \end{array} \right.$$

A further word about خواستن : it can of course take an ordinary direct object, as " want " can in English :

I want an apple *sib mîkhâham*   ۱۳ سیب میخواهم

## تمرین

I. Translate :

1. Can he write Persian ?  Yes, he can.

2. Does he want to learn this ?  No, he doesn't (want).

3. Where do you want to sit ?

4. I can't wash (my) hands without water.

5. Why don't you want him to see your house ?

6. Nobody could tell me this.

7. Do you want dinner now ?

8. He wanted to sleep, but he couldn't.

9. Yesterday he was very ill and couldn't eat anything.

10. When did you want to see us ?  Are we to come
early ?

II. Put the infinitive on the left into the correct subjunctive form to fit the sentence on the right :

| | |
|---|---|
| نشـسـتن | ۱ میخواهد اینجا —— |
| شستن | ۲ بی آب نمیتوانم —— |
| دانسـتن | ۳ چه خواستید ——؟ |
| خواندن<br>نوشتن | ۴ حالا میتوانم فارسی —— و —— |
| دیدن | ۵ در این کتاب نمیتوانیم —— که اسمش چیست |

III. (a) Put into the Past Tense Ex. II Nos. ۱, ۲, ۴,
and ۵.

   (b) Put into the Present Tense Ex. II No. ۳.


## LESSON 20a

*To ask.*  The English verb " to ask " is translated into
Persian in two ways :

خواستن *khâstan* (to want) = to request, ask for something

پرسیدن *porsîdan* = to ask a question

They both take از *az* (from) with their personal object :

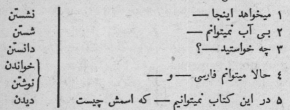

What did you ask of     از من چه خواستید؟
me ?           *az man ché khâstîd ?*

I asked him to come     از او خواستم تنها بیائید
alone             *az û khâstam tanhâ biâ'îd*

خواستن

| | | |
|---|---|---|
| What (question) did you ask me ? | از من چه پرسیدید؟<br>*az man ché porsîdîd ?* | پرسیدن |
| I asked you what this was | از شما پرسیدم که این چیست<br>*az shomâ porsîdam ké în chîst* | |

### Irregular Present Stems—verbs in ـدن- *-dan*

Verbs whose infinitive ends in ـدن- *-dan* fall into various groups :

(*a*) ـودن- *-ûdan* verbs are the second group of irregulars. See Lesson 18 for these.

(*b*) ـیدن- *-îdan* verbs are all regular, forming their present stems by dropping the ـیدن- *-îdan, except* those listed below under (*c*) and (*d*).

(*c*) The following verbs in ـدن- *-dan* have present stems in ـن- *-n-,* and occasionally other irregularities as well, which should be carefully noted :

| Infinitive | English | Present Stem |
|---|---|---|
| زدن *zadan* | hit | ـزن- *-zan-* |
| کردن *kardan* | do | ـکن- *-kon-* |
| آفریدن *âfarîdan* | create | ـآفرین- *-âfarîn-* |
| دیدن *dîdan* | see | ـبین- *-bîn-* |
| چیدن *chîdan* | arrange, lay out | ـچین- *-chîn-* |

(*d*) The following verbs in ـدن- *-dan* have present stems in ـو- *-v-* as well as a vowel change :

| Infinitive | English | Present Stem |
|---|---|---|
| شنیدن *shenîdan* | hear | ـشنو- *-shenav-* |
| شدن *shodan* | become | ـشو- *-shav-* |

*Compound Verbs.* You will probably have noticed that we have learned comparatively few verbs, so far. Persian has very few simple verbs; it uses simple verbs combined with other words, usually nouns or adjectives, making compound verbs.

*Compound Verbs formed with* کردن *kardan to do*

| | | |
|---|---|---|
| wait (for) | *sabr kardan (barâyé)* | صبر کردن (برای) |
| thank (*to* somebody) | *tashakkor k.* (*az kasî*) | تشکر کردن (از کسی) |
| speak | *sohbat k.* | صحبت کردن |
| work | *kâr k.* | کار کردن |
| accept, agree | *ghabûl k.* | قبول کردن |
| throw out, reject | *bîrûn k.* | بیرون کردن |
| prepare | *hâzer k.* | حاضر کردن |
| arrange | *dorost k.* | درست کردن |
| live (in a place) | *manzel k.* | منزل کردن |
| live (exist) | *zendegî k.* | زندگی کردن |
| move off | *harakat k.* | حرکت کردن |
| try | *sa'î k.* | سعی کردن |
| | *kûshesh k.* | کوشش کردن |
| open | *bâz k.* | باز کردن |
| find | *pêidâ k.* | پیدا کردن |
| think | *fekr k.* | فکر کردن |
| help (*to* somebody) | *komak k. (bé kasî)* | کمک کردن (بکس) |
| change | *'avaz k.* | عوض کردن |

Compound verbs form all the usual tenses, by inflecting the verb half of the compound, *which is never separated.* The Subjunctive, and hence also the Imperative, of a Compound Verb has no ـب *bé-* prefix; compare

۱ میتوانم اینرا بکنم

*mîtavânam înrâ békonam* I can do this

with

۲ میتوانم فارسی صحبت کنم

*mîtavânam fârsî soḥbat konam* I can speak Persian

Let us examine a typical Compound Verb, تشکر کردن *tashakkor k.* " to thank " in all its parts, as an example :

Infinitive :  تشکر کردن *tashakkor k.* to thank
Past Stem :  تشکر کرد- *t. kard-*
Pres. Stem :  تشکر -کن- *t. -kon-*
Pres. Tense :  تشکر میکنم *t. mîkonam* (etc.) I thank
Past Tense :  تشکر کردم *t. kardam* (etc.) I thanked
Subjunctive :  تشکر کنم *t. konam* (etc.) may I thank
Imperative :  تشکر کنید *t. konîd* Thank (someone)

The negative prefix -ن *nâ-* is added of course in the usual way to the verbal element of the compound. Remember that the non-verbal element of the compound *never changes and never separates itself from the verbal element.*

If we wish to suffix ش- -esh or شان- -eshân (him or them) as a direct object to a Compound Verb, we attach the suffix to the *non-verbal element*:

Throw it out ! *bîrûnesh konîd* بیرونش کنید

I didn't open them *bâzeshân nàkardam* بازشان نکردم

## TEXT

### صحبت

دیروز با یک آقا صحبت کردم که اسمش علی است و ازش پرسیدم که شما کجا منزل میکنید؟

من: علی من میدانم که شما چه کار میکنید ولی نمیدانم که شما کجا منزل میکنید

علی: چند وقت * پیش وقتیکه در شهر منزل کردم منزلم در خیابان * شاه بود ولی حال در شمیران در یک کوچهٔ کوچک منزل میکنم. اسم * این کوچه کوچهٔ تهران است

من: کوچهٔ تهران - صبر کنید - آن نه کوچهٔ کوچک نزدیک * دفتر * خودتان است؟

علی: بله. من خواستم برای * تابستان نه در خود * شهر که خیلی گرم است زندگی کنم و باین سبب منزل * خودم را عوض کردم. شما امشب وقت دارید بمنزل * من بیائید شام بخورید؟ خوب. پس امیدوارم شما را امشب ببینم

من: از التفات * شما خیلی تشکر میکنم و خوشوقتم که می آیم

علی: بامید * دیدار

## فرهنگ

| | |
|---|---|
| conversation صحبت *soḥbat* | don't mention it (lit. it's nothing) |
| to study درس خواندن *dars* | چیزی نیست *chîzî nîst* |
| salary حقوق *hoghûgh* | hope امید *omîd* |
| kindness التفات *eltefât* | I hope (I-am-hopeful) امیدوارم |
| for your kindness شما * از التفات | *omîdvâram* |
|     *az eltefât-ê-shomâ* | school مدرسه *madrasé* |
| | too much زیاد *zîâd* |

تمرین

I. Answer : جواب بدهید *javâb bédehîd*

۱ شما در کدام شهر منزل میکنید؟ وکجا کار میکنید؟

۲ وقتیکه کسی بشما اتفاق میکند – شما چه میگوئید؟

۳ میتوانید فارسی صحبت کنید؟

٤ در انگلستان چه زبان صحبت میکنند؟

۵ میتوانید شام * خودتـن را درست کنید؟

٦ کی ناهارتان را برای * شما حاضر میکند؟

۷ بگوئید که آیا شما در یک دفتر کار میکنید یا نه؟

۸ با حقوقتان میتوانید زندگی کنید؟

۹ در درستان کی بشما کمک میکند؟

۱۰ بگوئید که چند سال در مدرسه درس خواندید

II. Translate :

1. He moved.      4. Get the dinner ready.
2. Let him move.      5. Where do you live ?
3. Am I to speak ?

III. Give the Subjunctives of :

۱ میشوم      ۲ میکنم      ۳ زندگی میکنم

٤ صحبت نمیکنم      ۵ حاضر نمیکنند

IV. Translate, taking care with " ask " :

1. He asked me for an apple.
2. He asked me what the time was. (Time here = hour.)
3. Ask him where he lives.
4. Don't ask for money.
5. He asked too much for his fruit.

## LESSON 21

*Comparison of adjectives and adverbs.* There is no difference in form between adjectives and adverbs in Persian : خوب *khûb* = good OR well, بد *bad* = bad OR badly.

To form the comparative degree of adjectives and adverbs, we add the suffix تر- *-tar* to the simple form of that adjective or adverb. To form the superlative, we suffix ترین- *-tarîn* to the simple form.

Examine :

| | | | | |
|---|---|---|---|---|
| big | بزرگ *bozorg* | small | کوچک *kûchek* |
| bigger | بزرگتر *bozorgtar* | smaller | کوچکتر *kûchektar* |
| biggest | بزرگترین *bozorgtarîn* | smallest | کوچکترین *kûchektarîn* |
| | bad, badly | بد *bad* | |
| | worse | بدتر *badtar* | |
| | worst | بدترین *badtarîn* | |

There are only *two* irregular comparisons :

| | | | | |
|---|---|---|---|---|
| good, well | خوب *khûb* | very, much { | زیاد *zîâd* |
| better | بهتر *behtar* | | خیلی *khêilî* |
| best | بهترین *behtarîn* | more | بیشتر *bîshtar* |
| | | most | بیشترین *bîshtarîn* |

Note : (*a*) The comparative form of the adjective follows the noun it qualifies, and behaves exactly like the simple (positive) form, taking the *ézâfé*, etc. :

a big house *manzel-é-bozorg* منزل * بزرگ

a bigger house *manzel-é-bozorgtar* منزل * بزرگتر

some good place *jâ'î khûb* جائی خوب

some better place *jâ'î behtar* جائی بهتر

(*b*) The superlative adjective always *precedes* the noun it qualifies, and there is no *ézâfé*. We can, of course, because of its meaning, never have an indefinite suffix ـی - *î* associated with the superlative. The superlative always means *the* best, *the* biggest, etc. :

این بزرگترین منزل است

This is the biggest house

*în bozorgtarîn manzel ast*

آن کوچکترین پسر است

That is the smallest boy

*ân kûchektarîn pesar ast*

(c) than = از *az* or تا *tâ*:

این کتاب گرانتر از آن یکی بود

This book was dearer than that one

*în ketâb gerântar az ân yekî bûd*

" *too much* " *and* " *too* ". These English expressions such as in " too much money " and " too good ", are not easily expressed in Persian. As a rule we use, for

too much money
$$\begin{cases} \text{پول * زیاد} \quad \textit{pûl-é-zîâd} \\ \text{OR} \\ \text{پول * خیلی زیاد} \quad \textit{pûl-é-khêilî zîâd} \end{cases}$$

too good      *khêilî khûb*   خیلی خوب

Both these Persian expressions really only mean *very much* and *very*. Nevertheless, we have to make do with them, as they are the nearest we can get to the English idea.

*Numbers* 11–20 :

| Cardinal | | | | Ordinal | | |
|---|---|---|---|---|---|---|
| 11 | ۱۱ | یازده | *yâzdah* | 11th | یازدهم | *yâzdahòm* |
| 12 | ۱۲ | دوازده | *davâzdah* | 12th | دوازدهم | *davâzdahòm* |
| 13 | ۱۳ | سیزده | *sîzdah* | 13th | سیزدهم | *sîzdahòm* |
| 14 | ۱٤ | چهارده | *chahârdah* | 14th | چهاردهم | *chahârdahòm* |
| 15 | ۱٥ | پانزده | *pânzdah* | 15th | پانزدهم | *pânzdahòm* |

| 16 | ۱۶ | شازده shânzdaḥ | 16th | شازدهم shânzdahòm |
| 17 | ۱۷ | هفده hevdaḥ | 17th | هفدهم hevdahòm |
| 18 | ۱۸ | هجده hejdaḥ | 18th | هجدهم hejdahòm |
| 19 | ۱۹ | نوزده nûzdaḥ | 19th | نوزدهم nûzdahòm |
| 20 | ۲۰ | بیست bîst | 20th | بیستم bîstòm |

More about the comparison of adjectives and adverbs.
Some complex adjectives and adverbs, as in English, do
not add suffixes but form their comparative and superlative
degrees with the use of :

more *bîshtar* بیشتر
most *bîshtarîn* بیشترین

Thus :

pleasant (lit. pleasure-bringing) *neshât-âvar* نشاط آور
more pleasant *bîshtar neshât-âvar*
بیشتر نشاط آور
most pleasant *neshât-âvar tarin* نشاط آور ترین
interesting (lit. worthy of note) *ghâbel-é-tavajjoh* قابل * توجه
more interesting *bîshtar gh.* بیشتر قابل * توجه .
most interesting *ghabel-é ta-tarvajjoh tarin* قابل * توجه ترین

In colloquial Persian, the superlative is often expressed
by using the comparative degree followed by از همه *az hamé*
" of all " or " than all ", especially when the adjective is
the complement of the verb *to be* :

این میز بزرگتر از همه است = این بزرگترین میز است
*în bozorgtarîn mîz ast = în mîz bozorgtar az hamé ast*
This table is the biggest

بهترین = بهتر از همه
بیشترین = بیشتر از همه

فرهنگ

good خوب *khúb*

better بهتر *behtar*

best بهترین *behtarín*

much زیاد *zíâd*

more بیشتر *bíshtar*

most بیشترین *bíshtarín*

happy خوشحال *khoshhâl*

stubborn سرکش *sarkash*

old (of people) پیر *pír* §

new { تازه *tâzé*
جدید *jadíd*

orange (colour) نارنجی *nâranjí*

difficult مشکل *moshkel*

expensive گران *gerân*

brown قهوه‌ای‌رنگ *ghahvé'i-rang*

blue { آبی *âbí*
گلابی *golâbí*

cold سرد *sard*

hot (water, food, etc.) داغ *dâgh*

tight تنگ *tang*

bright, alight, light (of colours) روشن *róushan*

out, extinguished (of lights, fires) خاموش *khâmúsh*

dark تاریک *târík*

empty خالی *khâlí*

heavy, thick سنگین *sangín*

excellent عالی *'âlí*

intelligent باهوش *bâhúsh*

Turkish ترکی *torkí*

Russian روسی *rúsí*

Italian ایتالیائی *ítâliâ'í*

Indian هندی *hendí*

forbidden ممنوع *mamnú'*

grateful { متشکر *motashakker*
ممنون *mamnún*

well-known معلوم *ma'lúm*

correct درست *dorost*

important مهم *mohemm*

lazy تنبل *tambal* (نب- -nb- is pronounced -mb-)

bad(ly) { بد *bad*
خراب *kharâb*

pleasant نشاط آور *neshât-âvar*

poor بیچاره *bíchâré*

rich دولتمند *dóulatmand*

tall, high بلند *boland*

young جوان *javân*

old (of things) کهنه *kohné*

red قرمز *ghermez*

black سیاه *síâh*

easy آسان *âsân*

cheap ارزان *arzân*

woollen پشمی *pashmí*

white سفید *sefíd*

little (adverb) کم *kam*

a little (adverb) کمی *kamí*

warm, hot گرم *garm*

loose شل *shol*

full پر *por*

thin, light (weight) سبک *sabok*

happy خوشحال *khoshhâl*

stupid بی‌فهم *bífahm*

Egyptian مصری *mesrí*

French فرانسوی *farânsaví*

German آلمانی *âlmâní*

§ پیر *pír* " old " always *precedes* its noun :

an old man *pír-é-mard* پیر * مرد

an old woman *pír-é-zan* پیر * زن

| | | |
|---|---|---|
| Pakistani پاکستانی *pâkestâni* | successful موفق *movaffagh* |
| American آمریکائی *âmrikâ'i* | famous معروف *ma'arûf* |
| kind, gentle ملتفت *moltafet* | ready, present حاضر *hâzer* |
| sorry متاسف *mota'assef* | absent غایب *ghâyeb* |
| Ali علی *'ali* | people مردم *mardòm* |
| cat گربه *gorbé* | always همیشه *hamîshé* |

تمرین

## I. Example :

این منزل بلند است؛ منزل * شما بلندتراست ولی منزلم بلندترین منزل است.

۱ من باهوش هستم؛ او — است ولی شما — هستید.

۲ کتاب * اول سبک است؛ کتاب * دوم — است ولی کتاب * سوم — است.

۳ علی چای * داغ میخورد؛ من چایم — میخورم ولی برادرم از همه — میخورد.

٤ من کم میگیرم؛ شما — میگیرید ولی این شخص * بیچاره — میگیرد.

٥ قرمز روشن است؛ زرد — است ولی سفید — رنگ است.

## II. Translate :

1. Who is the richest man in this town ?

2. Ali is rich, but you are much richer.

3. The eleventh chapter is more interesting than the third.

4. Which book was most important ?

5. Old people know better than young ones.

6. I can walk faster than you.

7. Can you give me a cheaper one than this ?

8. He always arrives at the office earlier than you ;
does he have a faster car than yours ?

9. Why does the cat always sit on the most comfortable
chair ?

## LESSON 21*a*

کِ *relative*.  In the sentences :

(*a*) *The man who* came here yesterday was my friend.

(*b*) Give me *the book which* you bought.

(*c*) Did you go to *the place where* I sent you ?

the expressions *the man who*, *the book which*, and *the place
where* are called relative expressions.

They are all expressed in the same way in Persian :

۱ مردی که دیروز اینجا آمد دوست * من بود

*mardî ké dîrûz înjâ âmad âûst-é-man bûd*

The man who came here yesterday was my friend

۲ کتابی که خریدید به من بدهید

*kitâbî ké kharîdîd bé man bédéhîd*

Give me the book which you bought

۳ آنجائی که من شما را فرستادم رفتید؟

*ânjâ'î ké man shomâ râ ferestâdam raftîd ?*

Did you go to the place where I sent you ?

You will notice :

(*a*) We attach a ی- -*î* suffix to the noun beginning the
relative expression.  If the noun ends in a vowel, or if it
carries a ها- plural or را- definite direct object suffix, we put

a : *hamzé* on a bearer before the ی- -*î*, and pronounce a glottal stop.

Nouns already ending in ی- -*î*, like صندلی *sandali* a chair, do not add a further ی- -*î*.

(b) After the ی- -*î* or ئ -'*î* we have که *ké* which we have already met in Speech (Lesson 19a). The ی- -*î* or ئ -'*î* may be written together with the که *ké* as one word :

١ مردیکه دیروز آمد . . .

٢ کتابیکه خریدید . . .

٣ آنجائیکه من شما را فرستادم . . .

Here are some further examples of relatives :

٤ نوکریکه برای * ما کار میکند اسمش حسن است

*nôkariké barâ-yé-mâ kâr mîkonad esmesh hasan ast*

Hassan is the name of the servant who works for us

٥ وقتیکه من آنجا بودم اینرا بش گفتم . . .

*vaghtîké man ânjâ bûdam înrâ besh goftam . . .*

When I was there (" The time that I was there ") I said this to him . . .

٦ زنهائی را که اینجا منزل میکنند میشناسید؟

*zanhâ 'î-râ ké înjâ manzel mîkonand mîshenâsîd ?*

Do you know the women who live here ?

٧ آن کاردی را که من باو فروختم کجاست؟

*ân kârdî râ ké man bé-û forûkhtam kojâst ?*

Where is that knife (which) I sold to him ?

٨ هر جائی که میخواهید بروید

*har jâ'î ké mîkhâhîd béravîd*

Go wherever (" every place that ") you wish

You will notice that we have given وقتیکه *vaghtiké* and جائیکه *já'iké*, when and where respectively, as *relatives*. Do not confuse these *relative* words with کی *kéi ?* when ? and کجا *kojá ?* where ? which are both *interrogative, question-*words. The relatives وقتیکه when and جائیکه where mean " at the time that . . . " and " at/to/from the place that . . . " respectively. The interrogatives کی when ? and کجا where ? mean " at what time ? " and " at/to/from what place ? " respectively.

Distinguish between :

| Interrogative | Relative |
|---|---|
| شما کی اینجا هستید؟ | ۱ وقتی که شما اینجا هستید . . . |
| *shomá kéi injá hastid ?* | *vaghtiké shomá injá hastid . . .* |
| When (at what time) will you be here ? | When (at the time that) you are here . . . |
| بمن بگوئید که از کجا میائید | |
| *béman bégû'id ké az kojá miá'id* | ۲ از جائیکه من میایم . . . |
| | *az já'iké man miáyam . . .* |
| Tell me where (what place) you're coming from | The place I am coming from . . . |
| شما کجا بودید . . . | |
| *shomá kojá bûdid ?* | ۳ آنجائیکه من بودم . . . |
| | *ánjá'iké man bûdam . . .* |
| Where (at what place) were you ? | The place I was at . . . |

The relative does occur without ی-*i* or ی-*'i*, in rare examples. We shall deal with these later.

### *Irregular Present Stems—4th Group : f-b*

Verbs whose infinitive ends in افتن -*áftan*, یفتن- -*iftan*, and وفتن- -*úftan* take present stems in اب- -*áb-*, یب- -*ib-*, and وب- -*úb-* respectively :

| Infinitive | English | Present Stem |
|---|---|---|
| تافتن tâftan § | twist/shine | -تاب- -tâb- |
| يافتن yâftan | find | -ياب- -yâb- |
| فريفتن farîftan | deceive | -فري -farîb- |
| كوفتن kûftan § | beat, pound | -كوب- -kûb- |
| رفتن roftan (short vowel) | sweep | -روب- -rûb- |

§ تافتن tâftan and كوفتن kûftan have also formed infinitives derived from their present stems: تابيدن tâbîdan and كوبيدن kûbîdan.

There are two exceptions to the rule governing this class of irregulars. The following verbs in افتن- -âftan have regular present stems in -âf- -اف-:

بافتن bâftan, -bâf- to weave باف-

شكافتن shekâftan, -shekâf- to split شكاف-

## عبارات 'ebârât

چرا! chêrâ (lit. why ?) But yes! (after a negative question)

درست است dorost ast That's right

ببخشيد bébakhshîd Excuse me

از التفات * شما خيلى ممنونم
az eltefât-é-shomâ khêilî mamnûnam
Thank you very much for your kindness

درست است؟ dorost ast ?   } (rising tone)
اينطور نيست؟ întôur nîst ?   } Isn't that so ?

عجب 'ajab !   Strange ! How odd !

چيزى نيست chîzî nîst   Don't mention it

چه كار كنم؟ ché kâr konam ?   What (on earth) am I to do ?

متأسفم mota'assefam   I'm sorry

*Polite Speech.* (*a*) When speaking respectfully of somebody (i.e. somebody whom we would normally call آقا *âghâ*
Mr. or خانم *khânom* Mrs. or Miss) we use the 3rd person
*plural* of the verb :

آقا اینجا هستند ؟ âghâ *înjâ hastand ?*

Is (lit. are) the gentleman here ?

Madame didn't come *khânom nâyâmadand* خانم نیامدند

آقای * تهرانی امروز کار نمیکنند

*âghâ-yé-tehrânî emrûz kâr nâmîkonand*

Mr. Tehrani isn't (" aren't ") working today

and in such circumstances we correspondingly use ایشان
*îshân* they instead of the less polite او *û* he or she :

او آمد *û âmad* becomes ایشان آمدند *'îshân âmadand*

He/she (lit. they) came

(*b*) When speaking *to* such people, we tend to substitute
for the verb گفتن to say, and for many other verbs when
used in Compound Verbs—especially *kardan* in this case—
the verb

فرمودن (-فرما-) *farmûdan, -farmâ-* to command

e.g. :

What did you say (lit. command) sir ? چه فرمودید آقا ؟
*ché farmûdîd âghâ ?*

Mrs. T. said (commanded) that . . . . . . خانم * تهرانی فرمودند که
*khânom-é-tehrânî farmûdand ké . . .*

ممنونم از التفاتیکه فرمودید

I am grateful for the favour that you did (lit. commanded)
*mamnûnam az eltefâtîké farmûdîd*

And similarly we have the expression

بفرمائید *béfarmâ'îd* Command (me)

meaning " I am at your service. What can I do for you ? "
It is very often used when answering the telephone :

ببخشید – آقای \* و زیر هستند؟ بفرمائید آقا

*bébakhshîd — âghâyé vazîr hastand ? béfarmâ'îd âghâ*

Excuse me—is the Minister there ?—Yes, speaking ;
what can I do for you ?

(c) Conversely, when referring to what I say myself,
instead of گفتن *goftan* to say (and of course instead of فرمودن
*farmûdan* to command, which would be inexcusable
arrogance) I use the Compound Verb

عرض کردن *'arz kardan* lit. to petition, to beg

If I may say so, you are mistaken اشتباه که فرمودید عرض میکنم
(lit. I beg, you have commanded a mistake)

*'arz mîkonam ké eshtébâh farmûdîd* (اشتباه = error)

May I (be permitted to) say that . . . . . . که عرض کنم
*'arz konam ké . . .* (subjunctive)

پنج کیلو عرض کردم ولی آقا شش فرمودند
*panj kîlô 'arz kardam valî âghâ shesh farmûdand*
I said 5 kilos but the gentleman said 6

## فرهنگ

| | |
|---|---|
| to telephone تلفن کردن *telefon k.* | number شماره *shomâré* |
| message پیغام *péighâm* | Rafipour (surname) رفیعپور |
| director مدیر *modîr* | *rafî'pûr* |
| possible ممکن *momken* | |

بداند *bédânad* (subjunctive of دانستن *dânestan*) " so that he
should know " = in order to know. See text below.

In numerical series,

| | | | |
|---|---|---|---|
| " a " الف *alef* | | " b " ب *bé* |
| " c " ج *jîm* | | " d " د *dâl* |

بخوانید:

صحبت در تلفن

الف: ببخشید خانم — این شماره تهران ۳۳۰٤٥ (سی و سه صفر چهل و پنج) است؟

ب: بفرمائید خانم

الف: عرض کنم که خواستم با آقای * مدیر صحبت کنم

ب: متأسفم خانم حالا نیستند. ممکن است یک پیغام بفرمائید؟

الف: خیلی متشکر هستم. عرض کنم که بایشان بفرمائید که حسن رفیعپور تلفن کرد بداند چه ساعاتی ممکن است ایشان را ببیند.

ب: این روزهائی که آقا کار * زیاد دارند مشکل است خانم ولی عرض میکنم که بهتر است فردا صبح خودشان باآقای * مدیر تلفن بفرمایند چون امروز معلوم نیست چه روز و ساعتی آقا وقت دارند.

الف: خیلی خوب — فردا آقای * رفیعپور خودشان تلفن میفرمایند. خیلی ممنونم خانم

ب: خواهش میکنم خانم.

تمرین

I. Put the two sentences together to form one relative sentence, e.g.:

آن آقا را نمیشناسم + دیروز آمدند

= آن آقائی که دیروز آمدند نمیشناسم

۱ کتاب خریدید     + بمن بدهید

۲ بجائی رفت     + هیچکس نمیداند

۳ کاشیکاری * ایرانی خریدیم + قشنگ است

٤ مردی این را گفت     + دانا ست

۵ آقائی آمدند     + پدر * حسن هستند

II. Here are some sentences with relatives in them. In each case, *write* the underlined relative expression differently (the pronunciation remains unaltered, of course) :

e.g. مردیکه آمد becomes مردی که آمد . . . .

۱ زبانی که صحبت میکنم فارسی است

۲ جائیکه رفت اصفهان است

۳ بمن نفرمودید ساعت‌هائی که میتوانم بیایم

٤ صندلی که شکسته است دیدم

٥ آنهائی که دید از همه بهتر است

III. Translate your answers to Ex. I and II.

IV. Translate :

1. Where is the boy who broke the window ?

2. Wherever (Every place that) you go, you will be poor.

3. Timur the Lame (امیر تیمور گورکان *amîr têimûr gûrakân*) was the worst king who ever (هرگز *hargez*) lived.

4. They have sold that picture which you said was very beautiful.

5. A man who does that is not my friend.


## LESSON 22

More Compound Verbs :

(a) Formed with داشتن *dâshtan* to have :

| | | |
|---|---|---|
| to like | *dûst dâshtan* | دوست داشتن |
| remove, take away | *var d.* | ور داشتن |

| dare (+ subjunctive) | jor'at d.§ | جرأت داشتن |
| feel pain | dard d. | درد داشتن |
| to want something | mêil d. | میل داشتن |

(What would you like ? ché mêil dârîd ? (چه میل دارید؟)

§ The *hamzé* is written over the *alef*, which is pronounced short, *a*.
This is an Arabic word, spelt in the Arabic fashion. *Hamzé* never
occurs over *alef* in pure Persian.

(*b*) Formed with دادن *dâdan* to give :

| shake hands | dast dâdan | دست دادن |
| teach | dars dd. | درس دادن |
| give, cause trouble | zahmat dd. | زحمت دادن |
| give up, lose | az dast dd. | از دست دادن |
| give back | pas dd. | پس دادن |
| show | neshân dd. | نشان دادن |
| accomplish | anjâm dd. | انجام دادن |

(*c*) Formed with کشیدن *kashîdan* to draw :

| take pains, trouble | zahmat kashîdan | زحمت کشیدن |
| be ashamed (of) | khejâlat ksh. (az) | خجالت کشیدن (از) |
| to last, endure | tûl ksh. | طول کشیدن |
| revolt | sar ksh. | سر کشیدن |
| bring forward | pîsh ksh. | پیش کشیدن |

Note : Verbs formed with (*b*) دادن *dâdan* retain the
-بـ *bé*- prefix in the Subjunctive :

Show me that *ânrâ béman neshân bédéhîd* آنرا بمن نشان بدهید

### The Subjunctive of بودن *to be*

The stem of بودن *bûdan* from which we form the Subjunctive is -باش- -*bâsh*-. To this we add the usual endings,
omitting the customary -بـ *bé*- prefix. -بـ *bé*- is *never* prefixed
to any part of بودن *bûdan*.

### to be - Present Subjunctive

| | | | | |
|---|---|---|---|---|
| (1) | *bâsham* | باشم | *bâshîm* | باشیم |
| (2) | *bâshîd* | باشید | *bâshîd* | باشید |
| (3) | *bâshad* | باشد | *bâshand* | باشند |
| | *bâshad* | باشد | *bâshad* | باشد |

The usual negative suffix نـ *nà-* is added to make the Negative Subjunctive of this verb: نباشم *nàbâsham,* *nàbâshîd*, etc.

The stem ـباش- *-bâsh-* is in fact the original Present Stem of بودن *bûdan,* and there does exist a form of the Present Tense of بودن *bûdan* made regularly from this stem:

| | | | | |
|---|---|---|---|---|
| (1) | *mîbâsham* | میباشم | *mîbâshîd* | میباشیم |
| (2) | *mîbâshîd* | میباشید | *mîbâshîd* | میباشید |
| (3) | *mîbâshad* | میباشد | *mîbâshand* | میباشند |
| | *mîbâshad* | میباشد | *mîbâshad* | میباشد |

This form is rather rare and means *to exist* in everyday speech ; it is only used in rather formal speech in its original meaning *to be.*

*More about the Relative.* If in English the " whom ", " which ", or " that " beginning the relative clause is governed by a preposition :

(a) The box from which I got the money . . .

(b) The boy you spoke with (with whom you spoke) . . .

(c) The man to. (* رای *barâyé* here) whom I wrote the letter . . .

we say it thus in Persian :

۱ صندوقیکه من از آن پولرا گرفتم . . .

*sandûghîké man az ân pûlrâ gereftam . . .*

lit. The box *that from it* I took the money . . .

٢ پسریکه شما با او صحبت کردید . . .

*pesariké shomâ bâ û sohbat kardîd . . .*

lit. The boy *that with him* you spoke . . .

٣ مردیکه برای * او (برایش) من نامه را نوشتم . . .

*mardîké barâ-yé-û (barâyesh) man nâmérâ neveshtam . . .*

lit. The man who *to him* I wrote the letter . . .

You will notice :

(*a*) The یکه- or که ی- -*îké* which we met in the last lesson is *the only relative particle* used. There is no other one in Persian.

(*b*) We follow the یکه- -*îké* with the preposition, از or با or * برای or whatever it is, and آن *ân*, او *û*, ایشان *îshân* or آنها *ânhâ* as the case may be.

(*c*) In English it is possible to cast the sentence containing a relative in a different way, and omit the relative word " whom ", " which " or " that ". The examples above could read, with the same meaning :

    (*a*) The box I got the money from . . .
    (*b*) The boy you spoke with . . .
    (*c*) The man I wrote the letter to . . .

In Persian this is *not* possible : the relative word must *always* be present.

*Whose, of which, of whom.* These are possessive relatives and are expressed in Persian similarly to the prepositional relatives described above, but we use the *ezâfé* instead of a preposition :

(*d*) The man whose son goes to this school . . .

۴ مردی که پسر* او (پسرش) به این مدرسه میرود . . .

*mardî ké pesar-é-û* (OR *pesaresh*) *bé în madrasé mîravad* . . .

(literally) The man *who his son* goes to this school . . .

OR

The man *who the son of him* goes to this school . . .

(*c*) Those whose books are on the table can go

۵ آنهائیکه کتابهایشان روی* میز است میتوانند بروند

OR

۵ انهائیکه کتابهای* ایشان روی* میز است میتوانند بروند

*ânhâ'îké ketâbhâyeshân* (OR *ketâbhâ — yé-îshân*) *rûyé mîz ast*
*mîtavânand béravand*

(literally) Those *who their books* OR Those *who the books of*
*them* is on the table . . .

## فرهنگ

| | |
|---|---|
| so much آنقدر *ânghadr* | a well چاه *châh* |
| nail (iron) میخ *mîkh* | Bandar Shah (a port) بندر شاه |
| a port بندر *bandar* | *bandar-shâh* |

## تمرین

Translate :

1. Where is the book you found this in ?

2. The house I live in has a beautiful garden.

3. When Iran was the centre of civilization, she was very rich.

4. What is the name of the school your son goes to ? The one where they teach Russian and Turkish ?

5. The boat he spoke of in his letter arrived at Bandar Shah yesterday.

6. They draw the water we drink from wells.

7. Whose house is that ? It belongs to the gentleman who teaches my son.

8. Which one do you like more, the one I showed you or the one you found ?

9. I should like to thank the gentleman who took so much trouble with this work.

10. Does he have any pain in his foot (there) where the nail was that we found and removed yesterday ?

## LESSON 22*a*

How to translate -*ing* into Persian.

(*a*) The English continuous verbal forms " is talking ", " were going ", and so forth, cannot be exactly translated into Persian ; we use the simple Present and Past Tenses instead :

He talks, or is talking  او صحبت میکند  *û soḥbat mikonad*

We went, or were going  ما رفتیم  *mâ raftîm*

There is, however, an *Imperfect Tense*. This is used to denote an action which continued for some time but was interrupted, or a repeated past action. It is easy to form, We prefix می *mî* or ‐می *mî*- to the ordinary Past Tense :

من باصفهان میرفتم وقتی که اورا دیدم

*man bé-esfahân miraftam vaqtiké ûrâ dîdam*

I was going to Isfahan when I saw him

(i.e. my journey was interrupted by my seeing him)

معلم ما میگفت . . .

*mo'allem-é-mâ mîgoft . . .*

Our teacher used to say . . .

We can only use this device in the past. Examine :

۱ من دیروز کار میکردم وقتیکه او پیش * ... آ ... گفت ...

*man dîrûz kar mîkardam vaghtîké û pisheman âmad o goft ...*

I was working yesterday when he came to me and said . . .

۲ آنجائیکه دوستمان در آن وقت منزل میکرد تصادف شد

*ânjâ'iké dûstemân dar ân vaght manzel mîkard tasâdof shod*

(At the place) Where our friend was living at that time
there was an accident

(*b*) If the -*ing* word is a noun, the subject or object of a
verb, or if it is governed by a preposition, we use the
Persian *infinitive* :

Subject of a verb :

۳ فارسی صحبت کردن آسان است ولی خواندن و نوشتن مشکل است

*fârsî sohbat kardan âsân ast valî khândan o neveshtan
moshkel ast*

Speaking (to speak) Persian is easy, but to read and
write (reading and writing) is difficult

Object of a Verb :

٤ فارسی صحبت کردن را من دوست دارم ولی خواندن و نوشتنش را نمیدانم

*fârsî sohbat kardan râ man dûst dâram valî khândan o
neveshtanesh râ nàmîdânam.*

I like to speak (speaking) Persian but its reading
and writing (to read and write it) I don't know

-ing Governed by a Preposition :

۵ از پرسیدن * او میدانستم که ...

*az porsîdan-é-û mîdânestam ké . . .*

From his asking I knew that . . .

(*c*) If the -*ing* word is an adjective and is *not* preceded
by the verb " to be " in English (i.e. is not an English
Continuous Tense, see (*a*) above) then we use its exact
Persian equivalent, the Present Participle. The Present

Participle is an *adjective*, and is formed by adding the suffix ‌نده- -*àndé* (stressed) to the present stem of the verb.

Present Participle = Present Stem + نده- -*àndé*

Examples :

| doing | — | konàndé | کننده |
| working | | kâr konàndé | کار کننده |
| wishing | | khâhàndé | خواهنده |
| having, possessing | | dâràndé | دارنده |
| knowing | | dânàndé | داننده |
| coming | | âyàndé | آینده |

This adjectival Present Participle can be used as an adjectival noun :

دارندهٔ کلید بمن گفت ...

*dâràndé-yé-kelîd béman goft ...*

The possessor of (He having) the.key said to me ...

Used in this way, the نده- -*àndé* can take a plural ندگان- -*àndégân* or *andégán* :

Those running ⎫
The runners  ⎬ دوندگان *davandégân* (from
Those who run ⎭ دویدن (-دو-) *davîdan, -dav-* to run)

and you already know, from the verb *to fly* پریدن (-پر-) *parîdan, -par-* :

پرنده *paràndé* (= a flying thing) a bird

پرندگان *parandégân* (flying things) birds

which are used as nouns.

If the verbal adjective is in effect a relative expression, use the relative in Persian :

اشخاصی که در این ده منزل میکنند ...

*ashkhâsîké dar in deh manzel mîkonand ...*

The people who live in (living in) this village ...

The adjective آینده *âyàndé* " coming " is used to mean
" next " in expressions of time or of sequence :

next month *mâh-é-âyàndé* ماه \* آینده

(literally, the coming month)

next lesson *dars-é-âyàndé* درس \* آینده

next week *hafté-yé-âyandé* هفتة آینده

(هفته *hafté* = week)

the future *vaght-é-âyandé* وقت آینده

هیچکس نمیداند که در زمان \* آینده چه میگذرد

*hîhkas namîdânad ké dar zaman-é-âyandé ché mîgozarad*

**Nobody knows what will happen (pass) in the future**

Irregular Present Stems—Group 5 : *-ordan -âr*

Verbs whose infinitive ends in ردن- *-ordan* have present
stems in ـار- *-âr-* :

| Infinitive | English | Present Stem |
|---|---|---|
| شمردن *shomordan* | count | ـشمار- *-shomâr-* |
| سپردن *sepordan* | deposit, entrust | ـسپار- *-sepâr-* |
| فشردن *feshordan* | squeeze, press | ـفشار- *-feshâr-* |

There is one exception to this group : بردن (-بر-) *bordan*,
*-bar-* to carry ; this verb has a short *a* in its present stem
instead of a long *â*.

## فرهنگ

to ring a bell زنگ زدن *zang zadan*

a bell زنگ *zang*

Goodbye خدا حافظ *khodâ hâfez* (lit. God protect)

to get pleasure (from) لذت بردن *lezzat bordan* (az) (از)

God خدا *khodâ*

to happen اتفاق افتادن *ettefâgh oftâdan*

Tabriz (city in N.W. Iran) تبریز *tabrîz*

تمرین

I. In these sentences, put the bracketed verb into the
correct past tense (i.e. with or without the Imperfect
Prefix ‑می‎ *mî*-), e.g. :

پرویز از منزل بمدرسه میدوید وقتیکه ما را دید

Parvîz *was running* from home to school when he *saw* us

۱ وقتیکه من در تبریز (منزل کردن) این شخص را خوب (شناختن)

۲ دیروز کجا (رفتن) شما وقتیکه من شما را (دیدن)؟

۳ جنگ پنج سال (طول کشیدن)

٤ شما شام (خوردن) وقتیکه ایشان (زنگ زدن)؟

۵ او پول را (گرفتن) و (رفتن)

II. Translate :

1. Do you like working in the garden ?

2. Cooking is easy.

3. He gets a lot of pleasure from reading Italian.

4. Next month the bus coming from Tabriz will arrive
an hour later.

## LESSON 23

*The Relative—continued.*　When we have " whom ",
" that ", or " which " as a relative, and it is the object of
the verb following it :

　(*a*) This is the man (whom) I saw.

　(*b*) I gave you the book (which, that) I bought.

we can translate with یک‑ *-îkê* or که ی‑ *-î kê* as we have
already learnt :

*în hamân mardîst ké man dîdam* §　۱ این همان مردیست که من دیدم

*ketâbîké kharîdam bé-shomâ dâdam*　۲ کتابیکه خریدم بشما دادم

§ Literally " the *same* (همین) man who . . . "

*Relative without* ـِ *-î or* ـئ *- 'î.* We learned that the relative particle که *ké* does not usually occur without ی- *-î* or ـئ نـ. که *ké does* occur without ی- *-î* or نـ- *-'î,* but only in a rare and rather special kind of relative sentence. Compare :

*barâdarîké în ketâb râ kharîd . . .* . . . . برادری که این کتاب را خرید

(with ی- *-î*) The brother who bought this book . . .

with

*barâdar ké în ketâb râ kharîd . . .* . . . . برادرِ که این کتاب را خرید

(without ی- *-î*) The brother, who bought this book . . .

In (*a*) we have what is called a *limiting relative* : it is implied that there are several brothers, but " *that* one who bought the book . . . ", etc.

In (*b*) the relative که *ké* " who " does not limit the antecedent " brother " ; there is only one brother, and he (incidentally) bought this book.

If you find this distinction a difficult one to grasp at first, work to this rule, until you get the habit of distinguishing :

If we *cannot* reasonably place a comma before the relative " who ", " that ", " which ", etc., in the English, we need the suffix ی- *-î* or نـ- *-'î* in Persian.

If we *can* reasonably place a comma before the relative in English, we leave out the ی- *-î* or نـ- *-'î* in Persian.

More examples of limiting relatives:

١ كتابیکه من بیشتر دوست دارم دیوان * حافظ است

*ketâbîké man bishtâr dûst dâram dîvân-é-hâfez ast*

The book I like most is the " Divan " of Hafez

٢ شهریکه دیروز دیدیم قشنگ بنظر میاید

*shahrîké dîrûz dîdîm ghashang bénazar mîâyad*

The city we saw yesterday appears to be (lit. comes to the eye) beautiful

And of non-limiting relatives:

٣ کتاب * مثنوی که بزرگترین کتاب * رومی است. . .

*ketâb-é masnavî ké bozorgtarin kétâb-é rûmî ast . . .*

The book "Masnavi", which is the greatest book of Rûmî . . .

٤ شهری که قشنگ بنظر میاید سر * کوه واقع است

*shahri ké ghashang bénazar mîâyad sar-é-kûh vâghé' ast*

The city, which appears to be beautiful, is situated on the top of a hill

*Polite Speech.* (a) In formal speech it is considered more polite to refer to oneself not as من *man* " I ", but rather as بنده *bandé* " slave ". This word takes the 1st person singular of the verb, just as من *man* does:

I thank (you) *bandé tashakkor mîkonam* بنده تشکر میکنم

I should like to say that . . .    بنده عرض میکنم که . . .
*bandé 'arz mîkonam ké . . .*

(b) In similar circumstances we use instead of شما *shomâ* " you ", جناب * عالی *jenâb-é-âlî* " your excellency "—with the 2nd person of the verb, as with شما *shomâ*:

*jenâb-é-âlî farmûdîd ké* . . .    جناب * عالی فرمودید که . . .
You said (lit. Your Excellency commanded) that . . .

(c) When referring respectfully to somebody, we tend to avoid the use of آمدن *âmadan* to come and رفتن *raftan* to go. We use instead the noun تشریف *tashrîf* " presence " together with another verb, making a Compound Verb :

تشریف آوردن *tashrîf âvardan* = to bring one's presence
(i.e. to come)

تشریف بردن *t. bordan* = to take one's presence
(i.e. to go)

and also

تشریف داشتن *t. dâshtan* = to have one's presence
(i.e. to *be* somewhere)

Examples :

۱ دیروز تلفن کردم و خانم فرمودند که جناب * عالی تشریف ندارند
*dîrûz telefon kardam va khânom farmûdand ké jenâb-é-âlî tashrîf nâdârand*

Yesterday I telephoned and Madame said you were not in

۲ ٰ آقاک تشریف میبرند؟ When is Monsieur going ?
*âghâ kêi tashrîf mîbarand ?*

۳ خانم هنوز تشریف نیاورده اند Madame hasn't come yet
*khânom hanûz tashrîf nàyâvardéand*

These details of polite Iranian conversation may seem to the Western reader extravagant or servile, but the simple fact is that they are in everyday use by all classes of Iranians, and are therefore important. Iranians are generous people and will always forgive a foreigner for inadequacies of speech, but will always be careful to use the appropriate mode of speech themselves, and will naturally expect the same from a fluent foreigner.

فرهنگ

| | |
|---|---|
| storm توفان *tûfân* | travel مسافرت کردن *masâferat k.* |
| journey سفر *safar* | to fear (از) ترسیدن-ترس- *tarsîdan, -tars- (az)* |
| necessary لازم *lâzem* | |
| grandfather پدر بزرگ *pedarbozorg* | if اگر *agar* |
| space of time دوره *dôuré* | the past دورۀ گذشته *dôuré-yé-gozashté* |
| aeroplane هواپیما *havâpéimâ* | a few times چند دفعه *chand daf'é* |
| danger خطر *khatar* | some, a few چند *chand* |
| always همیشه *hamîshé* | . . . ago پیش . . . . . . *pîsh* |
| thief دزد *dozd* | Shiraz شیراز *shîrâz* (a city in S.W. Iran, home of the poets Hafez and Sa'adi) |
| airport فرودگاه *forûdgâh* | |
| dead مرده *mordé* | |
| to request خواهش کردن *khâhesh k.* | die مردن-میر- *mordan, -mîr-* |
| | mend تعمیر کردن *ta'amîr k.* |
| camel شتر *shotor* | moment موقع *môughé'* |
| so (much) آنقدر *ânghaar* | |

بخوانید :

<u>مسافرت کردن در ایران</u>

در دورۀ گذشته مسافت کردن در ایران مشکل و پر خطر بود. از
تهران باصفهان با اسب یا شتر یک هفته طول میکشید. پدر بزرگم وقتی که
جوان بود چند دفعه این سفر را کرد § وهمیشه از دزدان و طوفان که دو
تا از بزرگترین خطرهای بیابان است خیلی میترسیدند.

ولی امروز اگر بایران بروید مسافرت خیلی آسانتر است. از تهران
باصفهان هوا پیما هست که مسافرتش بجای یک هفته یکساعت وقت میگیرد.
چند هفته پیش برای دیدن دوستم به شیراز که یکی از قشنگترین شهرهای *
ایران است رفتم. ناشتائی در تهران خوردم – ناهار در فرودگاه * اصفهان –
و برای چای خوردن بشیراز رسیدم.

Note : From now on we will no longer mark the unwritten
*ézâfé* with an asterisk, but leave it entirely unmarked, as it
is in Persian writing and printing.

تمرین

I.

جواب بفرمائید :

۱ در دورهٔ گذشته مسافرت کردن در ایران آسان بود یا مشکل؟

۲ وقتی که در دورهٔ گذشته مسافرت میکردند از چه چیزها میترسیدند؟

۳ در انگلستان بیابان هست؟

۴ با شتر مسافرت کردن نشاط آور است یا نه؟

۵ امروز در ایران چطور مسافرت میکنند؟

۶ جناب عالی به ایران تشریف برده اید؟

۷ میل دارید که آنجا تشریف ببرید؟

۸ جنابعالی با هواپیما مسافرت فرموده اید ؟

۹ وقتی که در انگلستان سفر میکنیم آیا ما از چیزی میترسیم؟

۱۰ پدر بزرگتان زنده اند یا نه؟

II. Put into more polite forms :

۱ من فردا پهلوی شما نمیایم چون شما منزل نیستید

۲ چه بش گفتید؟

۳ گفتم من نمیتوانم بیایم

۴ این شخص آمد و خواهش کرد من بش شمارهٔ تلفن شما را بدهم

۵ برای شام شما چه میل دارید من حاضرکنم؟

III. Translate, giving particular attention to the relative :

1. The camel, which in the past was the most important animal in the desert, is now not so important for travelling.

2. Bring the chair which he has mended.

3. Have you travelled in the ship he was talking about ?

4. This picture, which they bought yesterday, is one of the most beautiful I have ever seen.

5. At that time (= moment) he lived in Shiraz, which is an Iranian city.

## LESSON 23*a*

The English language has two compound past tenses, formed with a part of " to have " and a Past Participle :

(*a*) I have written⎫   " have ", " had " is called the *auxiliary*
            ⎬   verb : " written " is the Past Par-
(*b*) I had written ⎭   ticiple of *to write*.

Tense 1 above is called in English the Perfect.

Tense 2 is called the Pluperfect or Past Perfect.

Persian can also form these two tenses. First, to form the Past Participle, we add ه or ‍ـه -*é* to the Past Stem of the verb. Thus, for two typical verbs :

| to write | نوشتن | Infin. | کردن | to do |
|---|---|---|---|---|
| | | ↓ | | |
| he wrote | نوشت | 3rd sing. Past | کرد | he did |
| | | ↓ | | |
| written | نوشته | Past | کرده | done |
| | *neveshté* | Participle | *kardé* | |

Having got the Past Participle in this way with any verb, we use it together with an auxiliary to get the Perfect and Pluperfect Tenses.

The auxiliary verb we use in English is *to have* : but in Persian (this is most important) it is :

بودن *bûdan* to *be*

I have written (lit. I *am* written) من نوشته ام *man neveshté am*
We have done (lit. we *are* done) ما کرده ایم *ma kardé îm*
I had written (lit. I *was* written) نوشته بودم *neveshte bûdam*
We haven't done (lit. we aren't done) نکرده ایم *nàkardé îm*
We hadn't done نکرده بودم *nàkardé bûdîm*

You will notice three points here : (*a*) in the Perfect Tense we use the short form of *to be* بودن, written not as a suffix but detached, i.e. with its own ا *alef*. Do not use the long form هستم *hastam*, هستید *hastîd*, etc., as an auxiliary. (*b*) We attach the negative prefix ـنـ- *-nà*- to the Past Participle, not to the auxiliary verb, and (c) the Past Participle does not change to indicate tense or person : the auxiliary does that. Use the Present of the auxiliary verb and you have the Perfect Tense ; use the Past of the auxiliary and you have the Pluperfect, or Past Perfect as it is sometimes called.

In Lesson 22 we gave the special Subjunctive Tense of بودن *to be* : باشم *bàsham*, باشید *bàshîd*, etc. This tense, used as an auxiliary, gives us the Perfect Subjunctive :

that I may have written که نوشته باشم *ké neveshté bàsham*
that you should have seen که دیده باشید *ké dîdé bàshîd*
that you might not have gone که شما نرفته باشید
*ké shomà nàrafté bàshîd*

Notice that in this tense, as in the two other Perfect tenses, the negative suffix is added to the participle and not to the auxiliary.

The Present Subjunctive of داشتن *dâshtan* " to have " is not used in modern Persian ; instead we always use the Perfect Subjunctive, but with present meaning :

(1) داشته باشم *dâshté bâsham* (that) I may have, let me have

(2) داشته باشید *dâshté bâshîd* may you have

etc.

۱ میخواهم که شما این را داشته باشید

*mîkhâham ké shomâ înrâ dâshté bâshîd*

I want you to have this (main verb in the Present)

۲ میخواستم که شما اینرا داشته باشید

*mîkhâstam ké shomâ înrâ dâshté bâshîd*

I wanted you to have this (main verb in the Past)

The first three tenses we learned in this book, the Present, Past, and Present Subjunctive, are by far the most common and most useful in Persian. The three Perfect Tenses we have learned in this lesson are rarely used in ordinary conversation ; but all the same it is necessary to know them, as they occur frequently in writing and occasionally in rather formal speech.

While we are on the question of the subjunctive, it would be as well to note that constructions of the following type require the next verb to be in the subjunctive, either the Present Subjunctive or the Perfect Subjunctive as the time-sequence may require :

| | | |
|---|---|---|
| it is possible (that) | *momken ast (ké)* | ممكن است (که) |
| it is not possible | { *ghêir-é-momken ast* | غیر ممکن است |
| | { *momken nîst* | ممکن نیست |
| it is not certain | *ma'lûm nîst* | معلوم نیست |
| one hopes that | *omîd ast (ké)* | امید است (که) |
| I hope | *omîdvâram* | امیدوارم |

These constructions can all, as in English, be followed by
" that " که ké. This is not obligatory. From the meaning
of these few phrases : *I hope that, it is not certain that, it is
possible that,* we can see that when an action or state of
affairs is uncertain, doubtful, or is an idea or hypothesis
rather than an established fact, we use the subjunctive to
express it.

Examine :

۱ امیدوارم که بیائید *omîdvâram ké bîa'îd*

I hope that you may come

(i.e. it is *not certain* that you will come)

۲ غیر ممکن است که کارتان موفق باشد
*ghêir-é-momken ast ké kâretân movaffagh bâshad*

It is impossible that your work should be successful

(i.e. the very *idea* of its being successful is impossible)

And similarly, after expressions of emotion, we use the
subjunctive :

۳ خیلی خوشحالم که دوستم آمده است
*khéilî khoshhalam ké dûstam âmadé ast.*

I am very glad that my friend has come

٤ متأسف بودیم که پولرا نداشتیم
*mota' assef bûdîm ké pûlrâ nàdâshtîm*

We were sorry not to have the money

(= that we did not have the money)

*Conjunctions and Prepositions.* Such prepositions as :

without بدون bedûn-é- apart from, except for غیر از ghêir az
for برای barâ-yé- with با bâ instead of بجای béjâ-yé-

after بعد از *ba'ad az*     before قبل از *ghabl az*

because of بسبب *bé sabab-é-*

in spite of با وجود *bâ vojûd-é-* (وجود *vojûd* = existence)

can be made into *conjunctions* (i.e. to introduce clauses) by
adding این که or اینکه *înké*. Compare :

| Preposition | Conjunction |
|---|---|
| except for me | apart from the fact that he came |
| غیر از من | غیر از اینکه آمد |
| *ghêir az man* | *ghêir az înké âmad* |
| after the war | after I went |
| بعد از جنگ | بعد از اینکه رفتم |
| *ba'ad az jang* | *ba'ad az înké raftam* |
| in spite of him, with him | although I went |
| با او | با اینکه رفتم |
| *bâ û* | *bâ înké raftam* |
| before the war | before I go |
| قبل از جنگ | قبل از اینکه بروم |
| *ghabl az jang* | *ghabl az înké béravam* |
| instead of him | instead of going, he . . . |
| بجای او | بجای اینکه برود |
| *béjâ-yé-û* | *béjâ-yé-înké béravad . . .* |

for him
برای او
*barâ-yé-û*

{ because I went
برای اینکه رفتم
*barâyé-înké raftam*
so that I should go (subjunctive)
برای اینکه بروم
*barâyé-înké béravam*

| because of that | because I went |
|---|---|
| بسبب آن | بسبب اینکه رفتم |
| *bésabab-é-ân* | *bésabab-é-înké raftam* |

| without them | unless they go |
|---|---|
| بدون ایشان | بدون اینکه بروند |
| *bedûn-é-îshân* | *bedûn-é-înké béravand* |

The *preposition* governs a noun or pronoun: the *conjunction* introduces a subject and its verb, i.e. a second clause.

فرهنگ

to weigh (-کش -) کشیدن *kashîdan, -kash-*

weight وزن *vazn*

think فکر کردن *fekr k.*

it seems (seemed) to him good . . . (آمد) . . . بنظرش خوب میآید *bé-nazaresh khûb mîâyad (âmad)* . . .

you seem to me to be . . . بنظرم . . . هستید شما *bénazaram shomâ . . . hastîd* (lit. to my eye نظر you are . . .)

Mustapha مصطفی *mostafâ* §

brother-in-law برادرزن *barâdarzan*

finish, end تمام کردن *tamâm k.*

return (-گرد- بر) برگشتن *bar gashtan, bar -gard-*

the same همین همان *hamîn, hamân*

kill (-کش-) کشتن *koshtan, -kosh-*

luggage اسباب *asbâb*

give permission اجازه دادن *éjâzé d., e. farmûdan* اجازه فرمودن

collect جمع کردن *jam' k.*

bag کیف *kîf*

willing مایل *mâyel*

family خانواده *khânevâdé*

remain (-مان-) ماندن *mândan, -mân-*

about راجع به *râje' bé*

gold زر *zar*

permission اجازه *éjâzé*

§ In some Arabic words a final ی *-é* is pronounced *â*.

تمرین

I.

ترجمه بفرمائید:

علی بابا

When Ali Baba had collected together all the gold, he
wished he had brought weights and a bag with him so that
he could weigh it. After he had thought about this for
some time, it seemed wise to him to go to his brother-in-
law's house to get some weights. Mustapha (which was his
brother-in-law's name) was willing to give him the bag and
the weights, and Ali went off to weigh his gold.

Some hours later, after Ali had finished the weighing of
his gold, he returned to Mustapha's with his things.
Although Mustapha was of the same family as Ali, he did
not love him. After taking the bag from Ali, he said:
" Before you go, Ali, tell me where your gold is. You
seem to me to be a very rich man, since there remains
some gold in this bag. All gold belongs to the king, and
in spite of being (" although I be ") your brother and your
friend, I will tell all I know unless you show me your
gold."

II. Fill in the blanks twice with the verb given in brackets,
first using the formal tense (i.e. one of the Perfects) and
then with the conversational tense (Present, Past, or
Present Subjunctive) : e.g. (تشریف بردن)

الف : بعد از اینکه آنجا تشریف برده بودید اسباب جمع کردند

ب : بعد از اینکه آنجا تشریف بردید اسباب جمع کردند

۱ میخواستم دیروز بمنزل دوستم (آمدن) ولی ممکن نبود

۲ ممکن نیست که برادرم این نامه را دیروز (نوشتن)

۳ معلوم نبود که هواپیما زود (رسیدن)

٤ خواهش میکردند که ما قبل از شام (نیامدن)

۵ امید وار بودم که جناب عالی برای این کار (اجازه فرمودن)

### LESSON 24

*Further uses of* خود *khod.* We learned in Lesson 15a that the particle خود *khod* "own" and its extended personal forms خودم *khodam* my own, خودتان *khodetân* your own, etc., are used as possessive pronouns when the possessor is the same person as the subject of the verb:

I took my (own) money

پول خودم را گرفتم  *pûl-é khodam râ gereftam*

The particle with its endings, م-, تان-, ش-, مان-, etc., has two other important uses. First, as a *reflexive* :

He deceived himself *khodesh râ farîft*  خودش را فریفت

از خودتان نترسید

Don't be afraid of yourself *az khodetân nàtarsîd*

از خودم خجالت میکشم

I am ashamed of myself *az khoda*m *khejâlat mîkasham*

بخودشان گفتند . . .

They said to themselves . . . *békhodeshân goftand* . . .

Note : را- *-râ* is never used in this construction.

Secondly, the particle is used as an *emphatic* word :

خودش گفت و رفت

He said it himself and went *khodesh goft o raft*

As the sentence پول خودش گرفت could be read *either* (*a*) *pûl-é-khodesh gereft* " He took his own money " OR (*b*) *pûl khodesh gereft* " He took the money himself " we can put the emphatic particle first, to avoid ambiguity, thus : خودش پول گرفت can only read *khodesh pûl gereft*, and must mean " He took the money himself ".

In the two uses of خود- *khod-* outlined above, reflexive and emphatic, the personal suffix م- *-am*, تان- *-etân*, ش- *-esh*, etc., must always be attached to the خود- *khod-*.

The Past Participle, ending in ده- *-dé* or ته- *-té*, can also be used by itself :

(*a*) As an absolute expression, doing the same work as a verb or a whole clause :

این را گفته و پول داده رفت *în râ gofté o pûl dâdé raft*

Having said this, and having paid the money, he went

(i.e. When he had said . . . etc.)

(b) As an adjective, in the usual manner of adjectives :

روی دیوار یک ساعت بزرگ آویخته است .

*rû-yé-dîvâr yek sâ'at-é-bozorg âvîkhté ast*

On the wall is hung (there hangs) a big clock

The Past Participle-adjective of the verb گذشتن (-گذر-)
*gozashtan -gozar-* to pass, to happen, is used to mean
" last " :

Time passes quickly *vaght zûd mîgozarad* وقت زود میگذرد

last month *mâh-é-gozashté* ماه گذشته

last week *hafté-yé-gozashté* هفتهٔ گذشته

last lesson *dars-é-gozashté* درس گذشته

last year *sâl-é-gozashté* سال گذشته

and a proverb :

گذشته که گذشته    *gozashté ké gozashté*

lit.: Past what (is) past (i.e. Let bygones be bygones)

*Must and may.* We have learned how to say " can " and
" want to ", using توانستن *tavânestan* and خواستن *khâstan* :

CAN متیوانم این کار را بکنم I can do this work
*mîtavânam in kârrâ békonam*

WANT TO میخواهید فردا بیائید؟ Do you want to come tomorrow?
*mîkhâhîd fardâ biâ'îd ?*

The verbs " must " and " may " both take the Subjunctive in the same way as do *can* and *want to*, but *must* and
*may* are *impersonal verbs* : they change for tense, but not
for person :

*must*, infinitive بایستن *bâyestan*, only has the two impersonal forms باید *bâyad* (Present) " it must be so " and
بایست *bâyest* (Past) " it had to be so ".

*may*, infinitive شایستن *shâyestan*, only has the impersonal forms شاید *shâyad* (Present) "it may be so" and شایست *shâyest* (Past) "it might be so". Examine:

(a) MUST :

I must do this *bâyad in kar râ békonam*    ۱ باید این کار را بکنم

(lit. It must be I do this)

You must come tomorrow *bâyad fardâ biâ'id*    ۲ باید فردا بیائید

(lit. It must be you come tomorrow)

(b) HAD TO (Past of MUST) :

I had to do this *bâyest in kâr râ békonam*    ۳ بایست این کار را بکنم

(lit. It had to be I do this)

۴ بایست دیروز بیائید

You had to come yesterday *bâyest dirûz biâ'id*

(It had to be you come yesterday)

(c) MAY :

He may come *shâyad biâyad*    ۵ شاید بیاید

(lit. It may well be he come)

I may do this *shâyad in kâr râ békonam*    ۶ شاید این کار را بکنم

(It may well be I do this)

(d) MIGHT (Past of MAY) :

He might have come *bâyest âmadé bâshad*    ۷ بایست آمده باشد

(It might be, he come)

Whether the impersonal verb is in the Present or Past form we normally use the Present Subjunctive of the verb following it, as you see from the examples above. If we use the Perfect Subjunctive of the second verb, we get the meaning " must have (done) ", " may have (done) " :

He must have gone *bâyad rafté bâshad*    ۸ باید رفته باشد

(i.e. Surely he has gone)

He may have gone *shâyad rafté bâshad* ٩ شاید رفته باشد
(i.e. Probably he has gone)

*Colloquial Pronunciation.* Colloquial Persian pronunciation differs in some respects from elevated pronunciation, which is the pronunciation we have been using throughout this book so far. Colloquial Pronunciation is not a matter of class difference : educated and uneducated Iranians alike use both styles of pronunciation, depending on the *occasion.* Colloquial is that used in ordinary conversation, Elevated is that used on formal occasions, by rich and poor alike. We must also remember that Colloquial can still be polite and grammatically correct : the Polite Forms we have learnt are just as frequently pronounced colloquially as in elevated pronunciation. Colloquial uses the same grammar, the same vocabulary, the same Polite Forms, and of course is spelled like Elevated ; there is only one standard Persian spelling.

The two principal things to learn are Elision and Vowel Change.

*Elision.*

    (a) In Colloquial, the present stems of the verbs

| | | | |
|---|---|---|---|
| دادن | *dâdan* to give | گفتن | *goftan* to say |
| آمدن | *âmadan* to come | رفتن | *raftan* to go |
| توانستن | *tavânestan* can | خواستن | *khâstan* to want to |
| | شدن | *shodan* to become | |

are shortened thus :

| | |
|---|---|
| -ده- -*deh*- becomes -*d*- : | میدهم *mîdam* I give |
| -گو- -*gû*- becomes -*g*- : | میگویند *mîgand* they say |

-ا- -â- becomes - :   میام *mîam* I come
بیائید! *bé'îd* come :   میائیم *mî'îm* we come
-رو- -rav- becomes -r- :   بروم *béram* let me go
-توان- -tavân- becomes -tûn-   نمیتوانیم *nàmîtûnîm* we can't
-خواه- -khâh- becomes -khâ-, and the short vowel *a*
disappears, thus : میخواهم *mîkhâm* I want. BUT
میخواهیم *mîkhîm*, میخواهید *mîkhîd*.
-شو- -shav- becomes -sh- : نشوم *nàsham* let me not become

(b) The د- -ad ending of the 3rd Person Singular Present
and Present Subjunctive becomes -é :

میکند *mîkonad* becomes *mîkoné* He does
بشود *béshavad* becomes *béshé*   Let him become

But note these exceptions to this rule :

میخواهد بخواهد *mîkhâd, békhâd* He wants. Let him want
م یاید بیاید   *mîâd, bîâd* OR
         *mîad, bîad* } He comes. May he come

The same is true of the negative forms of the above.

(c) است ast following a consonant is pronounced in
Colloquial as *é* :

دیر است *dîr é* It's late     باز است *bâz é* It's open

The pronunciations of هست *hast*, نیست *nîst*, and ست *ast* or -st
following a vowel, remain unchanged.

(d) The only Past Stem which is colloquially shortened
is that of توانستن *tavánestan*, which, like the Present Stem
(see (a) shortens -avâ- to -û- :

میتوانم *mîtûnam* I can
میتوانستم *mîtûnestam*, توانستم *tûnestam* I could

*Vowel Change.*

(a) Before the nasals ن *n* and م *m*, long ا *â* becomes sometimes *û*, sometimes a short *u*, as in " pull " :

آن *ûn* or *un* that      آمد *ûmad* He came

میدانم *mîdûnam* I know      آقایان *âghâyûn* gentlemen

خودتان *khodetun* or *khodetûn* your own, yourself/ves

ماندن *mundan* or *mûndan* to remain

This does not *always* happen. The Colloquial Pronunciation of تهران is the same as the Elevated, *tehrân*. The form *tehrûn* is dialect..

(b) When the negative particle ن *nà-* precedes می *mî-* it is often pronounced *nè* :

نمیکنم *némîkonam* I'm not doing

نمیگوید *némîgé* He isn't saying

but when not followed by می *mî-* it remains unchanged. In all cases the ن *nà-* or *nè-* is *stressed*.

تمرین

I. Write in each of two columns on the right the (i) elevated and (ii) colloquial pronunciations of the following phrases : e.g.

| Persian نمیگوید | Elevated *nàmîgûyad* | Colloquial *nèmîgé* |
|---|---|---|

1. آنجا میروم      2. نمیتوانند

3. زود میاید      4. باشد

5. نمیدانستم      6. نکند

7. چه میگوئید؟      8. بنده باید بروم

9. نمیکنند      10. کارتان آسان است

II. Translate:

1. I can speak Persian well.
2. I want to speak Persian well.
3. I must speak Persian well.
4. I may speak Persian well.
5. I had to speak Persian well.
6. I wanted to speak Persian well.
7. I could speak Persian well.
8. I might speak Persian well.
9. I must have spoken Persian well.
10. I may have spoken Persian well.

III. Translate:

۱ این مرد خودش را کشت
۲ خودتان فارسی بـ ، میکنید؟
۳ باید خودمان آن را درست کنیم
٤ شاید خودشان رفته باشند
۵ خودتان را نفریبید

## LESSON 24*a*

The following conjunctions usually take the verb
following them in the Subjunctive:

مگر اینکه *magar înké* unless

با اینکه *bâ înké* although    با وجود اینکه *bâ vojûd-é-înké* although

۱ مگر اینکه بمن حقیقت را بگوئید بشما کمک نمیکنم
*magar înké béman haghîghat râ béguîd béshomâ komak
némîkonam*
Unless you tell me the truth I shan't help you

۲ با اینکه این اسب خوب باشد من نمیتوانم سوار آن بشوم

*bâ înké în asb khûb bâshad man némîtavânam savâr-é-ân
béshavam*

Although this horse is (" be ") good, I can't ride him

*bâvojûd-é-înké în mâshîn âlî bâshad némîtavânam ânrâ
békharam*

Although this car is (" be ") excellent, I can't buy it

The following conjunctions take either the Subjunctive
or some other tense, depending on certain circumstances :

اگر *agar* if     تا *tâ* so that/until

برای اینکه *barâyé înké* so that/because

اگر *agar* " if " takes the Subjunctive after it if the verb
is in the present or future time (i.e. if the *condition* is a
possible one) :

٤ اگر زود بیاید اتوبوس میگیرد – اگرنه نمیگیرد

*agar zûd bîyâyad otôbûs mîgîrad — agarnà, némîgîrad*

If he comes soon, he'll catch the bus—if not, he won't

In this example, he may yet come in time : it is still a
possibility.

But if the verb following the اگر *if* is a *Past* verb (of any
tense), then obviously the condition is impossible. In this
case :

٥ اگر زودتر میامد اتوبوس را میگرفت

*agar zûdtar mîâmad otôbûsrâ mîgereft*

If he had come sooner he would have caught the bus

we use the IMPERFECT (the Past with ـمی *mî-* prefixed) in
both parts of the sentence.

تا *tâ* has two meanings : (i) *so that, in order that* (when
it usually takes the Subjunctive), and (ii) *until*, when it

takes the Subjunctive when referring to the future, and
the Past Tense when referring to the past :

*injâ sabr konîd tâ man biâyam*    اینجا صبر کنید تا من بیایم
       Wait here until I come

*injâ sabr kard tâ man âmadœm*    اینجا صبر کرد تا من آمدم
       He waited here till I came

The conjunction وقتی که *vaghtîké* " when " (see Lesson 21*a*,
Relative expressions) takes the Past Tense when we wish
to translate an English Perfect Tense :

*vaghtîké âmad înrâ besh bédîd*    وقتی که آمد این را بش بدهید
       When he has come, give him this

برای اینکه or برای این که *barâyé înké*, when it means " so
that ", " in order that ", takes the Subjunctive. It can
also mean " because ", in which case it takes some non-
Subjunctive tense. Compare :

SO THAT . . .

      ۱ خوب کار کنید برای اینکه موفق باشید
     *khûb kâr konîd barâyé înké movaffagh bâshîd*
      Work hard so that you may be successful

with
BECAUSE . . .

      ۲ موفق بودم برای این که خوب کار کردم . . .
     *movaffagh bûdam barâyé înké khûb kâr kardam*
     I was successful because I (had) worked hard

No. ۱ uses the Subjunctive, No. ۲ uses some other tense,
in this case the Past. No. ۱ expresses a hypothesis, No. ۲
a fact.

*The Passive.* In English the Passive of verbs is formed

by using the past participle of the verb with the auxiliary
" to be " in the appropriate tense :

> I see  becomes  I am seen
>
> I saw  becomes  I was seen, etc.

In Persian the same rule applies, but the auxiliary used
is (-شو-) شدن *shodan, -shav-* " to become ", NOT بودن " to be ",
which, you will remember, forms Perfect tenses, not
Passives.

In Persian the Past Participle precedes the auxiliary,
in the Passive as in the Perfects which you have already
studied :

I see میبینم *mîbînam* becomes I am seen دیده میشوم *dîdé
mîshavam*

I saw دیدم *dîdam* becomes I was seen دیده شدم *dîdé shodam*

I have seen دیده ام *dîdé am*—I have been seen دیده شده ام *dîdé
shodé am*

let me see ببینم *bébînam*—let me be seen دیده بشوم *dîdé
béshavam* OR دیده شوم *dîdé shavam*

let me not see نبینم *nâbînam*—let me not be seen
دیده نشوم *dîdé nâshavam*

(Note : in the Passive, the negative is attached to the
*auxiliary*, not, as is usually the case, to the participle.)

We use the Passive *far less* in Persian than we do in
English.

*Passive of Compound Verbs.* (*a*) Verbs compounded with
کردن *kardan*, and a few others, drop their verbal element
and use شدن *shodan* instead, to give the Passive :

satisfy راضی کردن *râzî k.*　　　be satisfied راضی شدن *râzî sh.*

fill پر کردن *por k.*　　　be filled پر شدن *por sh.*

| | | | |
|---|---|---|---|
| empty خالی کردن *khâlî k.* | be emptied خالی شدن *khâlî sh.* |
| open باز کردن *bâz k.* | be opened باز شدن *bâz sh.* |
| extend (a thing) پهن کردن *pahn k.* | be extended پهن شدن *pahn sh.* |
| find پیدا کردن *pêidâ k.* | be found پیدا شدن *pêidâ sh.* |
| arrange درست کردن *dorost k.* | be arranged درست شدن *dorost sh.* |
| prepare حاضر کردن *hâzer k.* | be made ready حاضر شدن *hâzer sh.* |
| send ارسال داشتن *ersâl d.* | be sent ارسال شدن *ersâl sh.* |

(b) A few verbs compounded with داشتن *dâshtan* nge this verbal element to یافتن *yâftan* (" to find ") to form their Passives :

educate پرورش داشتن *parvaresh d.*    be educated پرورش یافتن *p. yâftan*

accomplish انجام داشتن *anjâm d.*    be accomplished انجام یافتن *anjâm yâftan*

(c) Verbs compounded with most other verbal elements put that element into the Past Participle and add the appropriate tense of the auxiliary شدن *shodan* in the normal way :

> It shows نشان میدهد *neshân mîdé*
> It is shown نشان داده میشود *neshân dâdé mîshavad*
> He took it away آنرا ور داشت *ânrâ var dâsht*
> He was taken away ور داشته شد *var dâshté shod*
> With the Passive, " by " = از *az.*
> By whom was this found ? این از کی پیدا شد؟
> *în az kî pêidâ shod ?*

In English, we have a curious habit of forming passives from verbs which have no Direct Object : I was given (i.e. *to me*, Indirect Object, was given . . . ). This is not possible in Persian. The passive equivalents of such verbs which take Indirect Objects, as, for example, گفتن to say, فرمودن command, دادن give, فروختن sell, پرسیدن ask, etc., can only be formed thus:

<table>
<tr><td rowspan="2">I was given</td><td>EITHER</td><td>(a)</td><td>They gave to me ... بمن دادند<br>béman dâdand</td></tr>
<tr><td>OR</td><td>(b)</td><td>To me was given ... بمن داده شد<br>béman dâdé shod</td></tr>
</table>

<table>
<tr><td rowspan="2">I am told</td><td>EITHER</td><td>(a)</td><td>They tell me ... بمن میگویند<br>béman mîgûyand</td></tr>
<tr><td>OR</td><td>(b)</td><td>To me it is said ... بمن گفته میشود<br>béman gofté mîshavad</td></tr>
</table>

<table>
<tr><td rowspan="2">We were asked</td><td>EITHER</td><td>(a)</td><td>They asked from us ...<br>az mâ porsîdand از ما پرسیدند</td></tr>
<tr><td>OR</td><td>(b)</td><td>From us it was asked ...<br>az mâ porsîdé shod از ما پرسیده شد</td></tr>
</table>

*Numbers.* Here are the remaining numbers:

| | Cardinal | | Ordinal |
|---|---|---|---|
| 21 | ۲۱ بیست و یک *bîst o yek* | | بیست و یکم *bîst o yekom* |
| 22 | ۲۲ بیست و دو *bîst o do* | | بیست و دوم *bîst o dovvom* |
| 23 | ۲۳ بیست و سه *bîst o sé* | | بیست و سوم *bîst o sevvom* |
| 24 | ۲٤ بیست و چهار *bîst o chahâr* | | (etc.) |
| 25 | ۲٥ بیست و پنج *bîst o panj* | | *Cardinal* |
| 26 | ۲۶ بیست و شش *bîst o shesh* | 27 ۲۷ بیست و هفت *bîst o haft* | |
| 28 | ۲۸ بیست و هشت *bîst o hasht* | 29 ۲۹ بیست و نه *bîst o noḥ* | |
| 30 | ۳۰ سی *sî* | 31 ۳۱ سی و یک *sî o yek* | |
| 40 | ٤۰ چهل *cheḥel* | 50 ٥۰ پنجاه *panjâḥ* | |
| 60 | ۶۰ شصت *shast* | 70 ۷۰ هفتاد *haftâd* | |
| 80 | ۸۰ هشتاد *hashtâd* | 90 ۹۰ نود *navad* | |

100 ۱۰۰    صد *sad*     151 ۱۵۱ صد و پنجاه و یک *sad*
                              *o panjâh o yek*

200 ۲۰۰    دویست *devîst*

300 ۳۰۰    سیصد *sîsad*     400 ۴۰۰   چهارصد *chahâr sad*

500 ۵۰۰    پانصد *pânsad*     600 ۶۰۰   شش صد *shesh sad*

700 ۷۰۰    هفت صد *haft sad*   800 ۸۰۰   هشت صد *hasht sad*

900 ۹۰۰    نه صد *noh sad*   1000 ۱۰۰۰   هزار *hezâr*

1969 (year or numeral) ۱۹۶۹    هزار و نه صد و شصت و نه
                            *hezâr o noh sad o shast o noh*

2000 ۲۰۰۰    دو هزار *dô hezâr*

3000 ۳۰۰۰    سه هزار *sé hezâr*

1,000,000 ۱,۰۰۰,۰۰۰    ملیون *melyûn*

½ ¼ نصف *nesf*   50% ٪۵۰   پنجاه در صد *panjâh dar sad*

100% ٪۱۰۰   صد در صد *sad dar sad*

You will notice (*a*) Numbers from 21 to 29, 31 to 39, 41 to 49, etc., are formed by coupling the larger number (tens) to the smaller number (units) with و *o* " and ". (*b*) All *compound* numbers are formed in this way, right into the millions. (*c*) The tens, 30 to 90, are simple numerals, and irregularly formed. The only difference between سه *sé* 3 and سی *sî* 30 is the vowel. (*d*) 200, 300, and 500 have special words, دویست *devîst*, سیصد *sîsad*, and پانصد *pânsad*. Otherwise the hundreds are regularly compounded. (*e*) The Arabic word for " first ", اول *avval*, is not used for 21st, 31st, 101st, etc.—these are regularly formed by suffixing م- -*ćm* to the Cardinal number at the end of the compound.

When constructing any number, always work from greatest to smallest, and always connect separate elements with و which is pronounced *o*.

## فرهنگ

| | |
|---|---|
| to dance رقص کردن *raghs k.* | pass (by or over) گذشتن (ـ گذر-) |
| excellent عالی *'âlî* | (از) *gozashtan, -gozar- (az)* |
| understand فهمیدن *fahmîdan,* | to play بازی کردن *bâzî k.* |
| *-fahm-* | truth حقیقت *haghîghat* |
| bridge پل *pol* | heart دل *del* |
| hungry گرسنه *gorosné* | dog سگ *sag* |
| also, as well همچنین *hamchonîn* | happy خوشحال *khoshhâl* |
| as far as (preposition) تا *tâ* | bone استخوان *ostokhân* |
| be lost گم شدن *gom sh.* | lose گم کردن *gom k.* |
| tooth دندان *dandân* | slowly, gently آهسته *âhesté* |
| already هم *ham* | cast one's eyes نظر . . . انداختن |
| like, similar to مثل *mesl-é* | *nazar . . . andâkhtan* |
| animal حیوان *hêivân,* Arabic | alone تنها *tanhâ* |
| plural حیوانات *hêivânât* | |

بخوانید :

## سگ گرسنه و استخوان

یکروز سگی گرسنه خوشحال بود که استخوانی بزرگ پیدا کرده بود.
سگ استخوان را به دندان گرفت تا آزرا تنها بخورد بدون اینکه حیوانات دیگر
ببیند. از آنجا تا منزل بایست از پلی که زیر آن رود خانه ای بود بگذرد.
وقتیکه به پل رسید براست و چپ خوب نگاه کرد چون نمیخواست هیچکس
آزاربیند. در حالیکه آهسته از روی پل میگذشت نظر پائین انداخت و دید
یک سگ مثل خودش یک استخوان بزرگ در دهان دارد. سگ بی فهم
نفهمید این استخوانی که در آب رود خانه دیده میشود مال خودش است و از
ته دل میل داشت این استخوان را هم داشته باشد.

ولی همینکه دهان باز کرد تا آن استخوانی را که در آب دیده میشد بدندان
گیرد استخوان در آب افتاد و گم شد — وبجای اینکه استخوانی دیگر پیدا
کرده باشد آن یکی را هم که خود داشت — گم کرد.

تمرین

I. Translate the last paragraph of the text (beginning

... ولی وقتیکه دندانهای خودش باز کرد).

II. Put the bracketed verb into the sentence in the right form :

۱ بدون اینکه او زود (آمدن) دیر میرسیم

۲ با اینکه دولتمند (بودن) خوشحال نیست

۳ راضی شدم از اینکه شما (تشریف آوردن)

٤ اگر سگ دندانهای خودش (باز کردن) استخوان میافتد

۵ اگر پول زیاد نداشته باشید بهتر است چیز ارزانتری (خریدن)

ایلیاتی از یکی از ایلات جنوبیِ ایران
*îliyâtî-az-yekî az îlât-é-jonûbî-yé îrân*
Tribesman from one of the
southern tribes of Iran.

## LESSON 25

*The Short Infinitive.* We have learnt that the infinitive of Persian verbs is that form ending in تن‍--*-tan* or دن‍--*-dan* :

   کردن *kardan* to do        ریختن *rikhtan* to pour

   شکستن *shekastan* to break    خوردن *khordan* to eat

There exists also a second, shorter infinitive, which is

formed in the same way as the Past Stem of the verb, by dropping the final ن- -an of the infinitive proper. There are no irregularly formed Short Infinitives. Thus:

کرد *kard,* ریخت *ríkht,* شکست *shekast,* خورد *khord*

The Short Infinitive is used in these *impersonal* expressions:

(i) After باید *bâyad* one must, نباید *nàbâyad* one must not, *bâyest* بایست one had to, and بنایست *nàbâyest* one had not to:

One must not do this thing ١ نباید این کار را کرد
*nàbâyad în kâr râ kard*

One must say that . . . . . . ٢ باید گفت که
*bâyad goft ké . . .*

One had to work well for that employer
٣ بایست برای آن کارفرما خوب کار کرد
*bâyest barâ-yé-ân kâr farmâ khûb kâr kard*

One had not to tell lies ٤ نبایست دروغ گفت
*nàbâyest dorûgh goft* (i.e. it was necessary not to . . .)

(ii) After the verb میشود *mîshavad* or *mîshé* meaning, here, "it is possible to . . .". This construction is only common in the Present:

٥ میشود گفت بفارسی سلام علیکم؟
*mîsharad goft béfârsî salâm 'alêikom ?*

Can one say (Is it possible to say) "Salaam aleikum" in Persian ? بله میشود *balé mîshavad*—Yes, one can.

And similarly after نمیشود *nàmîshavad* one can't, it is not possible to . . .:

٦ نمیشود در مسجد کفش پوشید
*nàmîshavad dar masjed kafsh pûshîd*
One cannot wear shoe(s) in the mosque

(c) After the forms ميتوان *mîtavân*, نميتوان *nàmîtavân*,
ميتوانست *mîtavânest*, and نميتوانست *nàmîtavânest* (one can, one
cannot, one could, one could not):

(*N.B.*—There is *no* personal ending at all on this form.)

٧ از اينجا ميتوان مسجد شاه را ديد

*az înjâ mîtavân masjed-é-shâh râ dîd*

One can see the Masjed-é-Shah from here

٨ ولى مسجد جامع را نميتوان ديد

*valî masjed-é-jâme' râ nàmîtavân dîd*

But one cannot see the Friday Mosque

There is no shortened Colloquial pronunciation for these
forms of توانستن *tavânestan* when they are used in these
impersonal expressions with the Short Infinitive.

The Short Infinitive is also used after a special form of
the verb خواستن *khâstan* to wish:

Take the verb خواستن *khâstan* and conjugate it in the
Present Tense, DROPPING THE -مي *mî-* PREFIX. We get:

| | | | |
|---|---|---|---|
| (1) | خواهم *khâham* | خواهيم *khâhîm* | |
| (2) | خواهيد *khâhîd* | خواهيد *khâhîd* | |
| (3){ | خواهد *khâhad* | خواهند *khâhand* | |
| | خواهد *khâhad* | خواهد *khâhad* | |

Add to each of these forms the Short Infinitive of a verb,
and we have a Future Tense. Thus, for كردن to do and
گفتن to say:

| | | | |
|---|---|---|---|
| (1) | خواهم كرد *khâham kard* | خواهم گفت *khâham goft* | |
| | I shall do | I shall say | |
| (2) | خواهيد كرد *khâhîd kard* | خواهيد گفت *khâhîd goft* | |
| | you will do | you will say | |

|   |   |   |
|---|---|---|
| (3) | خواهد کرد *khâhad kard*<br>he/she will do | خواهد گفت *khâhad goft*<br>he/she will say |
|   | خواهد کرد *khâhad kard*<br>it will do | خواهد گفت *khâhad goft*<br>it will say |
| (1) | خواهیم کرد *khâhîm kard*<br>we shall do | خواهیم گفت *khâhîm goft*<br>we shall say |
| (2) | خواهید کرد *khâhîd kard*<br>you will do | خواهید گفت *khâhîd goft*<br>you will say |
| (3) | خواهند کرد *khâhand kard*<br>they will do | خواهند گفت *khâhand goft*<br>they will say |
|   | خواهد کرد *khâhad kard*<br>they will do | خواهد گفت *khâhad goft*<br>they will say |

About this tense : (a) Do not confuse it with خواستن *khâstan* with -می *mî-* prefixed in the Present, used with the Subjunctive of the verb, giving the meaning " I wish to do something ".  Compare :

این را خواهم کرد *înrâ khâham kard* (Future)    with    میخواهم این را بکنم *mîkhâham înrâ békonam*

I shall do this                    I want to do this

(b) In this future tense, the stress is always on the operative part of the verb which is the Short Infinitive— the auxiliary is only lightly pronounced :

خواهم رفت *khâham ràft* I shall go

(c) This Future Tense is only, or almost only, used in formal speech and in writing.  In conversation we normally use the Present Tense for future time, unless there is a risk of ambiguity, for example :

۹ نمیگویم که اینجاست میگویم که زود خواهد بود

*nàmîgûyam ké înjâst, mîgûyam ké zûd khâhad bùd*

I am not saying he is here, I am saying that he soon
will be

Whenever it is perfectly obvious that the action is a
future one, we use the Present :

Tomorrow I'll go *fardâ mîravam* فردا میروم

(*d*) There is no special Colloquial pronunciation for خواستن
*khâstan* when it is used in this construction.

(*e*) The negative prefix نـ *nà-* is attached to the auxiliary,
not to the Short Infinitive :

I shall not say *nàkhâham goft* نخواهم گفت ۱۰

He will not come *nàkhâhad âmad* نخواهد آمد ۱۱

When, therefore, is the long infinitive, the infinitive given
in all the dictionaries, used ?  Its sole use in sentences is
(see Lesson 22*a*) as a noun, i.e. as the subject of a verb :

۱۲ پختن تخم مرغ آسان است

*pokhtan-é-tokhm-é-morgh âsân é*

Cooking (to cook) eggs is easy

or as the object of a verb :

۱۳ من رادیو شنیدن را دوست دارم

*man râdiô shenîdan-râ dûst dâram*

I like listening (to listen) to the radio

or governed by a preposition :

۱٤ برای خواندن وقت ندارم

*barâyé khândan vaght nàdâram*

I have no time for reading (for to-read)

*Thou.* Up to now we have constantly used one pronoun

for *you*, شما *shomâ*. Strictly speaking, this is the *plural* form of you. There is also a *singular* form

"thou" تو *to*

with its secondary forms بتو *bé-to* to thee, ترا *torâ* (تو) thee, direct object—and so forth.

This form of *you* is only used as is "tu" in French or Italian, or "du" in German, i.e. to *one* person with whom one is on *very familiar terms indeed*. It even happens that father and son will address each other as شما *shomâ*. In some cases the use of تو *to* implies a familiarity almost verging on contempt. The foreigner is well advised *never* to use it; but it should be known, as it is sometimes heard, and is used in literature. The verb with تو *to* as its subject is the same as the شما *shomâ* form in all tenses, but with the final د- *-d* taken off:

| شما ئید | تو ئی | شما رفتید | تو رفتی |
|---|---|---|---|
| *shomâ îd* | *to î* | *shomâ raftîd* | *to raftî* |
| you are | thou art | you went | thou didst go |

| شما دارید | تو داری | دیده باشید | دیده باشی |
|---|---|---|---|
| *shomâ dârîd* | *to dârî* | *dîdé bâshîd* | *dîdé bâshî* |
| you have | thou hast | you may have seen | thou mayest have seen |

But for the *imperative* we drop the ید- *-îd* of the شما *shomâ* imperative form:

| بیائید | بیا | ننویسید | ننویس |
|---|---|---|---|
| *biâ'îd* | *biâ* | *nànevîsîd* | *nànevîs* |
| (you) come | (thou) come | don't (you) write | don't (thou) write |

The corresponding possessive suffix is ت- -at (this is the original singular of تان- -etân):

| پدرت | پدرتان | منزلت | منزلتان |
|---|---|---|---|
| *pedarat* | *pedaretân* | *manzelat* | *manzeletân* |
| thy father | your father | thy house | your house |

| خودت | خودتان | دوستهایت | دوستهایتان |
|---|---|---|---|
| *khodat* | *khodetân* | *dûsthâyat* | *dûsthâyetân* |
| thy own, thyself | your own, yourself/ves | thy friends | your friends |

*Colloquial Pronunciation.* In the Subjunctive and Imperative of some verbs, the بـ *bé-* becomes *bo-* when the next pronounced vowel is *o, ô,* or *û*:

$$\left.\begin{array}{l} \text{بکن} \quad bòkon \\ \text{بکنید} \quad bòkonîd \\ \text{بکنیم} \quad bòkonîm \end{array}\right\} \text{from کردن } kardan \text{ to do}$$

because the next pronounced vowel is *not o, ô,* or *û.*
$$\left.\begin{array}{l} \text{بگو} \quad bògû \\ \text{BUT} \\ \text{بگوئید} \quad bégîd \\ \text{بگویم} \quad bégam \end{array}\right\} \text{from گفتن } goftan \text{ to say}$$

$$\left.\begin{array}{l} \text{بگذر} \quad bògozar \\ \text{بگذرید} \quad bògozarîd \\ \text{بگذرند} \quad bògozarand \end{array}\right\} \text{from گذشتن } gozashtan \text{ to pass}$$

And note especially the pronunciation of the تو *tô* imperative in:

the و is pronounced *ô* here — برو ! *bòrô !*
$$\left.\begin{array}{l} \text{but as -av here, where the next } \left\{ \begin{array}{l} \text{بری, } béri, \\ \text{بروی. } béravî \end{array}\right. \\ \text{vowel is not pronounced } o, ô, \text{ or } û \end{array}\right\} \text{from رفتن } raftan$$

and similarly with شدن *shodan*: نشو ! *nàshô !*

**BUT**

| نشوید | nàshavîd,<br>nàshîd | نشود | nàshavad,<br>nàshé | بشود | béshavad,<br>béshé |

In both Elevated and Colloquial the following pronunciations are the only possible ones:

برو **bŏrô !** go!　　　　　نرو **nàrô !** don't go!

شو **shô !** be (in passives)　نشو **nàshô !**

*Irregular Present Stems—Group 6, âsh-âr.*

Verbs whose infinitive ends in اشتن- *-âshtan* have Present Stems in ار- *âr-*. There are no exceptions to this rule.

| Infinitive. | English. | Present Stem. |
|---|---|---|
| داشتن *dâshtan* | have | دار- *dâr-* |
| انگاشتن *angâshtan* | consider, suppose | انگار- *angâr-* |
| پنداشتن *pendâshtan* | consider, reflect | پندار- *pendâr-* |
| کاشتن *kâshtan* | sow, cultivate | کار- *kâr-* |
| گماشتن *gomâshtan* | appoint, set over | گمار- *gomâr-* |
| گذاشتن *gozâshtan* §<br>(گذاردن *gozârdan* also) } | place, set | گذار- *gozâr-* |

§ Distinguish between (گذر-) گذشتن *gozashtan*, *-gozar-* meaning *to pass by* (short *a*, no Direct Object) and its derivative given above (گذار-) گذاشتن *gozâshtan*, *-gozâr-* meaning *to place* (long ا *â*, takes a Direct Object).

تمرین

I. Put the bracketed verbs into the Future Tense:

۱ عرض کردم که ما هفتهٔ آینده کار زیاد (داشتن)

۲ او اسباب را (گذاشتن)

۳ آموزگار فرمودند که فردا کلاس (نبودن)

٤ نمیدانند آیا ایشان (تشریف آوردن) یا نه

۵ او زود یاصفهان (رفتن)

II. Put into the singular (تو *to*) form:

٣ خودتان      ٢ دستان      ١ بودید

٦ نروید      ۵ بروید    ٤ بگوئید! (imperative)

٩ چه میگوئید؟   ٨ نکنید! (imperative)   ٧ زود باشید! (imperative)

١٠ میخواهید

III. Write the pronunciation, thus:

| Orthography | Elevated | Colloquial |
|---|---|---|
| e.g.   بگویم | *bégûyam* | *bégam* |
| ٣ بگذاریم | ٢ نمیتوانم | ١ بکن |
| ۵ نروید | ٤ بگوئید | |

ترجمه بفرمائید:

IV. Translate:

1. One must not talk in the mosque.
2. One can always try; but one cannot always say whether one will succeed.
3. It is not possible to say who did this.
4. One shouldn't tell lies.
5. What must one say instead of " من "? One must say " بنده ".

## TEST PAPER—VERBS

A. 1. Give the Past Participles of:

۵ گذشتن    ٤ شدن    ٣ کردن    ٢ یافتن    ١ خواستن

2. Give the Present Participles of:

۵ زدن    ٤ آموختن    ٣ آمدن    ٢ گفتن    ١ رفتن

3. Give the Short Infinitives of :

۵ خواهش کردن    ٤ فرمودن    ۳ افزودن    ۲ بودن    ۱ رفتن

4. Conjugate completely in the Present Tense :

۵ بستن    ٤ داشتن    ۳ نشستن    ۲ آمیختن    ۱ نمودن

5. Put these forms into the Past Tense :

۵ میامیزد    ٤ میتابد    ۳ کیست؟    ۲ نمیروید    ۱ میخرم

6. Give the (*a*) Perfect, (*b*) Pluperfect, and (*c*) Perfect
   Subjunctives of these forms :

۵ پختم    ٤ شمردم    ۳ خواندم    ۲ گرفتم    ۱ کردم

B. Fill in the blanks with the correct form of the verb given
   in the column on the left :

| | |
|---|---|
| آمدن | ۱   اینجا صبر کنید تا من —— |
| رفتن | ۲   حسن میخواهد فردا بتهران —— |
| خواندن | ۳   کدام یکی از شما خواهد ——؟ |
| بودن | ٤   در تهران پایتخت ایران امروز زیاد دکانها —— |
| گفتن – بودن | ۵   نباید —— که او دزد —— |
| رسیدن | ۶   از این کوچه میتوانم بخیابان اصفهان ——؟ |
| نیامدن | ۷   چه گفت؟ گفت که چرا شما دیروز ——؟ |
| حس کردن | ۸   در دست چپ نمیتوانم هیچ چیز —— |
| بیرون شدن | ۹   آن شخص گفت که از اینجا نمیشود —— |
| نوشتن – رسیدن | ۱۰   اگر فردا —— نامه —— اگرنه نه |

C. Give the (*a*) Short Infinitive, (*b*) Full Infinitive, (*c*) 3rd
   person singular Subjunctive, (*d*) 3rd person singular
   Imperfect, and (*e*) 3rd person singular Present Tense
   of the Persian verb meaning

*to tell lies*

Put the form (*a*), (*b*), (*c*), (*d*), or (*e*) as appropriate into each of the blanks in the following sentences :

این شخص را دوست ندارم برای اینکه همیشه ——.

۲ همیشه —— و باین سبب هیچ کس او را قبول نمیکرد.

۳ —— بد است.

٤ نمیشود ——.

٥ اگر کسی —— هیچ کس او را قبول نخواهد کرد.

D. Distinguish, by translating or explaining, between :

$$
\left.\begin{array}{r}
\text{خواهیم دید} \\
\text{میخواهیم ببینیم}
\end{array}\right\} \text{۲}
\qquad
\left.\begin{array}{r}
\text{تا آمدم} \\
\text{تا بیایم}
\end{array}\right\} \text{۱}
$$

$$
\left.\begin{array}{r}
\text{باید عرض کنم} \\
\text{باید گفت}
\end{array}\right\} \text{٤}
\qquad
\left.\begin{array}{r}
\text{اگر برود} \\
\text{اگر میرفت}
\end{array}\right\} \text{۳}
$$

$$
\left.\begin{array}{r}
\text{گم کرد} \\
\text{گم شد}
\end{array}\right\} \text{٦}
\qquad
\left.\begin{array}{r}
\text{شاید اشتباه کنم} \\
\text{شاید اشتباه کرده باشم}
\end{array}\right\} \text{٥}
$$

$$
\left.\begin{array}{r}
\text{نکن} \\
\text{نکنی}
\end{array}\right\} \text{۸}
\qquad
\left.\begin{array}{r}
\text{دیده ام} \\
\text{دیده میشوم}
\end{array}\right\} \text{۷}
$$

$$
\left.\begin{array}{r}
\text{گذشته} \\
\text{گذاشته}
\end{array}\right\} \text{۱۰}
\qquad
\left.\begin{array}{r}
\text{نمیتوانستند بیایند} \\
\text{نمیتوانست آمد}
\end{array}\right\} \text{۹}
$$

# PART THREE

## Words

## لغات

*Word-building.* By the use of suffixes we can form many derivative words in Persian :

(a) If we take the Present Stem of some verbs and add the suffix ش- -*esh* (یش- -*yesh* after vowels), we form abstract nouns of quality or of activity :

سر *sar*        head⎫ سرزنش *sarzanesh*
زدن (-زن-) *zadan,* -*zan*- beat ⎭    = punishment

کوشیدن (-کوش-) *kûshîdan,* -*kûsh*- to strive :

کوشش *kûshesh* effort

ورزیدن (-ورز-) *varzîdan,* -*varz*- to exercise :

ورزش *varzesh* sport, exercise

Similarly, from obvious sources, آمیزش *âmîzesh* mixture ; آموزش *âmûzesh* learning, knowledge ; نمایش *namâyesh* exhibition, show ; دانش *dânesh* knowledge ; آزمایش *âzmâyesh* experiment, test ; and many others.

(b) If we add to any adjective (including participles) ending in ه- -*é* the suffix گی- -*gî*, we get the abstract noun of the activity concerned :

راننده *rânàndé* driving (ad.) رانندگی *rânandégî* (noun)
خسته *khasté* tired خستگی *khastégî* fatigue
بسته *basté* bound بستگی *bastégî* bond, link, connexion
گرسنه *gorosné* hungry گرسنگی *gorosnégî* hunger

(c) Many words of activity are formed by coupling together the Past and Present Stems of a verb, or two Past Stems :

from گفتن goftan : گفتگو (گفت و گو) goftogû quarrel

جستن jostan to search : جستجو jostojû search

آمدورفت âmadoraft or آمدوشد âmadoshod traffic

(d) If we add the suffix بان- -bân (rarely, وان- -vân) to a noun, we get the name of the person tending the place or thing :

باغ bâgh garden :          باغبان bâghbân gardener

شتر shotor camel :          شتربان shotorbân ⎫
                           شتروان shotorvân ⎬camel-driver

در dar door :          دربان darbân concierge, janitor

پاس pâs watch :          پاسبان pâsbân watchman, policeman

(e) The suffix ستان- -stân, -estân, means " place of " :

گل gol rose :          گلستان golestân rose-bower

انگلستان englestân England

لهستان lehestân Poland

شهر shahr city :          شهرستان shahrestân a county

پاکستان pâkestân Pakistan          هندوستان hendûstân India

افغانستان afghânestân Afghanistan

عربستان 'arabestân Arabia          ترکستان torkestân Turkestan

(f) The suffix گاه- -gâh also means " place " :

ایستگاه îstgâh station          دانشگاه dâneshgâh university

نمایشگاه namâyeshgâh theatre          فرودگاه forûdgâh airport

آزمایشگاه âzmâyeshgâh laboratory          باشگاه bâshgâh club

بنگاه bongâh society, office

(g) The word خانه khâné " house " is used as a suffix, for a place where things are kept or where a certain activity is pursued :

کتابخانه *ketâbkhâné* library     کارخانه *kârkhâné* workshop

آشپزخانه *âshpazkhâné* kitchen     مریضخانه *marîzkhâné* hospital

مهمانخانه *mehmânkhâné* hôtel

(*h*) A few abstract nouns of quality or condition are made by adding the suffix ار- -*âr* :

from   رفتن *raftan* :     رفتار *raftâr* behaviour

from   گرفتن *gereftan* :     گرفتار *gereftâr* affliction

from   گفتن *goftan* :     گفتار *goftâr* speech, talk

from   کردن *kardan* :     کردار *kerdâr* action (vowel
                                                      change here)

(*j*) We can add, to adjectives of quality, the suffix ا- -*â* to give the abstract quality, a noun :

پهن *pahn* wide, broad     پهنا *pahnâ* width, breadth

گرم *garm* warm     گرما *garmâ* warmth

(*k*) Many abstract nouns are also formed by adding ی- -*î* (ئی- -*î* after vowels) to other words :

آشپز *âshpaz* a cook     آشپزی *âshpazî* cuisine

باغبان *bâghbân* gardener     باغبانی *bâghbânî* gardening

نقاش *naghghâsh* painter     نقاشی *naghghâshî* painting

دانا *dânâ* wise     دانائی *dânâ'î* wisdom

بزرگ *bozorg* great     بزرگی *bozorgî* greatness

And, from equally obvious sources :

زیباشناسی *zîbâshenâsî* aesthetics

کاشیکاری *kâshîkârî* tilework, mosaic

نامنویسی *nâmnevîsî* registration

وزن کشی *vaznkashî* weighing

(*l*) Finally, for this lesson at least, a colloquial suffix denoting the operator or handler of something. This suffix چی- -*chî* is taken from the Turkish -*ci* or *çi* :

تلفنچی *telefonchî* telephone operator

نفتچی *naftchî* oil-seller

تفنگچی *tofangchî* rifleman (تفنگ *tofang* = rifle)

*Colloquial Pronunciation.* In the verb گذاشتن (-گذار-) *gozâshtan, -gozâr-* " to place ", it is common practice to omit in speech the syllable -*go*- *only when it is preceded by a prefix* :

میگذارم *mîzâram* I put اینجا بگذارید *înjâ bézârîd* Put it here.

**BUT**

آنرا کجا گذاشتید؟ *ânrâ kojâ gozâshtîd?* Where did you put it?

## تمرین

I. Form workers from :

١ باغ      ٢ در      ٣ پاس

places from :

٤ گل      ٥ عرب      ٦ مهمان      ٧ بودن      ٨ دانش

abstracts of activity from :

٩ آشپز      ١٠ باغبان      ١١ راندن      ١٢ بستن

and redoubled compounds from :

١٣ جستن      ١٤ گفتن

II. Translate and explain the construction of :

١ بستگی      ٢ دانشگاه      ٣ نقاشی کردن      ٤ نمایش      ٥ نامنویسی شدن

III. Translate :

   1. to do the cooking.

   2. to be painted.

   3. a quarrel, to quarrel. There was (= شدن) a quarrel between them.

4. the policeman, the police, traffic.
5. theatre, library, county.

## LESSON 26a

*Wordbuilding.* We form CAUSATIVE VERBS in Persian thus :

(*a*) By taking the Present Stem and adding اندن- -*ândan* or انیدن- -*ânîdan* to make the new verb, which is then regular : رفتن ـرو- *raftan*, *-rav-* to go ; روانه کردن *ravânék*, ـروان- -*ravân-* (also راندن *rândan*, ـران- -*rân-*) to make it go, to drive something along.

رسیدن ـرس- *rasîdan*, *-ras-* to arrive ; رساندن *rasândan*, ـرسان- -*rasân-* or رسانیدن -*rasân-* رسانیدن *rasânîdan*, -*rasân-* to make it arrive, to bring it up.

گردیدن *gardîdan*, ـگرد- -*gard-* (also گشتن *gashtan*, ـگرد- -*gard-*) to become ; گردانیدن ـگردان- *gardânîdan*, -*gardân-* to make something become so.

سوختن ـسوز- *sûkhtan*, *-sûz-* to blaze, be on fire ;
سوزانیدن ـسوزان- *sûzânîdan*, -*sûzân-* to make it burn.

(b) By changing a root short *a* (unwritten) to long -ا- -*â*-;

گذشتن - گذر- ‎ *gozashtan, -gozar-* to move, go past;

گذاشتن - گذار- ‎ *gozâshtan, -gozâr-* to pass something, to place it, to make it move past.

گذردن - گذر- ‎ *gozardan, -gozar-* = *gozashtan* above;

گذاردن - گذار- ‎ *gozârdan, -gozâr-* = *gozâshtan* above.

Note : گذردن - گذر ‎ *gozardan, -gozar-* also forms the Causative گذراندن - گذران- ‎ *gozarândan, -gozarân-* (by rule (i) above), meaning to spend or pass time.

In each of the cases above, the original verb does not take an object, but itself performs the action of the verb. The Causative derivative takes an object and causes it to do the action. Examine :

کاغذ سوخت ‎ *kâghaz sûkht* The paper burned

کاغذ را سوزانیدم ‎ *kâghaz râ sûzânîdam* I burned the paper

*Time.* The hour is given with the word ساعت ‎ *sâ'at* meaning (1) hour (as here) and (2) clock or watch :

    one o'clock   ساعت یک ‎ *sâ'at-é-yek*

    three o'clock  ساعت سه ‎ *sâ'at-é-sé*

    eleven o'clock ساعت یازده ‎ *sâ'at-é-yâzdah*

Time up to the half hour is given by adding the minutes to the last hour, using و pronounced *o* :

1.10  *sâ'at-é-yek o dah daghîghé* ساعت یک و ده دقیقه

2.15  *sâ'at-é-do o rob'* ساعت دو و ربع

3.25  *sâ'at-é-sé o bîstopanj daghîghé* ساعت سه و بیست وپنج دقیقه

4.30  *sâ'at-é-chahâr o nîm* ساعت چهار و نیم

## فرهنگ — وقت

hour, clock, watch, ساعت *sâ'at*

half an hour نیم ساعت *nîmsâ'at*

quarter of an hour ربع ساعت *rob' sâ'at*

a.m. صبح *sobh*

noon ظهر *zohr*

forenoon قبل از ظهر *ghabl az zohr*

sunset غروب *ghorûb*

year سال *sâl*

week هفته *hafté*

minute دقیقه *daghîghé*

half نیم *nîm*

quarter ربع *rob'*

p.m. بعد از ظهر *ba'ad az zohr*

midnight نصف شب *nesf-é-shab*

sunrise طلوع *tolû'*

second (of time) ثانیه *sânîyé*

month ماه *mâh*

day روز *rûz*

*Days of the Week.* Iran is a Moslem country and the weekly day of rest is Friday. The day after that, Saturday, is called after the Jewish Sabbath. From then on the days are numbered in order after Saturday:

Saturday   شنبه *shambé* (-نب- = *mb*)

Sunday یکشنبه *yekshambé*

Monday دوشنبه *doshambé*

Tuesday سه‌شنبه *séshambé*

Wednesday چهارشنبه *chahârshambé*

Thursday پنجشنبه *panjshambé*

Friday     جمعه *jom'é* or آدینه *âdîné* (less commonly)

To all these names we may prefix روز *rûz-é-* (day).

*The Calendar,* تقویم *taghvîm.*

Three calendars are known in Iran:

(a) *The Arab (Moslem) lunar calendar,* 354–5 days long, is only used to mark religious occasions. It is not necessary for us to learn it, merely to know it exists.

(b) *The Iranian national calendar* is solar and lasts 365–6 days. It begins exactly on the Spring Equinox which,

depending on the year, falls on our 20th, 21st, or 22nd
March :

| | | | |
|---|---|---|---|
| بهار<br>*bahâr* Spring | 31 days<br>each | فروردین *farvardîn*<br>اردی بهشت *ordîbehesht*<br>خرداد *khordâd* | ۱<br>۲<br>۳ |
| تابستان<br>*tâbestân* Summer | 31 days<br>each | تیر *tîr*<br>مرداد *mordâd*<br>شهریور *shahrîvar* | ٤<br>۵<br>۶ |
| پائیز<br>*pâ'îz* Autumn | 30 days<br>each | مهر *mehr*<br>ابان, آبان *âbân*<br>آذر *âzar* | ۷<br>۸<br>۹ |
| زمستان<br>*zemestân* Winter | 30 days<br>each<br>29/30 days | دی *dêi*<br>بهمن *bahman*<br>اسفند *esfand* | ۱۰<br>۱۱<br>۱۲ |

*esfand* اسفند has 30 days every fourth (leap) year (سال کبیسه
*sâl-ê-kabîsê*). To each of these names we can suffix ماه- *-mâh*
" month ". This is especially common in the case of the
short names : تیرماه *tîrmâh*, مهرماه *mehrmâh*.

Both the Moslem and the Iranian years are reckoned
from the date of the Prophet's journey from Mecca to
Medina in 622 A.D., but because the solar year is longer
than the lunar year, the number of the year (and of course
the names of the months) differ.

1 Aug. 1968 A.D.=۱۰ مرداد ۱۳٤۷ 10 *mordâd* 1347 A.H. Iranian
(A.H. = anno hegirae, Year of the Flight)

(c) *The Christian Calendar* is used unofficially, especially
in commerce and international affairs. The months are
mostly pronounced as in French and transliterated so :

| French. | Persian. | French. | Persian. |
|---------|----------|---------|----------|
| juillet | ژویه | janvier | ژانویه |
| août (*ût*) | اوت | février | فوریه |
| septembre | سپتامبر | mars | مارس |
| octobre | اکتبر | avril | آوریل |
| novembre | نوامبر | mai | مه |
| décembre | دسامبر | juin | ژوئن |

Dates are given with Ordinal numbers and the *ézâfé* :

Saturday 16th Khordâd *shambé shânzdahòm-é-khordâd*

شنبه شانزدهم خرداد

1st March *avval-é-mârs* روز اول مارس or اول مارس or

*rûz-é-avval-é-mârs*

The year is quoted as a number, beginning with the
thousand : 1914   ۱۹۱٤   هزار و نهصد و چهارده

*hezâr o nohsad o chahârdah.*

## فرهنگ

| | |
|---|---|
| holiday *'éid* عید | solar (Iranian) year سال |
| sun آفتاب *âftâb*, خورشید *khorshîd* | *sâl-é-khorshîdî* خورشیدی |
| New Year's Day (1st Farvardin) | Zoroastrian زردشتی *zardoshtî* |
| عید نوروز*'éid-é-nô rûz* | Jew(ish) یهودی *yahûdî* |
| Moslem مسلمان *mosalmân* | Jesus § عیسی *'îsâ,* |
| Christian عیسوی *'îsavî* | حضرت عیسی *hazrat-é-'îsâ* |

§ حضرت *hazrat* = Lord ; Christ is honoured as a prophet by
Moslems. Similarly : حضرت پیغامبر *hazrat-é-péighâmbar* the Lord
Prophet (i.e. Mahomet محمد *mohammad*).

| | |
|---|---|
| card کارت *kârt* | to be born تولد یافتن *tavallod* |
| sweets شیرینی *shîrînî* | *yâftan*, متولد بودن (شدن) |
| send فرستادن (فرست-) *ferestâdan*, | *motovalled b., sh.* |
| *-ferest-* | this year امسال *emsâl* |
| congratulate, send best wishes | last year پارسال *pârsâl* |
| تبریک گفتن *tabrîk goftan* | the day after tomorrow پسفردا |
| تبریک عرض کردن *tabrîk 'arz k.* | *pasfardâ* |

| | |
|---|---|
| within (time) درظرف *dar zarf-é-* | the day before yesterday پریروز *parîrûz* |
| sometimes گاهی *gâhî* | |
| visit دیدن رفتن *dîdan raftan* | new (year) نو *nôu* |
| religion مذهب دین *dîn mazhab* | last night دیشب *dîshab* |
| birthday روز تولد *rûz-é-tavallod* | the night before last پریشب *parîshab* |

بخوانید :

### عید نوروز

در ایران بزرگترین عید سال عید نوروز است که روز اول سال —
به اول فروردین ماه می افتد. در این روز هرکسی که ایرانی باشد — مسلمان
عیسوی زردشتی و یهودی — عید میگیرد. باید هرکس در این روز بزرگ برای
دیدن دوستان برود و اول میروند بدیدن پدر و مادر. وقتی که کسی بدیدن
ما میاید ما باید با ایشان شیرینی و چای بخوریم. اگرکسی دوستان زیاد دارد که
نمیتواند در این روز اول بدیدن هریک برود پس سعی میکند در ظرف سیزده
روز اول سال (از اول تا روز سیزدهم فروردین ماه) دیدن برود. گاهی اتفاق
می افتد که کسی را نمیتوانیم ببینیم که در شهر یا شهرستان دیگر منزل میکند —
پس یک کارت کوچک میفرستیم که رویش نوشته شده است «برای سال
نو آقا وخانم (اسم) باقا وخانم (اسم) تبریک عرض میکنند».

**I.**

تمرین

جواب بفرمائید :

۱    بزرگترین عید در تقویم ایرانی کی اتفاق می افتد؟

۲    اسم این عید چیست ؟

۳    روز اول سال ایرانی در تقویم عیسوی کی اتفاق می افتد؟

٤    مسلمان هستید شما؟ دینتان چیست؟

۵   جناب عالی کی متولد شدید؟

۶   بنده روز ۲۰م ژوئیه سال ۱۹۳۳ عیسوی متولد شدیم. از جناب عالی
بزرگتر یا جوانتر هستم؟

۷   چای بیشتر دوست دارید یا قهوه؟

۸   در تقویم ایرانی روز اول فصل تابستان کی اتفاق می افتد؟

۹   در سال چند ماه هست؟

۱۰   امسال سال کبیسه است؟ و پارسال؟

## II. Complete :

امروز شنبه است. فردا   (۱) ── است و دیروز   (۲) ── بود. همچنین
پریروز   (۳) ── بود. از امروز تا یک هفته   (۴) ── خواهد بود. پسفردا
(۵) ── خواهد بود.

## III.

چه ساعتی است؟ :

۳              ۲              ۱

## IV. Write in full words :

بتمام حرفها بنویسید :

(ساعت):    (۱) ۳ ── ۲۰        (۲) ٤ ── ۱۷        (۳) ۸ ── ۳۰

(تقویم ایرانی):    (۴) ۱۳۳۵/۸/۲۰        (۵) ۱۳۳۶/۱۰/۳۰

## LESSON 27

*Wordbuilding.* Suffixes—continued.

We often use a suffix ی- *-î* (ئ- -'*î* after vowels,
گی- *-gî* after vocalic ه *h*) to form adjectives from other
parts of speech :

| | |
|---|---|
| ملت *mellat* nation | ملی *mellî* national |
| شاهنشاه *shâhenshâh* emperor | شاهنشاهی *shâhenshâhî* imperial |
| ایران *îrân* Iran | ایرانی *îrânî* Iranian |
| عراق *'erâgh* Iraq | عراقی *'erâghî* Iraqi |
| عرب *'arab* an Arab | عربی *'arabî* Arab, Arabic, Arabian |
| مذهب *mazhab* religion | مذهبی *mazhabî* religious |
| جمهور *jomhûr* republic | جمهوری *jomhûrî* republican |
| شب *shab* evening, night | شبی *shabî* evening's, nocturnal |
| هفته *haftê* week | هفتگی *haftegî* ⎫ weekly |
| دوهفتگی *dohaftegî* bi-weekly | هرهفتگی *harhaftegî* ⎭ |

*Adjectives and Adverbs* are usually identical in form :
bad(ly) بد *bad* ; good/well خوب *khûb* ; better بهتر *behtar* ;
but certain adverbs, usually of Manner or Time, borrowed
from Arabic, keep their Arabic form ending in the curious
orthography ً or *-an.*

This is not a Persian letter ; it is an Arabic double
letter, and all we need to know about it is that it is
pronounced *-an,* short *a* even if there is an ا *alef* there.
Learn these essential ones, derived from adjectives :

| | |
|---|---|
| اول *avval* first | اولاً *avvalan* firstly |
| معمولی *ma'amûlî* general | معمولاً *ma'amûlan* generally |
| سابق *sâbegh* former | سابقاً *sâbeghan* formerly |

مثل mesl-é similar to     مثلاً masalan for example

فعل fe'l fact     فعلاً fe'lan in fact

اصل asl origin     اصلاً aslan actually

خصوصی khosûsî special     خصوصاً khosûsan specially

Persian abstract nouns in ه -é and ت -at come from Arabic nouns ending in ة (ه dotted and pronounced -at). In some cases the Persians have dropped the dots and pronounce ه -é :

Arabic دفعة daf'at a time, Persian دفعه daf'é

and in others they have kept the pronunciation -at and re-spelled with ت :

Arabic ندرة nodrat rarity, Persian ندرت nodrat

The original Arabic forms also make adverbs as above :

دفعةً daf'atan suddenly ندرةً nodratan rarely

Remember to keep the -an short in all these adverbs.

The adverb for at last, finally is the Arabic بالاخره belakheré (medial ا alef short here).

*Compound Nouns and Adjectives* are often formed by running together a noun + a Present Stem :

| | | |
|---|---|---|
| خوش khosh pleasant<br>گو gû say | } | خوشگو khoshgû sweet-tongued, full of sweet speech |
| بد bad bad<br>گو gû say | } | بدگو badgû evil-mouthed, slanderous |
| سر sar head<br>باز bâz game | } | سرباز sarbâz soldier (one who risks his head, his life) |
| آش âsh stew<br>پز paz cook | } | آشپز âshpaz cook |
| سر sar head<br>کش kash pull | } | سرکش sarkash obstinate, stubborn, head-strong (used especially of horses) |

پیغام *pêighâm* message ⎱ پیغامبر *pêighâmbar* prophet
بر *bar*   carry ⎰

قالی *ghâlî* carpet ⎱ قالیفروش *ghâliforûsh* carpet-seller
فروش *forûsh* sell ⎰

شهر *shahr* city ⎱ شهردار *shahrdâr* municipality
دار *dâr* possess ⎰ شهرداری *shahrdârî* civic

دندان *dandân* tooth ⎱ دندانساز *dandânsâz* dentist
ساز *sâz* make ⎰

رنگ *rang* colour ⎱ رنگزن *rangzan* painter (of houses, etc.)
زن *zan* strike ⎰

خشک *khoshk* dry ⎱ کاغذ خشک کن *kâghaz-ê-khoshk-kon*
کن *kon*   do ⎰   blotting-paper

پاك *pâk* clean ⎱ پاکنویس *pâknevîs* fair copy
نویس *nevîs* write ⎰

*Nouns of agent* are formed by adding the suffix کر *-kar*,
گر *-gar*, کار *-kâr*, or گار *-gâr* :

درو *derôu* harvest : دروگر *derôugar* harvester

آهن *âhan* iron : آهنگر *âhangar* ironmonger, blacksmith

کار *kâr* work : کارگر *kârgar* worker, workman

آموختن *âmûkhtan* to teach : آموزگار *âmûzegâr* primary teacher

The prefix هم *ham-* (cognate with Latin " cum ") gives
us the additional meaning " together " :

کار *kâr* work : همکاری کردن *hamkârî k.* co-operate.

سایه *sâyé* shade, shadow : همسایه *hamsâyé* neighbour (i.e.
one who shares the same shade).

چنین *chonîn* like this : همچنین *hamchonîn* just like this,
likewise, also, as well (as).

هم *ham-* is also used as an intensifying prefix in :

همین *hamîn* this very one, the same

همان *hamán* that very one, the same

هيمنجا *hamînjâ* just here

هامنجا *hamânjâ* just there

Its meaning as a word is (*a*) emphatic, as above :

من هم ميروم ولی شما بايد بمانيد

*manham mîravam valî shomâ bâyad bémânîd*

I'm going, but you've got to stay

با اين صندوق کهنه چه کار کنم؟ کدام؟ اين هم

*bâ în sandûgh-é-kohné ché kâr konam ? kodâm ? înham*

What am I to do with this old box ? Which one ? This one.

(*b*) already :

They had already left. *anhâ ham rafté bûdand* آنها هم رفته بودند

(*c*) also :

I'm going too. *man ham mîravam* من هم ميروم

*All.* There are various ways of translating *all* into Persian :

(*a*) meaning " everything " : همه چيز *hamé chîz* or همش *hamash.*

(*b*) meaning " the whole of " : تمام *tamâm-é-.*

(*c*) meaning " all " in the plural : همه *hamé-yé-.*

(*d*) meaning " each " in the singular : هر *har* or همه *han é* (with *no ézâfé*).

Examples of these :

(*a*) He forgot everything

همه چيز را فراموش کرد

*hamé chîz râ farâmûsh kard*

(*b*) The whole world loves peace

تمام دنيا صلح دوست دارد

*tamâm-é-donyâ solh dûst dârad*

(c) All the boys were sorry to see you go

همهٔ پسران متأسف بودند که میروید

*hamé-yé-pesarân mota'assef bûdand ké mîravîd*

(d) Each of these workmen complained

هریکی از این کارگران شکایت کرد

*har yekî az în kârgerân shekâyat kard*

*Time—continued.* Time after the half hour is given by using به *bé* " to " followed by the next hour, as in English:

1.45  یک ربع به دو *yek rob' bé do*

3.52  هشت دقیقه به چهار *hasht daghîghé bé chahâr*

Or else we can use the phrase از . . . گذشته *az . . . gozashté* " past . . . " with the last hour, as in English:

4.50  پنجاه دقیقه از چهار گذشته *panjâḥ daghîghé az chahâr gozashté*

This construction is used equally often for time before the half hour:

6.07  هفت دقیقه از شش گذشته *haft daghîghé az shesh gozashté*

8.15  ربع ساعت از هشت گذشته *rob' sâ'at az hasht gozashté*

*Arabic Plurals.* We do not propose to spend long describing the complications of Arabic plurals which occur in Persian. As we have said before, it is always acceptable to suffix a Persian plural in ها- *-hâ* or ان- *-ân* to an Arabic word borrowed into Persian. Here, briefly, are some of the commonest Arabic plural forms used in Persian:

(a) ات- *-ât* (after ه *-é*, جات- *-jât*):

| | | | |
|---|---|---|---|
| حیوان *hêivân* | animal | حیوانات *hêivânât* | |
| میوه *mîvé* | fruit | میوه‌جات *mîvéjât* | |
| روزنامه *rûznâmé* | newspaper | روزنامه‌جات *rûznâméjât* | |
| دانشکدهٔ ادبیات *dâneshkadé-yé-adabîyât* Faculty of Letters | | | |

(*b*) medial -ا- -*â*- (sometimes also an initial ا short *a*) :

| وقت *vaght* | time | اوقات *óughât* |
| طرف *taraf* | direction | اطراف *atrâf* |
| مسجد *masjed* | mosque | مساجد *masâjed* |
| منزل *manzel* | house | منازل *manâzel* |
| شخص *shakhs* | fellow | اشخاص *ashkhâs* |
| خطر *khatar* | danger | اخطار *akhtâr* |
| سبب *sabab* | cause, reason | اسباب *asbâb*, which means " luggage " |

(*c*) medial -و- -*û*- :

| ظرف *zarf* pot, bowl | ظروف *zorûf* |
| حرف *harf* letter | حروف *horûf* |
| فصل *fasl* season | فصول *fosûl* |

(*d*) ین- -*în* :

مسافر *mosâfer*   traveller   مسافرین *mosâferîn*

*Orthographic Signs.* We learned, as long ago as Lesson 11, the last of the letters used to write Persian. We have also, later in the book, met the sign ٴ *hamzé* :

ميگوئيد *mîgû'îd* you say   آنهائيك *ânhâ'îké* those who

There are a few other signs, none of them in common use ; you should always rely on reading and writing Persian without their help.

First, three short vowels. They are :

(*a*) *e* or *é*, called *kasré*. It is placed just below the consonant it follows :

مثل *mesl* similar     سن *senn* age

The only time you are likely to see it used is to mark an

*ezâfé* after a final consonant (the *é* we marked with an
* asterisk in the texts earlier in this book) :

مِثْل شاه *mesl-é-shâh* like an emperor

منزلِ بزرگِ این شخص *manzel-é-bozorg-é-în shakhs*
       this fellow's big house

Even so, it is rarely used.

(*b*) (This and the signs following are even more rarely
used.)

˘ short *a*, called *fathé* and written just over‛ the consonant it follows :

مَرد *mard* man     مَن *man* I     زَن *zan* woman

(*c*) ˘ *o*, called *zammé*, and written just over the consonant which it follows : ·

پُر *por* full     کُل *koll* chief     پُل *pol* bridge

(*d*) ˘ or ˘ called *sokûn*, or *jazm*. It shows that the
consonant over which it is written has no vowel pronounced after it, but runs straight into the next consonant :

کشتی *kashtî* boat     مَرد *mard* man

·(*e*) ˘ called *tashdîd*. It shows that the consonant over
which it is placed is doubled in pronunciation. It is not
important to write the ˘ *tashdîd*, but it *is* most important
to pronounce the consonant doubled, as in Italian :

اما *am-mâ* but     بنا *ban-nâ* builder

نجّار *naj-jâr* carpenter

تمرین

I. Form adjectives from :

١ ملت     ۲ عراق     ۳ شهردار

٤ جمهور     ٥ خورشید

II. Give the Persian for :

1. bi-weekly
2. monthly
3. former, formerly
4. finally
5. for example

6. in fact
7. worker
8. slanderous
9. a fruit-seller
10. a greengrocer

ترجمه بفرمائید :

III.

1. This man is both rich and happy.
2. The Prophet teaches us to love God.§
3. They travelled in the same bus as I.
4. Persia is a land full of beautiful buildings.
5. Now that you can speak Persian, you must visit Iran and read as much as ( خوشبختانه *baxchfohadr*) you can—newspapers, books, anything (= everything).

§ God—Arabic الله *allāh*, Persian خدا *khodā*. The Persian is more common in everyday speech.

IV. Give the two plural forms for each of these important words. They are not all Arabic words :

٣ منزل     ٢ میوه     ١ مسجد

٦ شخص     ٥ سبب     ٤ روز نامه

٩ حرف     ٨ طرف     ٧ ظرف

V. These are Arabic plurals of words familiar to you. Give (a) the singular, (b) the meaning, singular and plural, of :

٥ اخطار     ٤ اسباب     ٣ فصول     ٢ مسافرین     ١ اوقات

VI. Write in the signs ˌ kasré, ˊ fathé, ˋ zammé, and ˘ tashdíd :

۱ طلوع آفتاب چیز قشنگی است

۲ روز نامهٔ امروز رسیده است؟

۳ نمیفهمم چرا نمیتوانید زبان فارسی را بخوانید و بنویسید

٤ شهر اصفهان پر از عمارت‌های بزرگ و مهم است

## KEY TO EXERCISES

### LESSON 1

II. (a) آن نان   (b) آن آب   (c) آن بنا   (d) با نان   (e) با آب

V. (a) That builder with that water.

    (b) That water with that bread.

    (c) with the builder.

    (d) water with bread.

### LESSON 2

II. (a) نانش   (b) نانشان   (c) آش با نان   (d) سنش

V. (a) his stew.        (c) water, his water.

    (b) their bread.    (d) water with his bread.

### LESSON 3

II. (a) دمش   (b) نامش   (c) شامان   (d) نانشان   (e) شام   (f) آمان

V. (a) The builder came with that water.

    (b) my age, his age, our age, their age.

    (c) my water, his water, our water.

    (d) his name, their name.

    (e) my dinner, his dinner, our dinner, their dinner.

## LESSON 4

**II.** (a) میایم    (b) میاید

**V.** (a) I am coming to that water.
    (b) He is coming to this water.
    (c) water with this stew.
    (d) This builder is coming, that builder came.

## LESSON 5

**II.** (a) شام سرد است    (b) این نان بد است
    (c) آن مرد ایرانی نیست    (d) آب نیست

**III.** (a) I have a horse.      (c) This horse isn't Iranian.
    (b) I saw a horse.      (d) That is a door.
    (e) This bread is bad.
    (f) I am coming with you as far as the door.
    (g) The water is cold.

## LESSON 6

**II.** (a) با اسب دوستم آمدم    (b) این مرد دزد است
    (c) زن این مرد ایرانی نیست    (d) روی آن مرد را دیدم
             (e) بایران میایم

**III.** (a) I have some cold water.
    (b) That horse isn't bad.
    (c) Why did he come?
    (d) This horse's name is Rustam.
    (e) This man's friend came.

## LESSON 7

**II.** (a) در در دست چپ است    (b) هر سه از شما را در شهر دیدم
    (c) در شیشه من آب نیست    (d) هر شیشه آب دارد

III. (a) On the left hand is my mother and on the right
       hand is my father.

  (b) I am giving you everything.

  (c) Our brother comes to town every month.

LESSON 8

II. (a) من باوچه میدهم؟     (b) باو نان وکره میدهم

  (c) او پول دارد؟ نه ولی کار دارد    (d) او بکار میاید؟ بله میاید

III. (a) He came to work.

  (b) This flower is in the water.

  (c) Everyone comes to town on horseback.

  (d) I have no money.

LESSON 9

II. (a) من خوب میخوابم     (b) آن جا بد است

  (c) او چه چیز در دست دارد؟    (d) آب گرم نیست

III. (a) I have a request.     (c) This man is very good.

  (b) Tomorrow is Friday.    (d) This is a good place.

  (e) The sum of three and four is seven.

LESSON 10

II. 1. پول نخواست

  2. سه تا شیشه آب گرم دارد و دو تا آب سرد دارد

  3. باو نان وکره دادم

  4. در دست سه تا نان دارد

III. 1. Six and four are ten.    3. Everybody came.

  2. I have three flowers.    4. He wanted warm water.

LESSON 11

II. (a) s: ث ص   ذ ض ظ: z   ا د ذ ر ز ژ و (b)

  t: ط   h: ح   (c) (i) س   (ii) ز   (iii) ت

  (iv) ه ء   (d) ا   (e) consonant. (ʃ) ء

III. 1. دوستم از پل آمد.     2. من قبل از شما میایم.

3. نان و آب دارد.     4. من باو چه چیز دادم؟ هیچ چیز.

VI. 1. I gave you these three loaves of bread and that
water.

2. I have none other than this (nothing but this).

3. A friend came from Tehran.

4. In this town the water isn't good OR there is no
good water.

5. He will come to the bridge with some money
tomorrow.

## LESSON 12

II. 1. ما در شهریک دوست با اسبش دیدیم     2. شما بآن مرد نان دادید

3. او نان و آب گرفت     4. ایشان نان باکره خوردند

5. باو هرچیز دادم

V. 1. I saw a horse in town.

2. We ate fish with water and bread and butter.

3. That man got three horses in town.

4. They ate and drank that water and bread.

5. The carpenter took some money.

6. We saw a horse.

7. I gave some money to the man.

8. This horse drank some water.

9. I saw everything in Tehran.

10. They saw two people.

## LESSON 12a

I. (1) رفتیم    رفتم      گرفتیم    گرفتم

(2) رفتید    رفتید      گرفتید    گرفتید

(3) { گرفتند   گرفت   رفتند   رفت

    گرفت   گرفت   رفت   رفت

II. (1)   من آمدم   ما آمدیم   من بودم   ما بودیم   (—بود)

(2)   شما آمدید   شما آمدید   شما بودید   شما بودید

(3) { او آمد   ایشان آمدند   او بود   ایشان بودند

    آن آمد   آنها آمد   آن بود   آنها بود

V.

دیروز من بدفتر دیر رفتم. هوا در تهران خیلی گرم بود و اتوبوس دیر آمد.
شب من بمنزل رفتم و شام خوردم.

## LESSON 13

I. 1. پدرم بمن پول نداد

2. بمن پول را نداد

3. دیروز برادرم هیچ جا نرفت

4. باو هیچ چیز ندادم

5. مادرم بخواهرم هیچ چیز نداد

6. دخترش هیچ وقت بدفتر نیامد

7. هیچ کس نرفت

8. دیروز پدرش بدفتر دیر آمد

9. آن اتوبوس هیچ وقت زود نمیاید

10. اتوبوس را دیدم. ما اتوبوس دیدیم

II. 1. I gave him nothing.

2. Did you come by bus ?

3. The weather wasn't very warm.

4. I have never been in this town.

5. He went to Iran.

6. I saw nobody in town.

7. You didn't eat dinner.

8. I never took his money.

9. His daughter and his brother were in town
   yesterday.
10. They didn't see this thing anywhere.

IV. (1)   من نگرفتم   ما نگرفتیم   من نخوردم   ما نخوردیم

(2)   شما نگرفتید   شما نگرفتید   شما نخوردید   شما نخوردید

(3) {   او نگرفت   ایشان نگرفتند   او نخورد   ایشان نخوردند

  آن نگرفت   آنها نگرفتند   آن نخورد   آنها نخوردند }

V. 1. هیچ جا   3. هیچ وقت   2. هیچ کدام

4. هیچ چیز   5. هیچکس

## Lesson 13a

IV. 1. دیروز هیچ کس نیامد؟

2. دیدم کجا رفت. کجا رفت؟ آنجا رفت

3. چطور بمنزل رفتند؟ اینطور رفتند؛ با اتوبوس و با تاکسی

4. من هیچ وقت در تهران نبودم. شما آنجا بودید؟

5. شما کدام اتوبوس را گرفتید؟ این یکی یا آن یکی؟

6. من این شخص را در دفتر هیچوقت ندیدم. من آنجا هیچوقت
   هیچکس ندیدم

7. برادرش در آن وقت کجا بود؟ برادرش در آن وقت در تهران بود

## Lesson 14

I. زنان (زنها) ــ پرندگان ــ سگها ــ درختها ــ باغها ــ قلمها ــ
مدادها ــ (منازل) منزلها ــ کتابها ــ آقایان ــ بچهها ــ اتوبوسها ــ
ماشینها ــ خطها ــ گربهها ــ اسبها ــ این سگها ــ آن گربهها ــ
اینها ــ آنها

II. 1. شما نامه نوشتید؟    2. این آقایان اینجا آمدند
نه ما نامه ننوشتیم. ایشان نامه بدوستان نوشتند

3. در منزلها (منازل) برادرامان بودند    4. کتابها را بپدران دادند

5. دوستامان بتهران رفتند و بما نامهها نوشتند

6. پسرها خیلی بد نوشتند    7. این سگها خیلی بد بود(ـند)

8. ‫در باغهایمان درختها بود‬

9. ‫باغها خیلی بزرگ بود. منزلها خیلی کوچک بود‬

10. ‫خط این نامه‌ها خیلی بد بود.‬

‫نخواندیم. شما آنها را خواندید؟ نه نامه‌ها را نخواندیم‬

III. 1. ‫شما نامه‌ها را خواندید؟ کدام نامه‌ها را؟ اینها.‬

2. ‫کتابهایم خیلی بزرگ نبود‬

3. ‫او قلم کاغذ و مداد بدفتر برد‬

4. ‫دیروز یک نامه نوشتم. کدام نامه؟ این یکی‬

5. ‫این بچه‌ها دیر آمدند. چطور آمدند با اتوبوس یا با ماشین؟‬

6. ‫این منزلها بزرگ بود ولی آنها کوچک بود‬

7. ‫در درختها پرندگان را دیدم‬

8. ‫این پسرهای بد دم آن سگ را کشیدند‬

9. ‫با یک مداد بزرگ یک خط کشید‬

10. ‫سگش و گربه ما در باغان رفت (رفتند)‬

VI. 1. ‫بود‬    2. ‫آمد (ند-)‬    3. ‫رفت‬    4. ‫ننوشت‬

5. ‫بود‬    6. ‫رفتند‬    7. ‫نبود‬    8. ‫نوشتند‬

9. ‫نوشت‬    10. ‫آمد؛ آمدند‬

VII. 1. *é.*   2. *yé.*   3. *é.*   4. *é.*   5. *yé.*

VIII. 1. unwritten.     2. ‫ی-‬     3. unwritten.

4. ‫ی-‬       5. unwritten.

## LESSON 14a

III. 1. ‫بود‬    2. ‫بودید‬    3. ‫بود‬    4. ‫بودند؟‬    5. ‫بود‬

IV. 1. ‫فردا من زود در دفتر هستم‬

2. ‫دیروز دو آقا در منزل داشتم‬

3. ‫من پول را نداشتم – شما داشتید؟‬

4. ‫این اطاق چهار پنجره و یک در دارد. پنجره‌ها هریک شش تا شیشه دارد‬

5. ‫اینها کتابهایم نیست. کجاست؟ آنها را هیچ جا ندیدم‬

V. 1. این مرد دوستم نیست    2. آن زن مادر خوبی نیست.

3. من خیلی وقت اینجا نیستم

4. آب نیست؟     5. ایرانی نیستید

## LESSON 15

I. 1. بنائی    2. آقائی    3. روئی    4. گاهی    5. کسی

6. کتابی    7. درختی    8. کوچهٔ or کوچه‌ای    9. چیزی

10. مردی    11. بچهٔ or بچه‌ای    12. صندلی

II. 1. آن مردرا دیروز دیدم. در دست کتابی داشت

2. کدام اتوبوس دیر آمد؟ ندیدم — گاهی اتوبوسها دیر است، گاهی زود.

3. امروز آقائی بمنزل آمد

4. شما از میز چیزی برداشتید؟ نه آقا هیچ چیز ندیدم و نگرفتم

5. این کیست؟ برادرش نیست کسی دیگر است

V. 1. Is there anybody else in this house? No sir, there
is nobody else.

2. Why does this man have no friends? This man is
a bad man and nobody is his friend.

3. I went nowhere else from the office yesterday.

4. Why didn't you go home? I hadn't any time.

5. Have you got a good book? What book? I haven't
got any book.

## LESSON 15a

I. 1. خود    2. خود، ـیشان    3. خود    4. خود    5. خود

II. 1. از باغ خودش گذشت    2. از باغش گذشتم

3. از باغ خودم گذشتم    4. از باغم گذشت

5. از باغش گذشت

## LESSON 16

I. 1. ‏این عمارت * بزرگ * قشنگ مال * بانک * ملهٔ ایران است‏

2. ‏زبان * فارسی آسان نیست‏

3. ———

4. ‏حسن * شوفر شوفر * خوبی است‏

5. ———

6. ‏در خیابان‌های * مختلف * شهر * تهران ماشین‌های * زیاد هست‏

7. ‏این اسب مال * کیست؟ مال * برادر * این آموزگار است‏

8. ‏سیب گلابی و گیلاس میوهٔ خوب است‏

9. ‏یک پرندهٔ بزرگ در درخت دیدم‏

10.

III. 1. ‏آن ماشین مال کیست؟ کدام؟ آن یکی‏

2. ‏آن ماشین وزیر فرهنگ است‏

3. ‏تهران پایتخت ایران است. شهری بزرگ است‏

4. ‏در ایران زیاد شهرهای بزرگ نیست ولی دههای کوچک زیاد هست‏

5. ‏چون ماشین از خیابان‌های اصفهان گذشت چیزی قابل توجه دیدیم‏

IV.

| Apposition | Noun + Adjective | Possession |
|---|---|---|
| ‏۱ حسن *‏<br>‏شوفر‏ | ‏۲ این عمارت *‏<br>‏بزرگ چیست‏<br>‏۳ اسب *‏<br>‏قشنگ است‏<br>‏۵ نقاشیهٔ قشنگ‏ | ‏۳ اسب *‏<br>‏این آقا‏<br>‏٤ چراغهای *‏<br>‏این ماشین‏ |

## LESSON 16a

I. 1. ‏خسته ام‏     2. ‏مینویسید؟‏

3. ‏میروید؟‏     4. ‏نمیخواند‏

5. خوشحالیم       6. میروند

7. آمدند       8. کی می‌بیند؟

9. چه می‌گذرد؟       10. میدهید

II. 1. میروم    2. می‌بینیم    3. کی می‌گذرد؟    4. میخورند

5. مینویسد    6. میخوانید    7. نمی‌بیند

8. میرود    9. میخوابند    10. میگیرد

III. (1) میگیرم    میگیریم    می‌بینیم    می‌بینیم

(2) میگیرید    میگیرید    می‌بینید    می‌بینید

(3) { میگیرد    میگیرند    می‌بیند    می‌بینند

    میگیرد    میگیرد    می‌بیند    می‌بیند

IV. 1. تازه ام    2. بلدند    3. کجائید؟

4. در آبند    5. خسته ایم

V. 1. نمیخواند    2. میرود    3. مینویسیم    4. می‌گذرد    5. میابند

## LESSON 17

I. 1. روی میز یک بشقاب یک کارد و یک فنجان هست

2. چه نزدیک میز است؟

3. در این منزل سه نفر هست. بیرون منزل یک باغ هست و توی باغ گلهاست

4. شما کلید را در در دیدید؟ بله در در بود ولی آن را بیرون کشیدم.

5. برای ناهار شما هر روز چه میگیرید؟

6. شما با ناشتائی قهوه میخورید؟ در انگلستان چای از فنجان میخورند ولی در ایران از لیوان میخوریم

7. کی پشت در ایستاد؟

8. دیروز دوست خودم را با پدرش دیدم

9. این را پهلوی شما گفت؟

10. نه بدوستان خودش بیرون گفت

11. داخل این منزل اثاثه زیاد هست

12. منزل او نزدیک سفارت واقع است

13. اثاثه او از چه عبارت است؟ از صندلی میز و تخت خواب

14. او بدون من (بی من) سر کار میرود ولی جای کارش خیلی نزدیک است

15. بخاری نزدیک درب واقع است؟ بله پشت درب واقع است

16. طرف (بطرف) مسجد رفتم

17. برادرم در بانک نشسته بود. در دست یک کتاب داشت

18. هیچوقت کلاه بر سر ندارم

19. کی نقش را روی آن دیوار نزدیک پنجره زیر چراغ گذاشت؟

20. ما قالیچه را از روی قالی برداشتیم و زیر ان پول خود را گذاشتیم

21. این اطاق شماست و این تخت خواب بزرگ برای شماست

II. 2. در میان * این بچه‌ها   4. از زیر * زمین   3. توی * اطاق
6. بطرف * تهران   8. از پشت * درب   7. بدون * اضافه

## Lesson 17a

II. 1. آرد و آب و نمک را میامیزد و توی فنجان میریزد. این را روی آتش میزد.

2. نزدیک در می‌ایستد

3. آتش خوب میسوزد

4. شما چه میکنید؟ آن را میفروشید؟

5. آن مرد را میشناسم. پسر من زبان فارسی میاموزد

6. چرا این کاغذ را بیرون انداخت؟ خودم آن را پرداختم

7. نقش را روی دیوار میاوریزد

8. کی ماشین خودش را فروخت؟

III. 1. میپردازید   2. میسوزد   3. میشناسم   4. می ایستم
5. میزد   6. میاندازند   7. میاورند   8. میفروشیم

## Lesson 18

I. 1. ایشان میگویند   2. کی میاید؟   3. میشناییم
4. میفزاید   5. میفرمائید؟   6. میگوید
7. نمیگوئیم   8. نمینماید   9. نمی آزماید

III. 1. میفرمائید؟    2. نمیایند    3. نمیاموزد
     4. میائیم    5. میگزیند

## LESSON 18a

I. (a) $۶ = ۳ \times ۲$    (b) $۱۰ = ۳½ + ۶½$    (c) ۶م ۷م و ۸م

II. (a) هشتم    (b) اول    (c) دوم    (d) سوم

III. 1. تا؛ تا    2. تا    3. نفر    4. نفر    5. تا

## LESSON 19

I. 1. بروم    2. نیایم    3. بپرسید    4. بکنند
    5. بگوید    6. نخوریم    7. بنویسیم    8. نکشد
    9. بپردازیم    10. نپزد

II. 1. روم    3. نپرسید    4. نکنند
     5. نگوید    7. ننویسیم    9. نپردازیم

III. 2. بیایم    6. بخوریم    8. بکشد    10. بپزد

IV. 1. بیرون بروم؟    2. چه بگویم؟
     3. اینجا بیائید    4. او کجا برود؟
     5. ببینیمش    6. پولش را نگیرید
     7. پول خودش را نگیرد    8. این را با من بگوئید
     9. چرا نپردازم؟    10. امشب شاعرا در نپزید

V. 1. چرا ندیدیدش؟    2. بش گفتم    3. بش نگوئید
    4. رویش بود    5. تویش نرود

VI. 1. Why didn't you do it?     3. Don't tell him.
     2. I said to him.     4. It was on that.
     5. Let him not go into the room.

## LESSON 19a

II. 1. نمیدانم که اسمش چیست
     2. آیا گفت که کجا میروم؟

٣. بش بگوئيد برود      ٤. حسن گفت که کسی را در ده
ديدم ولي نميدانم که کيست

٥. بش بگوئيد که دستهايش را بشويد

III. 1. (a) I asked him " Why are you here ? "
    (b) I asked him why he was here/there.

2. (a) He commanded them " Come ".
    (b) He commanded them to come.

3. (a) The man thought " This fellow is mad ".
    (b) The man thought that the fellow was mad.

4. (a) He said " It is late ".
    (b) He said that it was late.

5. (a) Today we learned " Some years ago Iran was
        the centre of civilization ".
    (b) Today we learned that some years ago Iran was
        the centre of civilization.

## LESSON 20

I. 1. او ميتواند فارسی بنويسد؟ بله ميتواند

2. او ميخواهد اين را بياموزد؟ نه نميخواهد

3. شما کجا ميخواهيد بنشينيد؟

4. دستها را نميتوانم بدون آب بشويم

5. چرا نميخواهيد او منزل شما را ببيند؟

6. هيچ کس نتوانست اين را بمن بگويد

7. حالا شام ميخواهيد؟

8. خواست بخوابد ولي نتوانست

9. ديروز خيلی مريض بود و هيچ چيز نتوانست بخورد

10. شما کی خواستيد مارا ببينيد؟ زود بيائيم؟

II. 1. بنشيند     2. بشوم     3. بدانيد؟

4. ببينيم     5. بخوانم و بنويسم

III. (a) 1. بی آب نتوانستم بشورم    2. خواست اینجا بنشیند

در این کتاب نتوانستیم ببینیم ... 5.    پس توانستم ... 4.

(b) 3. چه میخواهید بدانید؟

## LESSON 20a

II. 1. من صحبت کنم؟    3. حرکت کند    2. حرکت کرد

شما کجا منزل میکنید؟ 5.    شام را حاضر کنید 4.

III. 1. بشوم    2. بکنم    3. زندگی کنم

حاضر نکنند 5.    صحبت نکنم 4.

IV. 1. از من سیب خواست

2. از من پرسید که ساعت چیست

3. ازش بپرسید که کجا منزل میکند

4. پول نخواهید

5. برای میوهٔ خودش زیاد پول خواست

## LESSON 21

I. 1. سبکتر – سبکترین    2. بیشتر با هوش – با هوش ترین

3. داغتر – داغترین    4. کمتر – کمترین

5. روشنتر – روشنترین

II. 1. در این شهر دولت مند ترین مرد کیست؟

2. علی دولت مند است ولی شما خیلی بیشتر دولتمند هستید

3. فصل یازدهم از فصل سوم خیلی بیشتر قابل توجه است

4. کدام کتاب مهمترین کتاب بود؟

5. مردم پیر از جوانان بهتر میدانند

6. من میتوانم تندتر از شما راه بروم

7. میتوانید یکی ارزانتر از این بمن بدهید؟

8. همیشه زودتر از شما به دفتر میرسد؛

آیا ماشین سریع تر از مال شما دارد؟

9. چرا گربه همیشه در (روی) راحت ترین صندلی مینشیند؟

LESSON 21a

I. 1. ‏کتابی که خریدید بمن بدهید‏

2. ‏بجائی که هیچ کس نمیداند رفت‏

3. ‏کاشیکاری ایرانی که خریدیم قشنگ است‏

4. ‏مردیکه این را گفت داناست‏

5. ‏آقائی که آمدند پدر حسن هستند‏

II. 1. ‏زبانیکه‏　　2. ‏جائی که‏　　3. ‏ساعتهائیکه‏

4. ‏آنهائیکه‏　　5. ‏صندلیکه‏

III. 1. Give me the book you bought.

2. He went to a place which nobody knows.

3. The Iranian mosaic we bought is beautiful.

4. The man who said this is wise.

5. The gentleman who came is Hassan's father.

1. The language I am speaking is Persian.

2. The place he went to is Esfahan.

3. You didn't tell me the time when I can come.

4. I saw the chair which is broken.

5. The ones you saw are the best of the lot.

IV. 1. ‏پسریکه پنجره را شکست کجاست؟‏

2. ‏هرجا که بروید بیچاره خواهیدبود‏

3. ‏امیر تیمور گورکان بدترین پادشاهی بود که پادشاهی کرد‏

4. ‏آن نقشی را که شما گفتید قشنگ است فروختند‏

5. ‏مردیکه چنین کاری میکند دوستم نیست‏

LESSON 22

I. 1. ‏کتابی که توی آن این را پیدا کردید کجاست؟‏

2. ‏منزلیکه من آنجا منزل میکنم باغی قشنگ دارد‏

3. ‏وقتیکه ایران مرکز تمدن بود خیلی غنی بود‏

4. مدرسه ایکه پسرتان آنجا میرود اسمش چیست؟

آن یکی که آنجا زبانهای روسی و ترکی میاموزند؟

5. کشتی که او از ش در نامهٔ خودش صحبت کرد دیروز به بندر

شاه رسید

6. آبی که ما میخوریم از چاه میکشند

7. آن منزل مال کیست؟ مال آقائی است که پسرم را درس میاموزد

8. کدام یکی را بیشتر دوست دارید آن یکی را که بشما نشان دادم یا

آن یکی را که پیدا کردید؟

9. میل دارم از آقائی که آنقدر زحمت برای این کار کشیدند تشکر کنم

10. آیا در پای خودش دردی دارد آنجائی که میخی بود که ما دیروز

پیدا کردیم و بیرون آوردیم؟

# LESSON 22a

I. 1. میرفتید – دیدم؟    2. منزل میکردم – میشناختم

3. میخوردید – زنگ زدند؟    4. طول میکشید

5. گرفت و رفت

II. 1. شما کار کردن توی باغ را دوست دارید؟

2. پختن آسان است

3. از خواندن زبان ایتالیائی خیلی لذت میبرد

4. در ماه آینده اتوبوسی که از تبریز میاید یک ساعت دیرتر میرسد

# LESSON 23

II. 1. بنده فردا پهلوی جناب عالی نمیایم چون جناب عالی منزل تشریف

ندارید

2. بایشان چه فرمودید؟    3. عرض کردم بنده نمیتوانم بیایم

4. این آقا تشریف آوردند و خواهش فرمودند بنده بایشان شمارهٔ تلفن

جنا بعالی را بدهم

5. برای شام جناب عالی چه میل میفرمائید بنده حاضر کنم؟

III. 1. شتر که در دورهٔ گذشته مهمترین حیوان در بیابان بود حالا برای مسافرت کردن آنقدر مهم نیست

2. صندلی که تعمیر کرد بیاورید

3. شما در کشتی که او ازش صحبت میکرد مسافرت کردید؟

4. این نقشکیه دیروز خریدند یکی از قشنگترین نقشهائی است که من دیدهام

5. در آن موقع در شیراز که از شهرهای ایران است منزل داشت

## LESSON 23a

I.

### علی بابا

وقتیکه علی بابا تمام زرها را جمع کرد از خدا میخواست که چند وزنه و یک کیسه با خودش آورده بود تا بتواند زرها را وزن کند. بعد از اینکه قدری راجع بان فکر کرد بنظرش رسید عاقلانه است که بمنزل برادرزن خود برود تا وزنهها را بگیرد. مصطفی (برادرزنش) مایل بود کیسه و وزنهها را باو بدهد و(داد) و علی رفت تا زر خود را بکشد.

چند ساعت بعد پس از آنکه علی کشیدن زر خود را تمام کرد با اسبابش بمنزل مصطفی برگشت. با وجود یکه مصطفی از همین خانواده علی بود او را دوست نداشت. بعد از آنکه کیسه وزر را از علی گرفت گفت: «علی قبل از آنکه بروید بمن بگوئید که زرتان کجاست کجاست بنظرم شما مردی خیلی دولتمند میآئید چون هنوز قدری زر در ته این کیسه هست. تمام زرها مال پادشاه است و هر چند من برادر و دوستان باشم آنچه میدانم میگویم مگر اینکه شما زر خودتان را نشان بدهید.

II. 1. (a) آمده باشم        (b) بیایم
    2. (a) نوشته باشد       (b) بنویسد
    3. (a) رسیده باشد       (b) برسد
    4. (a) نیامده باشیم      (b) نیائیم
    5. (a) اجازه فرموده باشید  (b) اجازه بفرمائید

**LESSON 24**

**I.**

| | Elevated | Colloquial |
|---|---|---|
| 1. | ânjâ mîravam | unjâ mîram |
| 2. | nàmîtavânand | nèmîtûnand |
| 3. | zûd mîâyad | zûd mîad/mîâd |
| 4. | bâshad | bâshé |
| 5. | nàmîdânestam | nèmîdûnestam |
| 6. | nàkonad | nàkoné |
| 7. | ché mîgûʼîd ? | ché mîgîd ? |
| 8. | bandé bâyad bèravam | bandé bâyad bèram |
| 9. | nàmîkonand | nèmîkonand |
| 10. | kâretân âsân ast | kâretûn âsûn é |

**II.** 1.    میتوانم خوب فارسی صحبت کنم

2.    میخواهم   »   »   »   »

3.    باید   »   »   »   »

4.    شاید   »   »   »   »

5.    بایست   »   »   »   »

6.    میخواستم   »   »   »   »

7.    میتوانستم   »   »   »   »

8.    شایست   »   »   »   »

9.    باید   »   »   کرده باشم

10.    شاید   »   »   »   »   »

**III.** 1. This man killed himself.

2. Do you speak Persian yourself ?

3. We must arrange it ourselves.

4. Perhaps they have gone themselves (he ... himself).

5. Don't deceive yourself.

LESSON 24a

I. 1. But when he opened his teeth, so that he might get
the bone seen in the water, the bone fell into the
water and was lost—and instead of having got a
second bone, he lost the one he had.

II. 1. بیاید　2. باشد　3. تشریف آوردبد

4. (باز بکند (کند　5. بخرید

LESSON 25

I. 1. خواهیم داشت　2. خواهد گذاشت　3. نخواهد شد

4. خواهد رفت　5. تشریف خواهند آورد

II. 1. بودی　2. دست　3. خودت

4. بگو!　5. بروی　6. رُوی

7. زود باش!　8. نکن!

9. چه میگرُی؟　10. میخواهی

III.　　Elevated　　　Colloquial

1. békon　　　bòkon

2. nàmîtavânam　　nèmîtûnam

3. bègozârîm　　bògozârîm

4. bègû'îd　　　bègîd

5. nàravîd　　　nàrîd

IV. 1. نباید (نمیشود) در مسجد صحبت کرد

2. میتوان همیشه سعی کرد ولی نمیشود گفت که آیا متیوان موفق شد

3. نمیتوان گفت کِی این کار را کرد

4. نبایست دروغ گفت

5. بجای «من» چه با ید گفت؟ باید گفت «بنده»

TEST PAPER—VERBS

A. 1.    ۱ خواسته ۲ یافته ۳ کرده ۴ شده ۵ گذشته

2.    ۱ رونده ۲ گوینده ۳ آینده ۴ آموزنده ۵ زنده

3.    ۱ رفت ۲ بود ۳ افزود ۴ فرمود ۵ خواهش کرد

4.   ۲ میامیزم

| | | | |
|---|---|---|---|
| (1) | میامیای | میامیزم | ۱ میامیئم | میامیزم |
| (2) | میامیائید | میامیزید | میامیئید | میامیزید |
| (3){ | میامیاید | میامیند | میامیزد | میامیزند |
| | میامیاید | میامیند | میامیزد | میامیزد |

۴ دارم

| | | | |
|---|---|---|---|
| (1) | مینشیم | مینشینیم | ۳ دارم | داریم |
| (2) | مینشینید | مینشینید | دارید | دارید |
| (3){ | مینشیند | مینشینند | دارد | دارند |
| | مینشیند | مینشینند | دارد | دارد |

۵

| | | |
|---|---|---|
| (1) | مینندم | میندیم |
| (2) | مینندید | مینندید |
| (3){ | مینندد | مینندند |
| | مینندد | مینندد |

5.    ۱ خریدم ۲ رفتید ۳ کی بود؟ ۴ تافت/تابید ۵ آمیخت

6.(a)    ۱ کرده ام ۲ گرفته ام ۳ خوانده ام ۴ شمرده ام ۵ پخته ام

(b)    ۱ کرده بودم ۲ گرفته بودم ۳ خوانده بودم ۴ شمرده بودم ۵ پخته بودم

(c)    ۱ کرده باشم ۲ گرفته باشم ۳ خوانده باشم ۴ شمرده باشم ۵ پخته باشم

B. 1. آمدم    2. برود    3. خواند    4. ست/هست
5. حس کنم    8. نیامدید؟    7. بپرسم؟    6. گفت – است/باشد
9. بیرون شد    10. میرسد –    بنویس/م/ید/د/یم/ند

C. (a) دروغ گفت    (b) دروغ گفتن    (c) دروغ گوید
(d) دروغ میگفت    (e) دروغ میگوید
1, e.. 2, d. 3, b. 4, a. 5, c.

D. 1. until I come ; so that I should come.
   2. we shall see ; we wish to see.
   3. if he goes ; if he had gone.
   4. I must say ; one must say.
   5. I may be mistaken ; I may have been mistaken.
   6. he lost ; he was lost.
   7. I have seen ; I am seen.
   8. don't ! ; that you may not do.
   9. they couldn't come ; one couldn't come.
  10. past, passed ; put, placed.

## Lesson 26

I. 1. باغبان    2. دربان    3. پاسبان    4. گلستان
   5. عربستان    6. مهمانخانه    7. باشگاه    8. دانشگاه
   9. آشپزی    10. باغبانی    11. رانندگی    12. بستگی
   13. جست وجو/جستجو    14. گفتگو/گفت و گو

II. 1. connexion, -gí abstract.
   2. university, -gâh place.
   3. to do the painting, -í abstract of activity made into a Compound Verb.
   4. show, -esh abstract.
   5. to be registered, -í abstract, Passive Compound Verb.

III. 1. آشپزی کردن    2. نقاشی شدن
   3. گفتگو. گفتگوکردن. بین ایشان گفتگو شد
   4. پاسبان. شهربانی. آمدورفت/آمدوشد
   5. نمایشگاه. کتابخانه. شهرستان

## LESSON 26a

II. 1. يكشنبه    2. جمعه    3. پنجشنبه    4. شنبه
5. دو شنبه

III. 1. ساعت دو
2. ساعت نه و بیست و پنج دقیقه
3. ساعت یک و ربع

IV. 1. ساعت سه و بیست دقیقه
2. ساعت چهار و هفده دقیقه
3. ساعت هشت و نیم
4. روز بیستم آبان (آبان) ماه هزار و سیصد و سی و پنج
5. روز سیم دی ماه هزار و سیصد و سی و شش

## LESSON 27

I. 1. ملی    2. عراق    3. شهرداری    4. جمهوری    5. خورشیدی
II. 1. دوهفتگی    2. ماهی    3. سابق، سابقاً
4. بالاخره    5. مثلاً    6. اصلاً    7. کارگر
8. بدگو    9. میوه فروش    10. سبزی فروش

III. 1. این مرد هم دولت مند هم خوشحال است
2. حضرت پیغامبر بما دوست داشتن خدا را میاموزد (میاموزد خدا را
دوست داشته باشیم)
3. در همان اتوبوس با من مسافرت کردند
4. ایران کشوریست پر از عمارت‌های قشنگ
5. حالا که میتوانید فارسی صحبت کنید باید ایران را دیدن کنید و
هر قدر که میتوانید روز نامه و کتاب و هرچیز دیگر بخوانید

IV. 1. مساجد مسجدها    2. میوه‌ها میوه جات    3. منزلها منازل
4. روزنامه‌ها روزنامه‌جات    5. سببها اسباب    6. شخصها اشخاص
7. ظروف ظرفها    8. طرفها اطراف    9. حروف حرفها

V. 1. (a) وقت     (b) time, times.
2. (a) مسافر     (b) traveller, travellers.

3. (a) فصل      (b) chapter/season, chapters/seasons.

4. (a) سبب      (b) cause/reason, luggage.

5. (a) خطر      (b) danger, dangers.

VI. 1.      ۱ طُلوعِ آفتاب چیزی قَشَنگ است

2.      ۲ روزنامهٔ اِمروز رِسیده است؟

3.      ۳ نِمیفَهمَم چِرا نِمیتَوانَند زَبان فارسی را بِخوانَند و بِنویسَند

4.      ٤ شَهر اِصفَهان پُر از عِبارَتهای بُزرگ وَ مُهِم است

## VOCABULARIES

In the following Vocabularies, all numbers and most proper names have been omitted, as they can be found through the Index. The abbreviations mean : *k.* کردن *kardan* (and forming a passive with شدن *shodan*) ; *b.* بودن *bûdan* ; *â.* آمدن *âmadan* ; *d.* داشتن *dâshtan* ; *dd.* دادن *dâdan* ; *ksh.* کشیدن *kashîdan*—which are the verbs used to form Compound Verbs from the words given, thus : " اجازه *ejâzé* permission *dd.*" means that اجازه *ejâzé* means permission, and that اجازه دادن *ejâzé dâdan* means to give permission, to permit.

آب *âb* water.

آب و هوا *-o havâ* climate

آبی *-i* blue

آتش *âtesh* fire

اتفاق افتادن *ettefâgh oftâdan* happen

اتوبوس *otôbûs* bus

اثاثه *asâsé* furniture

اجازه *ejâzé* permission dd.

آخر آخرین *âkher, -în* last

اداره *edâré* office

ارتش *artesh* army

آرد *ârd* flour

ارزان *arzân* cheap

از *az* from, than, by

آزمودن *âzmûdan* test

آسان *âsân* easy

اسب *asb* horse

اسباب *asbâb* luggage

اسلام *eslâm* Islam

اسم *esm* name

آش *âsh* stew

آشپز *-paz* cook

اشتباه *eshtebâh* error k.

اصل *asl* origin

اصلا *-an* actually

اطاق *otâgh* room

اطراف *atrâf* directions

آفتاب *âftâb* sun

آفریدن *âfarîdan* create

افتادن *oftâdan* fall

آقا *âghâ* Mr., gentleman

اگر *agar* if

البته *albatté* certainly

التفات *eltefât* kindness

اما *ammâ* but

آمدن *âmadan* come

امروز *emrûz* today

امسال *emsâl* this year

امشب *emshab* tonight

آموختن *âmûkhtan* teach

آمیختن *âmîkhtan* mix

امید *omîd* hope

امیدوار *-vâr* hopeful

آن *ân* that, it

اینجا *ânjâ* there

انداختن *andâkhtan* throw

آنطور *ântôur* like that

آنقدر *ânghadr* so (much)

آنها *ânhâ* those, they

او *û* he, she

آوردن *âvardan* bring

اوقات *ôughât* times

اول *avval* first

اولا- *-an* firstly

آویختن *âvîkhtan* hang

آهسته *ahesté* slowly

اهمیت *ahammîyat* importance

آهن *âhan* iron

آیا *âyâ* whether

ایستادن *îstâdan* stand, stop

ایشان *îshân* they

ایل *îl* tribe

این *în* this

اینجا *înjâ* here

آینده *âyandé* next

اینطور *întôur* like this

اینقدر *înghadr* so (much)

با *bâ* with

با اینکه *-înké* although

باد *bâd* wind

باران *bârân* rain

باز *bâz* open *k.*

بازی *bâzî* game

باشگاه *bâshgâh* club

باعث *bâ'es* cause

باغ *bâgh* garden

بافتن *bâftan* weave

بالاخره *belakheré* lastly

باهوش *bâhûsh* intelligent

باید *bâyad* must

بجای *béjâ-yé* instead of

بچه *bachché* child

بخاری *bokhârî* stove

بخشیدن *bakhshîdan* excuse

بد *bad* bad

بدون *bedûn-é* without

بدون اینکه *-înké* unless

برادر *barâdar* brother

برای *barâ-yé* for

برای اینکه *-înké* so that, because

بر خاستن *bar khâstan* arise

بردن *bordan* carry

برف *barf* snow

برق *bargh* lightning, electricity

برگ *barg* leaf

بر گشتن *bar gashtan* return

برنج *berenj* rice, brass

بریدن *borîdan* cut

بزرگ *bozorg* big, great

بس *bas* enough

بستگی د. با *bastegî d. bâ* depend on

بستن *bastan* close, tie

بسیار *besyâr* very

بشقاب *boshghâb* plate

بعد بعدا *ba'ad , -an* afterwards

بعد از *-az* after (preposition)

بعد از اینکه *-az înké* after (conjunction)

بعد از ظهر *-az zohr* afternoon

بعضی *ba'azî* some

بقیه *baghîyé* remainder

بلد *balad* knowledgeable

بلند *boland* tall, -*k.* raise

بله *balé* yes

بنا *bannâ* builder

بندر *bandar* port

بنده *bandé* (slave) I

بنظر *bénazar â.* appear

بنگاه *bongâh* establishment

بو *bû* smell *k.*

بودن *bûdan* be

به *bé* to

بها *bahâ* price

بهار *bahâr* Spring

بهتر *behtar* better

بهترین -*în* best

بی *bî* without

بیابان *biâbân* desert

بیچاره *bichâré* poor

بیدار *bîdâr* awake *k.*

بیرون *birûn-é* outside -*k.* throw out

بیشتر *bîshtar* more

بیشترین -*în* most

بیفهم *bîfahm* stupid

بیمارستان *bîmârestân* hospital

بین *bêin-é* between

بینی *bînî* nose

پا *pâ* foot

پادشاه *pâdeshâh* king

پارچه *pârché* cloth

پارسال *pârsâl* last year

پاسبان *pâsbân* watchman

پاک *pâk* clean

پایتخت *pâ-yé-takht* capital (city)

پائیز *pâ'îz* Autumn

پائین *pâ'în* low, below

پختن *pokhtan* cook

پدر *pedar* father

پذیرفتن *pazîroftan* receive (guests)

پر *por* full *k.*

پرداختن *pardâkhtan* pay

پرده *pardé* curtain

پرسیدن *porsîdan* ask

پرنده *parandé* bird

پریدن *parîdan* jump, fly

پریروز *parîrûz* day before yesterday

پریشب *parîshab* night before last

پزشک *pezeshk* doctor

پس *pas* then

پست *post* post

پسر *pesar* boy, son

پسفردا *pasfardâ* day after tomorrow

پشت *posht-é* behind -*bâm* roof

پشم *pashm* wool

پل *pol* bridge

پنبه *pambé* cotton

پنجره *panjeré* window

پنیر *panîr* cheese

پول *pûl* money

پوشیدن *pûshîdan* wear

پهلوی *pahlû-yé* at, " chez "

پهن *pahn* wide *k.*

پیاده *pîâdé* on foot

پیچ *pîch* screw

پیچیدن *pîchîdan* turn, wrap

پیدا *pêîdâ k.* find

پیر *pîr-é* old

پیش *pîsh-é* before

پیشنهاد *pîshnehâd k.* suggest

پیمودن *pêimûdan* measure

پیغام *pêighâm* message

پیغامبر *-bar* prophet

تا *tâ* piece, until, so that

تابستان *tâbestân* Summer

تابیدن *tâbîdan* twist, shine

تاریخ *târîkh* history

تاریک *târîk* dark

تافتن *tâftan* v. تابیدن

تازه *tâzé* new

تبریک *tabrîk* congratulations

تخت خواب *takht-é-khâb* bed

تخم *tokhm* seed

تخم مرغ *-é-morgh* egg

تربیت *tarbîyat* culture

ترجمه *tarjomé* translation *k.*

ترسیدن *tarsîdan* fear

تشکر *tashakkor k.* thank

تصادف *tasâdof* (road) accident

تعجب *ta'ajjob* surprise, *-k.* be surprised

تعمیر *ta'amîr k.* repair

تغییر *taghyîr k.* alter

تفنگ *tofang* rifle

تقدیم *taghdîm* gift

تقویم *taghvîm* calendar

تمام *tamâm* complete *k.*

تمبر *tambr* stamp

تمرین *tamrîn* exercise *k.*

تنبل *tambal* lazy

تنگ *tang* tight

تنها *tanhâ* alone

تو *to* thou

توانستن *tavânestan* be able

توجه *tavajjoh* attention *k.*

توفان *tûfân* storm

تولد یافتن *tavallod* birth *yâftan*

تومان *toman* = 10 rials (1s.)

توی *tû-yé* inside

ته *tah* end, bottom

ثانیه *sânîyé* a second

جا *jâ* place

جدا *jodâ* separate *k.*

جدید *jadîd* new

جز *joz* besides

| | |
|---|---|
| جستن *jostan* seek | حالا *hâlâ* now |
| جلوى *jelôu-yé* in front of | حركت *harakat k.* move off |
| جمع *jam'* together, sum, -*k.* collect | حرف *harf* letter (of the alphabet) |
| جمهور *jomhûr* republic | حروف *horûf* letters |
| جنس *jens* kind, sort | حس *hess* feeling *k.* |
| جنگ *jang* war | حساب *hesâb* reckoning *k.* |
| جنوب *jonûb* South | حفظ *hefz k.* protect |
| جواب *javâb* answer *dd.* | حقوق *hoghûgh* wages |
| جوان *javân* young | حقيقت *haghîghat* truth |
| جهان *jâhân* world | حمام *hammâm* bath |
| چاى *çhâi* tea | حيوان *hêivân* animal |
| چپ *chap* left-hand | خارج *khârej* ⎫ foreign |
| چرا *cherâ* why | خارجه *khârejé* ⎭ |
| چراغ *cherâgh* lamp | خاستن *khâstan* rise |
| چرم *charm* leather | خاك *khâk* dust |
| چشم *cheshm* eye | خالى *khâlî* empty *k.* |
| چطور *chétoûr* how | خاموش *khâmûsh* out (lights) |
| چقدر *chéghadr* how much/ many | خانم *khânom* Mrs., Miss, lady |
| چگونه *chégûné* what sort of | خانواده *khânevâdé* family |
| چند چندتا *chand, -tâ* how many, a few | خانه *khâné* house |
| چنگال *changâl* fork | خجالت *khejâlat ksh.* be ashamed |
| چوب *chûb* wood | خدا *khodâ* God |
| چون *chûn* as | خدا حافظ *khodâ-hâfez* goodbye |
| چه *che* what | خدمت *khedmat* service *k.* |
| چيدن *chîdan* arrange | خراب *kharâb* destroyed *k.* |
| چيز *chîz* thing | خريدن *kharîdan* buy |
| حاضر *hâzer* ready *k.* | خسته *khasté* tired |
| | خشك *khoshk* dry |

خصوص *khosûs* special

ـاً *-an* specially

خط *khatt* line, writing

خطر *khatar* danger

خندیدن *khandîdan* laugh

خواب *khâb* sleep

خوابیدن *khâbîdan* sleep

خوب *khûb* good

خوردن *khordan* eat, drink

خواستن *khâstan* want

خواندن *khândan* read

خواهر *khâhar* sister

خواهش *khâhesh* request *k.*

خود *khod* own, self

خورشید *khorshîd* sun

خوش خوشحال *khosh, -hâl* happy

خیابان *khîâbân* street

خیر *khêir* no

خیلی *khêilî* very

داخل *dâkhel-é* inside

دادن *dâdan* give

داشتن *dâshtan* have

داغ *dâgh* hot (food)

دانا *dânâ* wise

دانستن *dânestan* know

دختر *dokhtar* girl, daughter

در *dar* door

در *dar* in -*â.* enter

در آوردن *dar âvardan* produce

در ظرف *dar zarf-é* within

در میان *dar mîân-é* among

دربار *darbâr* court

درخت *derakht* tree

درد *dard* pain

درس *dars* lesson, *k.* study, *dd.* teach

درست *dorost* correct, *k.* arrange

دروغ *dorûgh* a lie

دریا *daryâ* sea

دزد *dozd* thief

دزدیدن *dozdîdan* steal

دست *dast* hand

ـمال *-mâl* handkerchief

دشت *dasht* a plain

دفتر *daftar* office

دفعه *daf'é* a time

دقیقه *daghîghé* a minute

دکان *dokkân* shop

دل *del* heart

دم *dom* tail, *dam-é* near, close

دندان *dandân* tooth

دنیا *donyâ* world

دوا *davâ* medicine

دور *dûr* far

دوره *dôuré* space of time

دوست *dûst* friend, *d.* like

دولت *dôulat* government

دویدن *davîdan* run

ده *déh* village

دیدن *dîdan* see

دیدن رفتن -*raftan* visit

دیر *dîr* late

دیروز *dîrûz* yesterday

دیشب *dîshab* last night

دیگر *dîgar* more, other

دین *dîn* religion

دینار *dînâr* 1/100 rial

دیوار *dîvâr* wall

دیوانه *dîvâné* mad

راجع به *râjé' bé* concerning

راحت *râhat* comfortable

راست *râst* right

راضی *râzî* satisfied *k.*

راندن *rândan* drive

راه *râh* road

راه آهن -*é-âhan* railway

راه رفتن -*raftan* walk

ربع *rob'* quarter

رساندن *rasândan* ⎱ bring up
رسانیدن *rasânîdan* ⎰

رسیدن *rasîdan* reach, arrive

رفتار *raftâr* behaviour

رفتن *raftan* go

رفتن *roftan* sweep

رقص *raghs* dance *k.*

رنگ *rang* colour

رو *rû* face

رود رودخانه *rûd, -khâné* river

روز *rûz* day

روزنامه -*nâmé* newspaper

روشن *rôushan* bright, alight *k.*

روی *rû-yé* upon

ریال *riâl* = approx. 1¼d.

ریختن *rîkhtan* pour

رئیس *ra'îs* director

زبان *zabân* tongue, language

زحمت *zahmat* trouble, -ksh.
    take trouble

زدن *zadan* strike

زر *zar* gold

زرد *zard* yellow

زمستان *zemestân* Winter

زمین *zamîn* ground

زن *zan* woman

زندگی *zendegî* life *k.*

زنگ *zang* bell

زنگ زدن -*zadan* ring

زود *zûd* early, soon, quick(ly)

زیاد *ziâd* very much, too
    (much)

زیبا *zîbâ* beautiful

زیر *zîr-é* under

سابق *sâbegh* former

سابقاً -*an* formerly

ساختن *sâkhtan* make

ساعت *sâ'at* hour, clock, watch

سال *sâl* year

سایه *sâyé* shadow

سبب *sabab* reason

سبز sabz green

سبزه sabzé grass

سبک sabok thin

سخت sakht hard

سر sar head

سرباز -bâz soldier

سرد sard cold

سریع sarî‘ fast

سعی sa‘î k. try

سفارت sefârai embassy

سفید sefîd white

سگ sag dog

سلام علیکم salâm ’alêikom good-
morning

سن senn age

سنگین sangîn heavy

سوختن sûkhtan burn

سوار savâr mounted, aboard

سوزانیدن sûzânîdan burn

سیاه sîâh black

سیب sîb apple

سیب زمینی -é-zamînî potato

شام shâm dinner

شاه shâh king, emperor

شاهنشاه -enshâh emperor

شاید shâyad perhaps

شب shab night

شتر shotor camel

شخص shakhs person

شخصی -î private

شدن shodan become

شراب sharâb wine

شرکت sherkat company

شروع shorû’ beginning k.

شستن shostan wash

شکایت shekâyat complaint k.

شکستن shekastan break

شل shol loose

شما shomâ you

شماره shomâré number

شمال shomâl North

شمردن shomordan count

شناختن shenâkhtan know

شهربانی shahrbânî police

شهرداری shahrdârî muni-
cipality

شهرستان shahrestân county

شیرینی shîrînî sweets

شیشه shîshé glass

صابون sâbûn soap

صاحب sâheb owner

صبح sobh morning

صبر sabr k. wait

صحبت sohbat talk k.

صدا sedâ voice, -k. call

صفحه safhé page

صلح solh peace

صندلی sandalî chair

صندوق sandûgh box

طرف taraf direction, -é
towards

طلوع tolû’ sunrise k.

طور *tôur* manner

طول *tûl* ksh. to last

ظرف *zarf* pot

ظروف *zorûf* pots

ظهر *zohr* noon

عاقلانه *âghélâné* wise, wisely

عالى *'âlî* excellent

عبارت از *'ebârat az* consisting of

عجیب *'ajîb* strange

عرض *'arz* petition k.

عزیز *'azîz* dear, beloved

عصر *'asr* evening

عکس *'aks* photograph

عمارت *'emârat* building

عوض *'avaz* change k.

عید *'eid* holiday

عیسوى *'îsavî* Christian

عینک *'éinak* spectacles

غروب *ghorûb* sunset k.

غنى *ghanî* rich

غیراز *gheir az* other than

غیرازاینکه *-az înké* except that

فارسى *fârsî* Persian language

فایده *fâyedé* advantage

فراموش *farâmûsh* k. forget

فرار *ferâr* k. escape

فردا *fardâ* tomorrow

فرستادن *ferestâdan* send

فرش *farsh* carpet

فرصت *forsat* chance

فرمودن *farmûdan* command

فرودگاه *forûdgâh* airport

فروختن *forûkhtan* sell

فرهنگ *farhang* education, vocabulary

فریفتن *farîftan* deceive

فشردن *feshôrdan* press

فصل *fasl* chapter, season

فصول *fosûl* pl. of فصل

فعل *fe'l* fact

فعلا *-an* in fact, presently

فکر *fekr* thought k.

فلان *folân* a certain

فنجان *fenjân* cup

فهمیدن *fahmîdan* understand

قابل *ghâbel-é* worthy of

قابل توجه *-tavajjoh* interesting

قاشق *ghâshogh* spoon

قالى *ghâlî* carpet

قالیچه *-ché* rug

قانون *ghânûn* law

قبل از *ghabl az* before

قبلا *ghablan* previously

قبل از ظهر *ghabl az zohr* a.m.

قبول *ghabûl* k. accept

قدیم *ghadîm* ancient

قرمز *ghermez* red

قسمت *ghesmat* share k.

قشنگ *ghashang* beautiful

قفل *ghofl* lock k.

قلم ghalam pen

قند ghand lump sugar

قهوه ghahvé coffee

قهوه‌ای رنگ '-é rang brown

قیچی ghêichî scissors

قیمت ghêimat price

کار kâr work k.

کارد kârd knife

کافی kâfî sufficient

کامل kâmel complete

کاملاً -an completely

کبریت kebrît a match

کاغذ kâghaz paper

کتاب ketâb book

کتابخانه -khâné library

کثافت kesâfat dirt

کثیف kesîf dirty

کجا kojâ where

کدام kodâm which ?

کردن kardan do

کره karé butter

کس کسی kas, -î person

کشتن koshtan kill

کشتی kashtî boat

کشور keshvar country

کشیدن kashîdan draw

کفش kafsh shoe

کل koll chief

کلاس kelâs class

کلاه kolâh hat

کلمه kalemé word

کلید kelîd key

کم kam little, -k. lessen

کمک komak help k.

کنار kanâr-é beside

کوبیدن kûbîdan pound

کوتاه :tâh short

کوچک kûchék small

کوچه ku é lane

کوزه kûzé jug

کوشش kûshesh attempt k.

کوفتن kûftan v. کوبیدن

کوه kûh mountain

که ké that, who, which

که koh v. کوه

کهنه kohné old

که kî who ?

کی kêi where ?

کیسه kîse bag

کیف kîf bag

گاو gâv ox, cow

گاه gâh place

گاهی -î sometimes

گدا gadâ beggar

گذاردن gozârdan

گذاشتن gozâshtan } place

گذراندن gozarândan spend
    time

گذشتن gozashtan pass

گران gerân expensive

گربه *gorbé* cat

گردیدن *gardîdan* become

گرسنه *gorosné* hungry

گرفتن *gereftan* get, take

گرم *garm* warm

گشتن *gashtan* v. گردیدن

گفتگو *goftogû* argument

گفتن *goftan* say

گل *gol* flower, rose

گلابی *golâbî* pear

گم *gom k.* lose

گنجه *ganjé* cupboard

گوسفند *gûsfand* sheep

گوش *gûsh* ear, -*k.* listen

گوشت *gûsht* meat

گوشه *gûshé* corner

گیلاس *gîlâs* cherry

لازم *lâzem* necessary, -*d.* need

لباس *lebâs* clothing

لذت بردن از *lezzat bordan az* enjoy

لغات *loghât* words

لغت *loghat* word

لوازم *lavâzem* necessities

لوله *lûlé* tube

لیوان *lîvân* a glass

ما *mâ* we

مادر *mâdar* mother

ماشین *mâshîn* car

مال *mâl-é* belonging to

ماندن *mândan* remain

ماه *mâh* moon, month

ماهی *mâhî* fish

متأسف *mota'assef* sorry

متشکر *motashakker* grateful

متولد *motævalled* born

مثل *mesl-é* like

مختلف *mokhtalef* various

مخصوص *makhsús* special

مخصوصاً *-an* specially

مداد *medâd* pencil

مدرسه *madrasé* school

مدیر *modîr* director

مذهب *mazhab* religion

مرا *marâ* me

مرد *mard* man

مردم *mardom* people

مردن *mordan* die

مرکز *markaz* centre

مرگ *marg* death

مریض *marîz* ill

مسافر *mosâfer* traveller

مسافرت *mosâferat k.* travel

مسجد *masjed* mosque

مسلم مسلمان *moslem, mosalmán* Moslem

مشرق *mashregh* East

مشکل *moshkel* difficult

معروف *ma'arúf* well-known

معلم *mo'allem* teacher

معلوم ma'lûm known

معمولی ma'amûlî general

معمولاً ma'amûlan generally

معنی ma'anî meaning

مغرب maghreb West

ملت mellat nation

مگس magas a fly

ملکه maleké queen

ملی mellî national

ممکن momken possible

مملکت mamlakat country

ممنوع mamnû' forbidden

ممنون mamnûn grateful

من man I

منزل manzel house, -k. live

موش mûsh mouse

موفق movaffagh successful

موقع môughé' moment

مهربان mehrabân kind

مهم mohemm important

مهمان mehmân guest

در میان ی v. dar mîân-é v.

میخ mîkh nail

میدان mêidân a square

میز mîz table

میل meil d. to like to do

میوه mîvé fruit

ناشتائی nâshtâ'î breakfast

نام nâm name

نامه nâmé letter

نان nân bread

ناهار nâhâr lunch

نتیجه natîjé result

نجار najjâr carpenter

نخیر nakhêir no

نزدیک nazdîk-é near

نشاط آور neshâtâvar pleasant

نشان neshân dd. show

نشانی neshânî address

نشستن neshastan sit

نصف nesf half

نقاش naghghâsh painter

نقش naghsh picture

نقره noghré silver

نگاه negâh k. look

نمره nomré number

نمک namak salt

نمودن namûdan show

نوروز nôurûz Iranian New
Year

نوشتن neveshtan write

نوکر nôukar servant

نه na no

نیز nîz also

نیم nîm half

و va, o and

واقع vâghé' situated

ور var d. remove

ورزش varzesh sport

وزارت vezârat ministry

وزن *vazn* weight

وزیر *vazîr* minister

وسیله *vasîlé* means

وقت *vaght* time

وقتیکه *-îké* when

ولی *valî* but

هر *har* every

هرگز *hargez* never

هفته *hafté* week

هم *ham* just, also

همان *hamân* that same

همچنین *hamchonîn* as well

همسایه *hamsâyé* neighbour

همکاری *hamkârî k.* co-operate

همه *hamé* every

همهٔ *hamé-yé* all of

همیشه *hamîshé* always

همین *hamîn* this same

هنوز . . . نـ- *hanûz . . . nà-* not yet

هوا *havâ* air, weather

هواپیما *-péimâ* aeroplane

هیچ *hîch* no, none

یا *yâ* or

یاد *yâd d.* remember

یخ *yakh* ice

یکی *yekî* a, one

یواش *yavâsh* slow(ly)

Note : The words given here in Persian are transliterated, in Persian alphabetical order, in the Persian–English part.

about راجع به

accept قبول كردن

accident تصادف

actually فعلاً

address نشانى

advantage فايده

aeroplane هواپيما

after(wards) بعداً
بعد

after (اينكه) بعد از

—noon بعد از ظهر

age سن

air هوا

—port فرودگاه

alight k. روشن

all تمام؛ همهٔ

alone تنها

also نيز ؛ هم

although با اينكه

always هميشه

among در ميان

ancient قديم

and و

animal حيوان

answer dd. جواب

appear بنظر آمدن

apple سيب

arrange چيدن

arrive رسيدن

as چون

be ashamed of خجالت كشيدن از

ask پرسيدن؛ خواستن

at پهلوى

attention k. توجه

autumn پائيز

awake k. بيدار

bad بد

bag كيسه — كيف

bank بانك

bath حمام

be بودن

beautiful زيبا؛ قشنگ

because براى اينكه

become شدن

bed تخت خواب

before (اينكه) قبل از

beginning k. شروع

behind پشت

bell زنگ

belonging to مال

| | |
|---|---|
| beside کنار | buy خریدن |
| —s جز | by از |
| best بهترین | calendar تقویم |
| better بهتر | call صداکردن |
| between بین | camel شتر |
| big بزرگ | can توانستن |
| bird پرنده | car ماشین |
| birth تولد | carpenter نجار |
| black سیاه | carpet فرش، قالی |
| blue آبی | |
| boat کشتی | carry بردن |
| book کتاب | cause باعث |
| born متولد | cat گربه |
| bottom ته | certainly البته |
| box صندوق | a certain فلان |
| boy پسر | chair صندل |
| bread نان | chance فرصت |
| break شکستن | change k. عوض، تغییر |
| —fast ناشتائی | |
| bridge پل | chapter فصل |
| bright روشن | cheap ارزان |
| bring آوردن | cheese پنیر |
| brother برادر | cherry گیلاس |
| brown قهوهای رنگ | chief کل |
| builder بنا | child بچه |
| building عمارت | Christian عیسوی |
| burn سوختن | class کلاس |
| bus اتوبوس | clean k. پاک |
| but اما؛ ول | climate آب و هوا |
| butter کره | clock ساعت |

close بستن

cloth پارچه

clothing لباس

club باشگاه

coffee قهوه

cold سرد

collect جمع کردن

colour رنگ

come آمدن

comfortable راحت

command فرمودن

company شرکت

complaint *k.* شکایت

complete کامل

—ly کاملاً

congratulations تبریک

consisting of عبارت از

conversation صحبت

cook آشپز؛ پختن

corner گوشه

correct *k.* درست

cotton پنبه

count شمردن

country کشور؛ مملکت

county شهرستان

cow گاو

create آفریدن

culture تربیت

cup فنجان

curtain پرده

cut بریدن

dance *k.* رقص

danger خطر

dark تاریک

daughter دختر

day روز

dear گران؛ عزیز

death مرگ

deceive فریفتن

depend on بستگی داشتن با

desert بیابان

die مردن

difficult مشکل

dinner شام

direction طرف

director رئیس

مدیر

dirt کثافت

—y کثیف

do کردن

doctor پزشک

dog سگ

door در

draw کشیدن

drink خوردن

drive راندن

dry خشک

dust خاک

ear گوش

early زود

East مشرق

easy آسان

eat خوردن

education فرهنگ

egg تخم مرغ

electricity برق

embassy سفارت

empty k. خالی

enjoy لذت بردن از

enough بس کافی

enter در آمدن داخل شدن

escape فرار کردن

every هر؛ همه

excellent عالی

except for جز

excuse بخشیدن

exercise k. تمرین

expensive گران

eye چشم

face رو

fact فعل

in— فعلاً

fall افتادن

family خانواده

far دور

father پدر

fear ترسیدن

feeling k. حس

a few کی

find پیدا کردن

fire آتش

first اول

—ly اولاً

fish ماهی

flour آرد

flower گل

fly پریدن

a fly مگس

foot پا

for برای

forbidden ممنوع

foreign خارج خارجه

forget فراموش کردن

fork چنگال

former سابق

—ly سابقاً

friend دوست

from از

in front of جلوی

fruit میوه

full k. پر

furniture اثاثه

game k. بازی

garden باغ

general معمولی

—ly معمولاً

gentleman آقا

get گرفتن

gift هدیه — تقدیمی

girl دختر

give دادن

glass شیشه

a glass لیوان

go رفتن

God خدا

gold زر

good خوب

—bye خدا حافظ

—morning سلام علیکم

government دولت

grass سبزه

grateful ممنون / متشکر

green سبز

ground زمین

guest مهمان

half نصف / نیم

hand دست

—kerchief دستمال

hang آویختن

happen اتفاق افتادن

happy خوشحال

hard سخت

hat کلاه

have داشتن

he او

head سر

heart دل

heavy سنگین

help *k.* کمک

here اینجا

high بلند

history تاریخ

hit زدن

holiday عید

hope امید

—ful امیدوار

horse اسب

hospital بیمارستان

hot داغ

hour ساعت

house خانه ؛ منزل

how چطور

— much چند ؛ چقدر

— many

hungry گرسنه

I من ؛ بنده

ice یخ

if اگر

ill مریض

importance اهمیت

important مهم

in در

increase افزودن

in order to تا ؛ برای اینکه

inside داخل

in spite of باوجود

| | |
|---|---|
| instead of بجای | lazy تنبل |
| intelligent باهوش | leaf برگ |
| interesting قابل توجه | leather چرم |
| iron آهن | left-hand چپ |
| Islam اسلام | lesson درس |
| it آن | letter حرف |
| jug کوزه | a lie دروغ |
| jump پریدن | life k. زندگی |
| just هم | like مثل |
| key کلید | to like دوست داشتن |
| kill کشتن | line خط |
| kind مهربان | listen کردن گوش |
| —ness التفات | little کوچک |
| a kind جنس؛ طور | a little کمی |
| جور | lock k. قفل |
| king شاه؛ پادشاه | long بلند |
| knife کارد | look at نگاه کردن |
| know دانستن؛ شناختن | look for جستن |
| known معلوم | loose شل |
| well-known معروف | lose گم کردن |
| lady خانم | low پائین |
| lane کوچه | luggage اسباب |
| lamp چراغ | lunch ناهار |
| language زبان | mad دیوانه |
| last آخر؛ آخرین | match کبریت |
| —ly بالاخره | me مرا |
| to last طول کشیدن | meaning معنی |
| late دیر | means وسیله |
| laugh خندیدن | measure پیمودن |
| law قانون | meat گوشت |

medicine دوا

message پیغام

minister وزیر

ministry وزارت

minute دقیقه

Miss خانم

mistake k. اشتباه

mix آمیختن

moment موقع

money پول

month, ماه

moon

more بیشتر

morning صبح

Moslem مسلم
مسلمان

mosque مسجد

most بیشترین

mother مادر

mountain که؛ کوه

mouse موش

move off حرکت کردن

Mr. آقا

Mrs. خانم

must باید

nail میخ

name نام؛ اسم

nation ملت

—al ملی

near نزدیک

necessary لازم

necessities لوازم

need لازم داشتن

neighbour همسایه

never هرگز؛ هیچوقت

new تازه؛ جدید

newspaper روزنامه

next آینده

night شب

no نه؛ خیر؛ نخیر؛ هیچ

noon ظهر

North شمال

not yet هنوز . . . نه

now حالا

number نمره؛ شماره

office دفتر؛ اداره

old کهنه؛ پیر

a one یکی

open k. باز

or یا

other دیگر

out (lights) خاموش

outside بیرون

own خود

owner صاحب

page صفحه

pain درد

painter نقاش

paper کاغذ

pass گذشتن

| | |
|---|---|
| pay پرداختن | quarrel گفتگو |
| peace صلح | quarter ربع |
| pen قلم | queen ملکه |
| pencil مداد | quick(ly) زود |
| people مردم | railway راه آهن |
| perhaps شاید | rain باران |
| permission dd. اجازه | raise بلند کردن |
| Persian language فارسی | reach رسیدن |
| person شخص | read خواندن |
| photograph عکس | ready k. حاضر |
| picture نقش | reason سبب |
| place جا | receive (guests) پذیرفتن |
| a plain دشت | reckoning k. حساب |
| plate بشقاب | red قرمز |
| pleasant نشاط آور | religion دین؛ مذهب |
| point اصل | remain ماندن |
| police شهربانی | remainder بقیه |
| poor بیچاره | remember یاد داشتن |
| port بندر | remove ور داشتن |
| possible ممکن | repair k. تعمیر |
| post پست | republic جمهور |
| pot ظرف | request k. خواهش |
| potato سیب زمینی | result نتیجه |
| pour ریختن | return برگشتن |
| press فشردن | rice برنج |
| price بها؛ قیمت | right راست |
| private شخصی | ring زنگ زدن |
| produce در آوردن | rise برخاستن |
| prophet پیغمبر | river رود؛ رودخانه |
| protect k. حفظ | road راه |
| put گذاشتن | roof پشت بام |

room اطاق

rose گل

rug قالیچه

run دویدن

salt نمک

satisfied k. راضی

say گفتن

school مدرسه

scissors قیچی

screw پیچ : پیچیدن

sea دریا

season فصل

a second ثانیه

see دیدن

seed تخم

self خود

sell فروختن

send فرستادن

separate k. جدا

servant نوکر

service k. خدمت

shadow سایه

share k. قسمت

she او

sheep گوسفند

shine تافتن

shoe کفش

shop دکان

short کوتاه

show نمودن نشان دادن

silver نقره

sister خواهر

sit نشستن

situated واقع

sleep خواب خوابیدن

slow(ly) یواش

smell k. بو

snow برف

so اینطور

— much اینقدر

— many

— that تا؛ برای اینکه

soldier سرباز

some بعضی

—times گاهی

son پسر

soon زود

sorry متأسف

sort جنس؛ طور

sound حرف

South جنوب

special خصوص

—ly خصوصاً

spectacles عینک

spend (time) گذراندن

spoon قاشق

sport ورزش

| | |
|---|---|
| spring بهار | teach آموختن |
| square میدان | er— معلم |
| stamp تمبر | test آزمودن |
| stand ایستادن | than از |
| station ایستگاه | thanks k. تشکر |
| steal دزدیدن | that آن؛ که |
| stew آش | then پس |
| stop ایستادن | there آنجا |
| storm توفان | these اینها |
| stove بخاری | they ایشان؛ آنها |
| strange عجیب | thief دزد |
| street خیابان | thin نازک |
| study درس خواندن | thing چیز |
| stupid بی فهم | think فکرکردن |
| successful موفق | this این |
| sugar قند | those آنها |
| suggestion k. پیشنهاد | throw انداختن |
| summer تابستان | out— بیرون کردن |
| sun خورشید؛ آفتاب | tie بستن |
| rise— k. طلوع | tight تنگ |
| set— k. غروب | time وقت |
| surprise | tired خسته |
| be —d k. تعجب | to به |
| sweep رفتن | today امروز |
| sweet(s) شیرینی | tomorrow فردا |
| table میز | tongue زبان |
| tail دم | tonight امشب |
| take گرفتن | too (much) (many) زیاد |
| talk صحبت کردن | tooth دندان |
| tea چای | towards طرف |

translation k. ترجمه

travel k. مسافرت

—ler مسافر

tree درخت

tribe ایل

trouble زحمت

   take — ksh.

try k. سعی؛ کوشش

tube لوله

twist تافتن پیچیدن

under زیر

—stand فهمیدن

unless بدون اینکه

upon روی

until تا

various مختلف

very خیلی بسیار

village ده

visit دیدن رفتن

vocabulary فرهنگ

voice صدا

wages حقوق

wait صبر کردن

walk پیاده رفتن راه رفتن

wall دیوار

want میل داشتن خواستن

war جنگ

warm گرم

wash شستن

watch ساعت

water آب

we ما

wear پوشیدن

weather هوا

weave بافتن

week هفته

weight وزن

West مغرب

what چه؛ چه چیز

when کی؛ وقتیکه

where کجا

whether آیا

which کدام

white سفید

who کی؛ که

why چرا

wide پهن

wind باد

window پنجره

wine شراب

winter زمستان

wise دانا

with با

—in در ظرف

—out بی؛ بدون

woman زن

wood چوب

wool پشم

word لغت؛ کلمه

work *k.* کار

world جهان؛ دنیا

worthy of قابل

wrap پیچیدن

write نوشتن

year سال

yellow زرد

yesterday دیروز

you شما

young جوان

# INDEX

264